MANCHESTER UNITED
THE OFFICIAL REVIEW 1998

MANCHESTER UNITED
THE OFFICIAL REVIEW 1998

Contributors

Alex Ferguson | **Brian Kidd** | **Jim Ryan** | **Eric Harrison**
Dave Williams | **Neil Bailey**
The players and staff at Manchester United

Lou Pepper | **Sam Pilger** | **Adam Bostock**
Matt Turner | **Andy Mitten** | **Daniel Mallerman**
Paul Davies | **Jim Drewett** | **Justyn Barnes**

Photographs (unless otherwise stated)
Action Images | **John Peters** | **Allsport**

Design
Tim Barnes | **Carol Briggs**

First published in 1998 by
Manchester United Books
an imprint of
VCI
76 Dean Street | London | W1V 5HA

in association with

Manchester United Football Club Plc
Old Trafford | Manchester | M16 0RA

CIP data for this title is available from the British Library

ISBN 0233 99154 9

Produced by **Zone Ltd**.

Printed and bound in Italy by **Editoriale Bortolazzi-STEI**.

CONTENTS

ALEX FERGUSON
1997/98

THE MANAGER'S VIEW

We reached the heights and we sank to the depths to experience all over again what I wrote here last year... buying a ticket for Manchester Unted is like booking a ride on a roller-coaster.

We opened brilliantly and yet finished without a major trophy to disappoint our fans as well as ourselves: second best to Arsenal for the Championship and beaten at the quarter-final stage of the European Champions' League.

It was a bitter pill to swallow, especailly as our European dreams crashed, and I have never felt so low in football. Our expectations were high, and justifiably so I believe, but we failed to deliver.

It is hard to comprehend when you look back to first half of the season. I doubt we have ever started in such sparkling form and it confirmed for me the feeling that we were equipped to go all the way in Europe and, at the same time, retain the Championship with a bit of luck.

And up to Christmas I wasn't the only one thrilled with our football. The critics and even rivals were heaping praise on our heads. One bookmaker, admittedly a bit of a United supporter, declared he would start paying out bets on us winning the Premiership.

Everyone was talking about us having a truly great side, and who wouldn't after watching us run up 13 goals in successive matches against Barnsley and Sheffield Wednesday starting in October. Andy Cole was in tremendous form, scoring for fun at the rate of a goal a game.

I was delighted to see us score five goals at Wimbledon, too. Not many other teams do that. And there was a real zing about the side when we scored five again to knock Chelsea out of the FA Cup in London in January.

It had also been highly satisfying to watch the way we topped our qualifying group in the Champions' League with five straight wins and only losing the final match against Juventus in Turin because we knew we had already qualified for the quarter finals.

I felt we had crossed the bridge to master what it takes to be successful in Europe. We opened with a useful 3–0 win against unknown opposition in Kosice and then notched a notable victory against Juventus in our first home tie, winning 3–2 in a game which we dominated much more than the scoreline might suggest.

Man U in the middle

The hearts of the players were in the right place for the big one. We went out to show that we had learned a thing or two following naive performances against the Italians the previous season.

It was one of the great memorable nights of European football at Old Trafford. The players showed maturity, discipline and tactical awareness.

Feyenoord were beaten 2–1 at Old Trafford and then 3–1 in Holland thanks to a splendid hat-trick from Andy Cole. A place in the last eight was assured when we finished off Kosice 3–0 at Old Trafford and the bookmakers declared we were 2–1 favourites to become European Champions.

We returned to the Premership to beat both Blackburn and Liverpool to become 1–4 favourites to retain our League title.

And all this had been achieved despite the early loss of Roy Keane who was out for the rest of the season with a serious cruciate injury. The team just rose above the injuries with a desire to win that swept all before them. They took the absence of the skipper in their stride, just as we had overcome the retirement of Eric Cantona.

But football can humiliate you, as we found out the hard way. You can ride with the injuries for so long before there comes a time when they begin to flatten you. The key to maintaining top form is being able to make consitent team selections. In the second half of the season, I was unable to do this.

I didn't hear any alarm bells until we started to pick up injuries around about March. We were without Peter Schmeichel, Gary Pallister and Ryan Giggs. At this vital stage of the season we had to tackle six major games in 15 days, and it was too much for us. We lost twice in the League, including a key defeat against Arsenal at OT, and we were knocked out of Europe by Monaco.

This really hurt because I felt we were a better team than the French and if we had a full side I'm sure we would have gone on. In retrospect, I should have tried harder to find cover for Ryan Giggs on the wing.

We will all learn from our mistakes and we will keep a disappointing season in perspective. After all, we have been phenomenally consistent over the last seven years, with four Championships and finishing as runners-up in the other three seasons, along with winning the FA Cup twice.

It's not a bad record. And don't worry, the players will be up for it again this season.

AUGUST

1 | 2 | 3 | 4 | 5 | 6 | 7 | 8 | 9 | 10 | 11 | 12 | 13 | 14 | 15 | 16 | 17 | 18 | 19 | 20 | 21 | 22 | 23 | 24 | 25 | 26 | 27 | 28 | 29 | 30 | 31

AUGUST

THE MONTH AHEAD

August saw the conclusion of the three-year-long soccer bungs trial with acquittal for defendants Bruce Grobbelaar, Hans Segers and John Fashanu. But as the summer drew to a close it was the blossoming love between Diana and Dodi which was soon to end so tragically that captured the headlines on a daily basis.

It's always hot in Spain in August, but it reached boiling point when the world transfer record was smashed by Real Betis who bought Brazilian international Denilson for £24 million from Sao Paulo, making Ronaldo's proposed £18-million move to Inter Milan seem a snip. Back home, the month kicked off with a rare win for the Tories as they managed to hold off Labour in the Uxbridge by-election, but it was defeat for the blues as the football season kicked off at Wembley. Chelsea may have taken the lead against United – featuring £3.5 million signing Teddy Sheringham for the first time – in the Charity Shield, but Ronny Johnsen's first-ever goal for the Reds and some cool heads in the penalty shoot-out earned United the first trophy of the season. David Beckham, England's

most exciting young player, was absent from the game until late in the second half. After last season's exertions (which included a trip with England to Le Tournoi as well as a high profile relationship with Posh Spice) Alex Ferguson had decided his young star needed a rest. "We want him to be a great player in five years time, not just now," said Fergie who kept him on the bench for the Charity Shield and the first few League games of the season.

Meanwhile, Ferguson's search for a centre back continued but Brazilian Silva's proposed move from Corinthians was blocked when he was denied a work permit. A £5-million swoop for Henning Berg was the solution, ten years after the Norwegian international had been released after an unsuccessful trial at Old Trafford. Berg's compatriot Solskjaer was injured

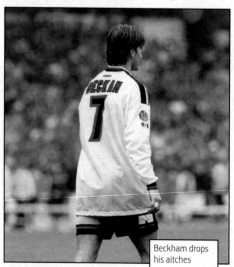

Beckham drops his aitches

Hello Henning

Au revoir, Eric.
Bonjour Teddy

for the first game of the new Premierhsip season, and what a game! The fixture computer had thrown up a potentially volatile meeting with Tottenham, Teddy Sheringham's old club, and the new United man received a viciously hostile welcome back at his old club. Matters were made worse when, to the delight of the home crowd, Sheringham struck a 61st minute penalty against the post. In the next few games, Sheringham's all-round play was exceptional and he showed his commitment to the club when he invested £350,000 in a two bedroom flat in a salubrious complex in Cheshire. Based here, he could pop round for tea with neighbours including *Coronation Street* stars and members of Oasis.

Elsewhere in the Premiership, man of the moment Chris Sutton fired in a hat-trick for Blackburn in their 4–0 triumph over Villa to send Rovers top. It was a dream start for the new man at Blackburn, coach Roy Hodgson, after his trials and tribulations in Italy with Inter Milan. Bolton hooked a former United target, South African's Mark Fish from Lazio and he was joined by Peter Beardsley, a £450,000 capture from Newcastle. Beardsley had been pushed out of the reckoning at St James' Park by the arrival of two promising 'youngsters' John Barnes from Liverpool and Ian Rush from

"I didn't expect it. Perhaps it was naive of me."

TEDDY SHERINGHAM ON THE ABUSE HE RECEIVED ON HIS RETURN TO SPURS

Leeds who were reunited with former Liverpool team-mate and manager, Kenny Dalglish. United's big summer signing Teddy Sheringham finally grabbed his first League goal for the club against Everton at Goodison Park in a 2–0 win which saw the Reds at their very best. And the month was rounded off with an impressive 3–0 victory over Coventry which took United into second behind Blackburn. Roll on September!

Englishmen abroad
at Le Tournoi

THAILAND 0
MANCHESTER UNITED 2

17 July 1997 | 5 pm | National Stadium | Att: 25,000

HOME TEAM

22. Chaiyong Kamplian
3. Tinnakorn Kamol
7. Natee Tongsukkaew
11. T. Damrngongtakul
12. S. Jaturapattarapong
14. Vitoon Kijmongkolsak
16. Surachai Jirastrichote
17. Dusit Chalermsan
19. Pongtorn Thiabthong
21. Sumet Akkarapong
23. Chaicharn Keawsaen

SUBSTITUTES

2. Krisda Plandit
8. A. Thaveechalermuit
24. Ronnachai Saymochai
26. Piyapong Pue-on

REFEREE

Pirom Umprasert

VISITORS

1. Peter Schmeichel
6. Gary Pallister
3. Denis Irwin
4. David May
16. Roy Keaneu
8. Nicky Butt
12. Phil Neville
18. Paul Scholes
14. Jordi Cruyff
9. Andy Cole
10. Teddy Sheringham

SUBSTITUTES

17. Rai Van Der Gouw
   Schmeichel | 66 mins
32. Michael Clegg
13. Brian McClair
15. Karel Poborsky
   Cruyff | 55 mins
20. Ole G Solskjaer

SCORERS

Butt | 57 mins
Tongsukkaew | og 87 mins

MATCH REPORT

In the opening game of the Far East tour, United produced a half-paced performance to beat the Thai national side 2–0 in Bangkok.

The spirited Thai side were far from out-classed, but United didn't move out of first gear.

In a game where every throw-in, corner and goal kick was cheered by a near-capacity crowd, Nicky Butt put the Reds ahead after 57 minutes when he rifled home a shot from 25 yards.

Good work by substitute Karel Poborsky resulted in a cross directed towards new signing Sheringham but Thai defender Tongsukkaew got there first and headed past his own keeper with three minutes to play.

Pictures from top:
The new captain steps out in Thailand | Teddy gets stuck in | Ole takes on South China | Red diamond meets the Red Diamonds

SOUTH CHINA 0
MANCHESTER UNITED 1

20 July 1997 | 3.30 pm | Hong Kong Stadium | Att: 36,611

HOME TEAM

1. Iain Hesford
5. Silva Aurelio
7. Au Wai Lun
9. Dale Tempest
10. Lee Bullen
11. Lee Kin Wo
12. Wu Qunli
14. Yau Kin Wai
16. Shum Kwok Pui
18. Sung Lin Yung
21. Ignjic Radislav

SUBSTITUTES

2. Poon Man Tik
4. Yeung Ching Kwong
8. Leslie Santos
13. Chan Chi Hong
15. Ng Chun Chung

VISITORS

1. Peter Schmeichel
12. Phil Neville
3. Denis Irwin
4. David May
5. Ronny Johnsen
16. Roy Keane
18. Paul Scholes
13. Brian McClair
20. Ole G Solskjaer
5. Karel Poborsky
10. Teddy Sheringham

SUBSTITUTES USED

27. Terry Cooke
32. Michael Clegg
11. Phil Mulryne
14. Jordi Cruyff
23. Ben Thornley

SCORERS

Cruyff | 75 mins

MATCH REPORT

New United captain Roy Keane made it two trophies in two games as the Reds chalked up a 1–0 victory over Hong Kong champions, South China.

The pace of the game was of typically slow pre-season standard but United created several good chances. Keane hit the crossbar, and Sheringham hit the post in the first half before Jordi Cruyff outjumped two defenders to head home United's first on 75 minutes.

With five Red substitutes to give more players a run-out, a dominant United held out for a one-goal win over an enthusaiastic home side.

URAWA RED DIAMONDS 1
MANCHESTER UNITED 2

22 July 1997 | 7 pm | Urawa Komaba stadium | Att: 17,642

HOME TEAM

16. Takita
19. Nijhuis
13. Yamada
29. Tabata
22. Jojo
6. Buchwald
35. Nagai
10. Beguiristan
7. Okano
24. Oshiba
2. Tsuchihashi

SUBSTITUTES

28. Sato
      Okano | 75 mins
1. Tschida
12. Nishiijo
8. Hirose
5. Hori

SCORER

Oshiba | 49 mins

VISITORS

1. Peter Schmeichel
32. Michael Clegg
12. Phil Neville
19. Ronny Johnsen
6. Gary Pallister
16. Roy Keane
14. Jordi Cruyff
8. Nicky Butt
11. Phil Mulryne
9. Andy Cole
20. Ole G Solskjaer

SUBSTITUTES

17. Rai Van Der Gouw
      Schmeichel | 45 mins
13. Brian McClair
      Johnsen | 45 mins
18. Paul Scholes
      Clegg | 57 mins
15. Karel Poborsky
      Cole | 57 mins
27. Terry Cooke

SCORERS

Solskjaer | 14/40 mins

MATCH REPORT

United saved their best performance of the Far East tour until the last game against Urawa Red Diamonds.

Solskjaer gave United the lead after just 14 minutes when he rose above two defenders to head home a Mulryne cross from the left.

The Norwegian added a second five minutes before the break after neat work from Cole and Butt cleared the way for him to drive the ball into the top-right corner.

Urawa were the more determined side in the second period and pulled a goal back through Oshiba on 49 minutes. Despite further pressure, United held on to their lead to make it three wins out of three in Asia.

INTER MILAN 1
MANCHESTER UNITED 1
27 July 1995 | 7.45 pm | San Siro | Att: 49,718

MANCHESTER UNITED 1
INTER MILAN 1
30 July 1997 | Old Trafford | Att: 48,579

HOME TEAM
1. Gianluca Pagliuca
4. Javier Zanetti
24. Luigi Sartor
7. Salvator Fresi
19. Massimo Paganin
3. Massimo Tarantino
14. Diego Simeone
13. Ze Elias
6. Youri Djorkaeff
10. Ronaldo
23. Maurizio Ganz

SUBSTITUTES USED

9. Ivan Zamorano
16. Taribo West
2. Giuseppe Bergomi
5. Fabio Galante
15. Benoit Cauet
8. Aron Winter
20. Alvaro Recoba
18. Nicola Berti
17. Francesco Moriero
11. Nwankwo Kanj

SCORER

Neville | 14 mins og

VISITORS
1. Peter Schmeichel
2. Denis Irwin
3. Phil Neville
6. Roy Keane
4. David May
5. Ronny Johnsen
7. Paul Scholes
8. Nicky Butt
11. Ryan Giggs
10. Teddy Sheringham
9. Ole G Solskjaer

SUBSTITUTES

13. Brain McClair
Irwin | 70 mins
12. Andy Cole
Solskjaer | 65 mins
16. Gary Neville
May | 38 mins
14. Jordi Cruyff
Giggs | 65 mins
15. Karel Poborsky

SCORER

Butt | 14 mins

MATCH REPORT

A simple pre-season friendly was turned into the unveiling of the world's most expensive player – Ronaldo. The Brazilian wonder boy attracted just under 50,000 fans into San Siro, only to be upstaged by United's kids. Ronaldo only stayed on the pitch for 17 minutes, and by that time Nicky Butt had already put the Reds ahead. An unfortunate own goal by substitiute Gary Neville in the 70th minute took the game to penalties.

PENALTIES:
United lost 4–1 on penalties. Teddy Sheringham was United's only penalty scorer

HOME TEAM
1. Peter Schmeichel
2. Denis Irwin
3. Philip Neville
4. Nicky Butt
5. Ronny Johnsen
6. Gary Neville
7. Paul Scholes
8. Karel Poborsky
9. Andy Cole
10. Teddy Sheringham
11. Ryan Giggs

SUBSTITUTES USED

12. Michael Clegg
15. Brian McClair
16. Ole G Solskjaer
14. Jordi Cruyff
17. Dante Poli
18. David Beckham
19. Kevin Pilkington

SCORER

Clegg | 67 mins

VISITORS
1. Gianluca Pagliuca
2. Giuseppe Bergomi
4. Javier Zanetti
5. Fabio Galante
14. Diego Simeone
8. Aron Winter
15. Benoit Cauet
18. Nicola Berti
16. Taribo West
9. Ivan Zamorano
20. Alvaro Recoba

SUBSTITUTES USED

23. Maurizio Ganz
3. Massimo Tarantino
21. Luca Mezzano
22. Massimo Paganin
23. Salvatore Fresi
24. Luigi Sator

SCORER

Ganz | 42 mins

MATCH REPORT

United's newest kid on the block spared the blushes of his senior colleagues in this patchy affair. Pitched in to shore up an injury-hit defence, second-half sub Michael Clegg headed United's equaliser from a corner.

Before that, Sheringham and Giggs missed gilt-edged chances; at least Poborsky and Neville could blame the skills of Inter keeper Pagliuca for their close-range failures. Without Djorkaeff and Ronaldo, Inter were below par but deserved their breakthrough when Simeone beat Johnsen to an aerial ball and unselfishly laid on a simple tap-in for Gainz.

Pictures from top:
Ronaldo gets mobbed | The return leg at Old Trafford | Terry Cooke: 21 today | Cole is a Slav to the game

SLAVIA PRAGUE 2
MANCHESTER UNITED 2

5 August 1997 | 8pm | Old Trafford | Att: 22,075

HOME TEAM

1. Rai Van Der Gouw
2. Gary Neville
3. Philip Neville
4. Dante Poli
5. Brian McClair
6. Gary Pallister
7. David Beckham
8. Karel Poborsky
9. Andrew Cole
10. Jordi Cruyff
11. Ryan Giggs

SUBSTITUTES USED

12. Ronny Johnsen
17. Ben Thornley
18. John Curtis
19. Phil Mulryne
16. Terry Cooke

SCORERS

Poborsky | 1 min
Cooke | 46 mins

REFEREE

E Lomas

VISITORS

1. Jan Sterjskal
2. Jiri Lerch
3. Lubos Kozel
4. Sladan Asanin
5. Pavel Rehak
6. Peter Vicek
7. Ivo Ulrich
8. Edvard Lasota
9. Karel Vacha
10. Pavel Horvath
11. Robert Vagner

SUBSTITUTES USED

12. Martin Hysky
13. Tomas Kuchar
14. Vladmir Labant
15. Jiri Vavra
16. Lucas Joarolim

SCORERS

Horvath | 50 mins (pen)
Asanin | 84 mins

MATCH REPORT

A fully rested David Beckham took his place in the centre of midfield, but the centre of attention was his girlfriend, Posh Spice, in the crowd.

Beckham lasted just 70 minutes before Fergie replaced him with Phil Mulryne. For Karel Poborsky, it was a personal success against his old club, when he scored a goal after just 34 seconds.

A quite uneventful game was brought to life when Terry Cooke on his 21st birthday put United in front with just 11 minutes to go. Slavia Prague spoiled the party when a controversial penalty and a fine curling shot by Pavel Horvath gave them a deserved equaliser.

MANCHESTER UNITED 1
CHELSEA 1

MAN UNITED

		RATING
1.	Peter Schmeichel	7
3.	Denis Irwin	8
5.	Ronny Johnsen	8
6.	Gary Pallister	9
12.	Phil Neville	7
16.	Roy Keane	8
8.	Nicky Butt	7
18.	Paul Scholes	7
11.	Ryan Giggs	6
9.	Andy Cole	6
10.	Teddy Sheringham	6

SUBSTITUTES

		RATING
7.	David Beckham	7
	Giggs | 73 mins	
14.	Jordi Cruyff	6
	Sheringham | 73 mins	
2.	Gary Neville	
15.	Karel Poborsky	
13.	Brian McClair	

SCORERS

Johnsen | 58 mins

REFEREE

Peter Jones | Leicester

CHELSEA

		RATING
1.	Ed De Goey	7
5.	Frank Leboeuf	6
20.	Frank Sinclair	7
6.	Steve Clarke	8
8.	Gustavo Poyet	7
28.	Jody Morris	7
7.	Dennis Wise	8
16.	Roberto Di Matteo	7
35.	Danny Granville	7
24.	Mark Hughes	8
25.	Gianfranco Zola	7

SUBSTITUTES

		RATING
2.	Dan Petrescu	6
	Morris | 45 mins	
9.	Gianluca Vialli	6
	Hughes | 76 mins	
21.	Paul Hughes	
4.	Ruud Gullit	
22.	Mark Nicholls	

SCORERS

Hughes | 52 mins

MATCH REPORT

The Charity Shield and the Premiership trophy are like a double act for United. They can't have one without the other.

Penalties decided this relatively even contest, but so assured were United's penalties and so wretched were Chelsea's, that United deserved to take the Shield back North for the fourth time in five years.

Dennis Wise snapped and snarled, Roy Keane 'welcomed' Chelsea's new Uruguayan Poyet to England and Teddy Sheringham attempted to ingratiate himself with United's fans by arguing with Wise.

Mark Hughes enjoys showing Alex Ferguson he was sold too early; his close-range header from Zola's cross gave Chelsea the lead.

Minutes later, Johnsen chose a good moment to score his first goal for United, by rising to head in a Beckham corner.

Schmeichel took advantage of the new goalkeeping laws, that allow him to move on his line before a penalty, to unnerve Frank Sinclair whose hopeless blast cannoned off him. Di Matteo lifted his penalty high over the bar while Irwin, Keane, Scholes and Butt calmly stroked in theirs to retain the Shield.

IN THE PAPERS

"This triumph may not have sent the same chilling warning which the Reds blasted out 12 months ago when they flattened Newcastle 4–0 but, nontheless, the sight of United with another piece of silverware was enough to send a shiver down the spines of some of the money-men in the Premiership."
MANCHESTER EVENING NEWS

"I feel like I've been here before"

Schmeichel saves from Sinclair

Johnsen equalises

TOTTENHAM HOTSPUR 0
MANCHESTER UNITED 2

HOME TEAM

1.	Ian Walker	6
3.	Justin Edinburgh	6
15.	Ramon Vega	5
23.	Sol Campbell	9
4.	David Howells	6
8.	Allan Neilsen	6
12.	Stephen Carr	7
14.	David Ginola	5
25.	Stephen Clemence	6
18.	Steffen Eversen	7
10.	Les Ferdinand	6

SUBSTITUTES

22.	Andy Sinton	6
	Clemence	75 mins	
13.	Espen Baardsen	
5.	Colin Calderwood	
17.	John Scales	
24.	Neale Fenn	

REFEREE

Graham Poll | Tring

VISITORS

		RATING
1.	Peter Schmeichel	7
3.	Denis Irwin	7
12.	Phil Neville	7
5.	Ronny Johnsen	9
6.	Gary Pallister	9
8.	Nicky Butt	8
16.	Roy Keane	8
18.	Paul Scholes	7
11.	Ryan Giggs	7
10.	Teddy Sheringham	7
14.	Jordi Cruyff	6

SUBSTITUTES

13.	Brian McClair	
10.	David Beckham	7
	Scholes	66 mins	
2.	Gary Neville	
15.	Karel Poborsky	
17.	Rai Van Der Gouw	

SCORERS

Butt | 81 mins
Vega | og 82 mins

MATCH REPORT

Homecomings are usually a happy occasion – except in football. Teddy Sheringham returned to White Hart Lane to be greeted with the sort of reception only seen before at public floggings.

Sheringham did manage to replace their vitrol with smiles when he missed a second-half penalty right in front of them. But it was the last thing they had to celebrate as Sheringham and United ran out comfortable 2–0 winners.

If only Tottenham could have mustered up the same passion their fans directed at Teddy. Their new signings, Ferdinand and Ginola must have wondered what they'd let themselves in for.

While United were nowhere near their best, they were too good for Spurs. Butt and Keane dominated the midfield and Giggs enjoyed a few jaunts down the left.

With ten minutes remaining, Nicky Butt found himself alone in the area with the ball at his feet and the goal in front of him. He paused before firing a shot over Ian Walker. The game was over just a minute later when Ramon Vega sliced a Beckham cross past Walker.

IN THE PAPERS

"Their rivals are already stuttering, but United are straight back into the groove. There might be a long season ahead but some things never change. Not that this victory was based on glory football we are accustomed to from United, but more with drive and grit."
DAILY STAR

"The depth of hatred and anger for Teddy Sheringham's defection from Spurs to Old Trafford finally surfaced at White Hart Lane yesterday. It's a tradition at this club to welcome back old boys of distinction before the kick-off, but there was no such privilege afforded to England's World Cup forward."
MIRROR

"United possess a collective will like few other teams, their solidity and strength of purpose assisted by thyeir relatively unchanged squad."
TELEGRAPH

Sol Campbell taunts Teddy

Butty Boy takes the lead

Did you miss me?

MANCHESTER UNITED 1
SOUTHAMPTON 0

HOME TEAM

		RATING
1.	Peter Schmeichel	7
3.	Denis Irwin	8
5.	Ronny Johnsen	8
6.	Gary Pallister	7
12.	Phil Neville	7
16.	Roy Keane	6
8.	Nicky Butt	7
18.	Paul Scholes	7
11.	Ryan Giggs	7
14.	Jordi Cruyff	6
10.	Teddy Sheringham	6

SUBSTITUTES

10.	David Beckham	8
	Scholes | 54 mins	
2.	Gary Neville	
15.	Karel Poborsky	
21.	Henning Berg	8
	Johnsen | 45 mins	
17.	Rai Van Der Gouw	

SCORERS

Beckham | 78 mins

REFEREE

G Barber | Surry

VISITORS

1.	Paul Jones	7
18.	Ulrich Van Gobbel	8
5.	Ken Monkou	7
15.	Frances Benali	6
3.	Lee Todd	7
8.	Matthew Oakley	6
4.	Jim Magilton	6
14.	Neil Maddison	7
11.	Robbie Slater	7
25.	Stig Johansen	6
10.	Egil Ostenstad	7

SUBSTITUTES

21.	Andy Williams	6
	Van Gobbel | 79 mins	
22.	Matthew Robinson	6
	Slater | 79 mins	
9.	Michael Evans	7
	Johansen | 56 mins	
13.	Maik Taylor	
16.	Kevin Davies	

MATCH REPORT

This is a game that will not linger long in the memory of those who frequent Old Trafford. United laboured to victory against an anonymous Southampton side, shorn of their only attraction, Le Tissier.

Teddy Sheringham and Jordi Cruyff looked an incompatible partnership, all nice touches and little penetration. Cole and Solskjaer's absence meant that United were bereft of any real pace up front. That was left up to Ryan Giggs along the left wing. Henning Berg's second-half debut slightly raised the game's interest value.

David Beckham is all pent-up frustration on the bench, and he's keen not to stay there for too long. This time he relinquished his place on the bench to come on and score the winner. Giggs cut the ball back and there was Beckham to turn and hit the ball beneath Paul Jones' legs. He enjoyed his celebration, sliding towards the fans at the Stretford End, although he could have done without a congratulatory kick from his captain.

IN THE PAPERS

"Alex Ferguson may as well concede with grace. For the second time in three days David Beckham, the player he most wants to shield from the early season Premiership competition, came off the bench to inspire Manchester United to an otherwise improbable win."
GUARDIAN

"Southampton, a side with a knack of interrupting United's momentum, were within 12 minutes of giving Dave Jones his first points at the club, when Ryan Giggs dismantled the right side of their defense and Beckham picked his way through the rubble to sweep home the only goal of the night."
INDEPENDENT

United in pole position

Big air

Jones thwarts Cruyff

LEICESTER CITY 0
MANCHESTER UNITED 0

HOME TEAM

1.	Kasey Keller	8
17.	Spencer Prior	8
5.	Steve Walsh	7
18.	Matt Elliott	8
15.	Pontus Kaamark	7
6.	Mustafa Izzet	7
7.	Neil Lennon	7
16.	Stuart Campbell	6
24.	Steve Guppy	6
20.	Ian Marshall	6
11.	Emile Heskey	7

SUBSTITUTES

14.	Robbie Savage	6
	Campbell	59 mins	
9.	Steve Claridge	6
	Marshall	59 mins	
21.	Graham Fenton	
10.	Garry Parker	
30.	Ian Andrews	

REFEREE

D Gallagher | Banbury

VISITORS   RATING

1.	Peter Schmeichel	8
3.	Denis Irwin	7
2.	Gary Neville	7
21.	Henning Berg	7
6.	Gary Pallister	8
8.	Nicky Butt	7
16.	Roy Keane	7
7.	David Beckham	7
11.	Ryan Giggs	8
10.	Teddy Sheringham	6
14.	Jordi Cruyff	6

SUBSTITUTES

18.	Paul Scholes	7
	Cruyff	8 mins	
12.	Phil Neville	
13.	Brian McClair	
28.	Phil Mulryne	
17.	Rai Van Der Gouw	

MATCH REPORT

It was a shame United's travelling support didn't wait for Teddy Sheringham's shot to hit the back of the net before they started celebrating – he hit the post from just three yards out with Kasey Keller on the ground.

For United, this game was a tale of hit posts: three times they found woodwork instead of the net. After Sheringham, both Scholes and Giggs struck the base of the post with Keller beaten.

But the rattling woodwork didn't mean United dominated this game. Far from it. Though they are a team without superstars, even in an age where the most mediocre of teams boasts a Serie A legend or two, Leicester are not a team to be dismissed lightly. Since their return to the Premiership, United have beaten Leicester only once in four games and the Foxes went into this game on the back of a win at Anfield.

Neil Lennon and Steve Walsh provided Leicester with a strong backbone, and Emile Heskey and Ian Marshall never stopped harrying up front. In fact, only some fine goalkeeping from Peter Schmeichel stopped Heskey from scoring.

IN THE PAPERS

"United still should have won, They passed Leicester to death, had greater staying power and better fitness but the post got in the way three times. Ryan Giggs managed it, so did Scholes and Sheringham amazingly proved it possible from three yards. Even for a well-capped, long-toothed international it was a miss to chill the blood."
SUN

"Once United got down to business on Saturday the game turned into a training session, with the Champions playing attack and Leicester defence. By the end of the afternoon every blue shirt was roadblocking the penalty area in a breathless effort to preserve a point."
GUARDIAN

"Alex Ferguson and the Manchester United public now know the truth – Teddy Sheringham is no Eric Cantona. Sheringham left Leicester last night with his face as red as his shirt after firing another blank. He failed to produce the midfield flair and artistry that was King Eric's trademark."
SUNDAY MIRROR

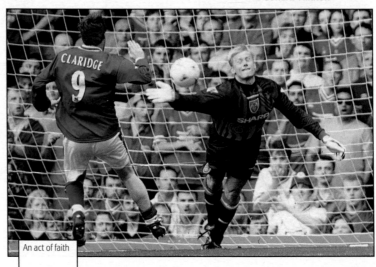

An act of faith

Berg makes his full debut for the Reds

EVERTON 0

MANCHESTER UNITED 2

HOME TEAM

		RATING
1.	Neville Southall	6
5.	David Watson	5
28.	Slaven Bilic	5
12.	Craig Short	6
2.	Earle Barrett	5
7.	Graham Stuart	6
4.	Daniel Williamson	6
10.	Gary Speed	7
6.	Terry Phelan	5
8.	Nick Barmby	6
9.	Duncan Ferguson	7

SUBSTITUTES

		RATING
13.	Paul Gerrard	
20.	Tony Thomas	6
	Barrett | 45 mins	
19.	John Oster	6
	Barmby | 67 mins	
17.	Gareth Farrelly	
16.	Michael Branch	5
	Short | 67 mins	

REFEREE

K Burge | Mid Glamorgan

VISITORS

		RATING
1.	Peter Schmeichel	7
3.	Denis Irwin	8
2.	Gary Neville	8
21.	Henning Berg	8
6.	Gary Pallister	8
8.	Nicky Butt	8
7.	David Beckham	7
16.	Roy Keane	8
11.	Ryan Giggs	9
10.	Teddy Sheringham	7
18.	Paul Scholes	8

SUBSTITUTES

		RATING
9.	Andy Cole	7
	Sheringham | 78 mins	
12.	Phil Neville	
13.	Brian McClair	
15.	Karel Poborsky	
17.	Rai Van Der Gouw	

SCORERS

Beckham | 28 mins
Sheringham | 50 mins

MATCH REPORT

After watching his side outplayed by Manchester United, Everton's manager Howard Kendall was ready to call off the whole Premiership programme "It was frightening for us tonight and, if that's the norm for United, then it's a one-horse race. It was as good a performance as I have seen for a long while." Rarely do rivals admit such inferiority.

Ryan Giggs was Everton's main tormentor. Given a free role behind the strikers, Giggs charged around the field terrifying Everton's defenders and opening up acres of space for Sheringham and Scholes. The evening's finest sight was provided by Giggs leaving Bilic for dead in a straight chase for the ball. It was a performance his team-mate Phil Neville simply called, "World-class."

Two goals seemed to be a meagre return on such a performance. The first one arrived through a mistimed Paul Scholes shot that looped up perfectly for David Beckham to head past Neville Southall. The second goal was due more to Giggs' craft. The Welshman jinked past Watson on the left and delivered a low cross for Teddy Sheringham to sweep in courtesy of a Slaven Bilic deflection.

IN THE PAPERS

"Maybe it was the smell of the incipient Champions' League but United gave a typically European-style performance, resisting early pressure, stilling the home crowd's early hope and then scoring twice on the break. Roy Keane was untouchable in midfield, his non-stop industry setting the benchmark for those in Red around him."
TELEGRAPH

"Sheringham had hit posts, defenders and sometimes the back of the stand as he marched through three and a half games searching for that elusive first goal. But 50 minutes into last night's victory the burden was lifted from his shoulders as Giggs set him up for what he hopes will be his first of many goals."
DAILY STAR

"A Manchester United team inspired by the second-half performance of Ryan Giggs eased Everton aside at Goodison Park with a nonchalance that did not bode well for those who would seek to wrestle the Premiership crown from them."
TIMES

Becks heads home

Giggs: "World-class"

Ted starts to finish

MANCHESTER UNITED 3
COVENTRY CITY 0

HOME TEAM

		RATING
1.	Peter Schmeichel	7
12.	Phil Neville	6
2.	Gary Neville	7
21.	Henning Berg	7
6.	Gary Pallister	7
8.	Nicky Butt	8
16.	Roy Keane	7
7.	David Beckham	6
11.	Ryan Giggs	8
10.	Teddy Sheringham	6
9.	Andy Cole	7

SUBSTITUTES

3.	Denis Irwin	7
	P. Neville	66 mins	
15.	Karel Poborsky	7
	Cole	66 mins	
13.	Brian McClair	
31.	John Curtis	
17.	Rai Van Der Gouw	

SCORERS

Cole | 2 mins
Keane | 71 mins
Poborsky | 89 mins

REFEREE

Gerald Ashby | Worcester

VISITORS

1.	Steve Ogrizovic	7
2.	Richard Shaw	6
3.	David Burrows	7
4.	Paul Williams	7
7.	Darren Huckerby	7
9.	Dion Dublin	8
11.	John Salako	7
12.	Paul Telfer	7
16.	Kevin Richardson	7
18.	Marcus Hall	6
23.	Roland Nilsson	7

SUBSTITUTES

13.	Magnus Hedman
14.	Tronde Soltvedt
15.	Kyle Lightbourne
19.	Martin Johansen
24.	Brian Borrows

MATCH REPORT

Coventry City are always the most accomodating guests. For the second successive season they conceded the lead within the first minute at Old Trafford.

Only 60 seconds into his first start of the season, Andy Cole played a one-two with Sheringham and fired in a shot from outside the area, which looped over Ogrizovic courtesy of a massive deflection from Richard Shaw.

The early goal certainly didn't inspire United, but rather sapped them for the rest of the game. They were fortunate Coventry did not exploit this lethargy. Dion Dublin was particularly unlucky to hit the post with a spectacular overkick.

United doubled their lead when an inswinging Beckham cross fortunately hit Roy Keane in the groin. The scoreline looked even more flattering when Poborsky made it three, scoring from a wonderful Giggs through ball.

Gordon Strachan spoke about the pride he had for his players afterwards. You sense there might be street parties in Coventry if they ever manage to win at Old Trafford.

IN THE PAPERS

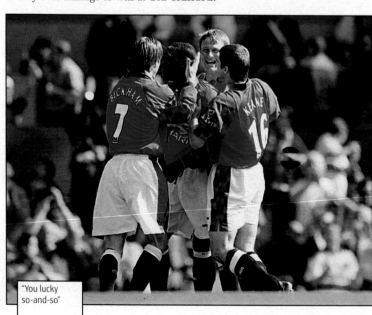

"You lucky so-and-so"

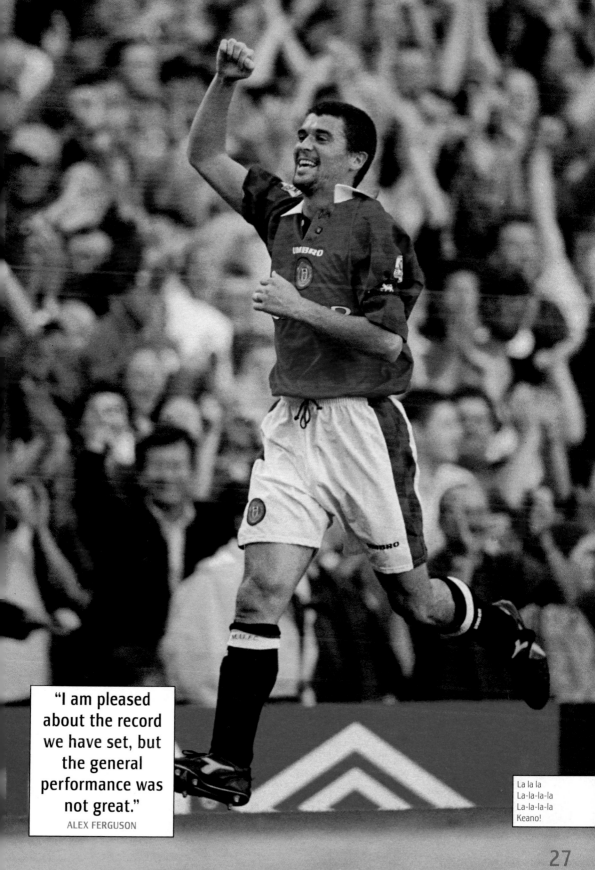

> "I am pleased about the record we have set, but the general performance was not great."
>
> ALEX FERGUSON

La la la
La-la-la-la
La-la-la-la
Keano!

August STATS

PLAYER RECORDS

■ PREMIERSHIP
■ COCA-COLA CUP ■ FA CUP

home | away

FULL APPEARANCE
CAME ON AS SUB

SCORER
SCORED AS SUB

#	Player	FULL APPEARANCES	SUB APPEARANCES	GOALS
1.	Peter Schmeichel	5	0	0
2.	Gary Neville	3	0	0
3.	Denis Irwin	4	1	0
4.	David May	0	0	0
5.	Ronny Johnsen	2	0	0
6.	Gary Pallister	5	0	0
7.	David Beckham	3	2	2
8.	Nicky Butt	5	0	1
9.	Andy Cole	1	1	1
10.	Teddy Sheringham	5	0	1
11.	Ryan Giggs	5	0	0
12.	Phil Neville	3	0	0
13.	Brian McClair	0	0	0
14.	Jordi Cruyff	3	0	0
15.	Karel Poborsky	1	1	1
16.	Roy Keane	5	0	1
17.	Rai Van Der Gouw	0	0	0
18.	Paul Scholes	3	1	0
20.	Ole Gunnar Solskjaer	0	0	0
21.	Henning Berg	3	0	0
22.	Erik Nevland	0	0	0
23.	Ben Thornley	0	0	0
24.	John O'Kane	0	0	0
25.	Kevin Pilkington	0	0	0
26.	Chris Casper	0	0	0
27.	Terry Cooke	0	0	0
28.	Phil Mulryne	0	0	0
30.	Ronnie Wallwork	0	0	0
31.	John Curtis	0	0	0
32.	Michael Clegg	0	0	0

PLAYER OF THE MONTH

Ryan Giggs

AVERAGE PERFORMANCE RATING: 7.8

FA CARLING PREMIERSHIP

as at 31 August 1997

	Pld	W	D	L	F	A	Pts	GD
Blackburn Rovers	5	4	1	0	15	4	13	11
Manchester United	5	4	1	0	8	0	13	8
West Ham United	5	3	1	1	9	6	10	3
Chelsea	4	3	0	1	14	5	9	9
Arsenal	5	2	3	0	9	5	9	4
Leicester City	5	2	2	1	6	5	8	1
Tottenham Hotspur	5	2	1	2	5	6	7	-1
Newcastle United	2	2	0	0	3	1	6	2
Crystal Palace	5	2	0	3	5	5	6	0
Barnsley	5	2	0	3	4	10	6	-6
Liverpool	4	1	2	1	5	4	5	1
Coventry City	5	1	2	2	6	10	5	-4
Bolton Wanderers	3	1	1	1	4	4	4	0
Leeds United	5	1	1	3	4	7	4	-3
Sheffield Wednesday	5	1	1	3	6	13	4	-7
Derby County	3	1	0	2	1	2	3	-1
Everton	3	1	0	2	3	5	3	-2
Southampton	5	1	0	4	4	9	3	-5
Aston Villa	5	1	0	4	3	9	3	-6
Wimbledon	4	0	2	2	3	7	2	-4

SEPTEMBER

1 | 2 | 3 | 4 | 5 | 6 | 7 | 8 | 9 | 10 | 11 | 12 | 13 | 14 | 15 | 16 | 17 | 18 | 19 | 20 | 21 | 22 | 23 | 24 | 25 | 26 | 27 | 28 | 29 | 30

SEPTEMBER

THE MONTH AHEAD

September was the month the nation united in mourning over the tragic deaths of Diana Princess of Wales and her boyfriend Dodi Fayed in a car crash in Paris. Incredible floral tributes lined the streets around Buckingham Palace and in city centres across the globe. Diana's funeral service at Westminster Abbey was transmitted to a television audience that ran into hundreds of millions of viewers world-wide.

Just over a week after Diana's death, England played Moldova on an emotional night at Wembley. Elton John's tribute song 'Candle in the Wind' was played before the game and the team responded with a heroic 4–0 win. Paul Gascoigne was the star of the show. He netted one and was joined on the score sheet by Ian Wright with two and the international find of recent years, United's very own Paul Scholes.

Greg Rusedksi failed to keep the red, white and blue ball rolling at the US Open Final, but it wasn't through lack of effort as he shot up to 11th in the rankings. Reaching the Final, he went down to Aussie Pat Rafter, narrowly missing out on becoming the first British male to win a Grand Slam trophy in 61 years.

Asprilla thrilla

Back at Old Trafford, United scraped a 2–1 win over West Ham after the Londoners had taken the lead. Roy Keane – with a little help from John Moncur – equalised and a header from Paul Scholes clinched victory. It was enough for United to go top but Ferguson was a relieved man at the end of the match: "They had two chances late on, so it was a good result for us," he said.

United couldn't afford to become complacent as Arsenal, among others, were breathing down their necks, with Ian Wright on top form. He broke Cliff Bastin's 50-year-old club record of 178 goals for Arsenal with a hat-trick at home to Bolton. He celebrated by ripping off his shirt to reveal a red '179' and later revealed even more to supporters after the game with an impromptu strip from a Highbury window overlooking the street.

Another record breaker was American Jade Kindar-Martin who walked over the Thames on an inch-thick, 1,000 feet long wire. Joined by fellow acrobat, Frenchman Didier Pasquette, their successful attempt was watched by a crowd of well over 10,000. Thankfully they kept their clothes on.

In Europe, United opened their Champions' League campaign with a comfortable 3–0 away win over Slovkia's FC Kosice. The Reds' performance was solid if not as exciting as fellow United's, Newcastle 3–2 home win over the Catalan giants Barcelona. Defenders Irwin and Berg were the unlikely

opening scorers before Cole wrapped it up at the death. Ominously, Juventus won 5–1 at home to Feyenoord. It's rare these days to view a local Manchester derby but United celebrated a victory of sorts over rivals City as famous City fans Mark and Lard were replaced on the Radio One Breakfast Show by celebrity Red Zoe Ball. And local rivalry was very much to the fore in the Greater Manchester derby at Bolton which threatened to spill over into violence but didn't bring any goals. Pallister earned a red card for his 'part' in a tussle with worked up Bolton striker Nathan Blake. The television cameras came to the rescue, however, as the FA looked at video evidence and subsequently cleared Pallister of any wrongdoing.

The midweek game against Chelsea at home was another fiery encounter. Ruud Gullit unusually losing his cool, angry at the assistant referee's decision not to give offside when Paul Scholes raced clear to equalise Henning Berg's own goal.

There were scuffles in the tunnel at half-time and Chelsea, fired up in the second half, raced to a 2–1 lead with former Old Trafford hero Sparky Hughes claiming the second goal. Super sub Ole Gunnar Solksjaer came off the bench to salvage the situation for United with a stunning equaliser.

The world of football was similarly stunned when Al Fayed, father of Dodi, owner of Harrods and successor to Jimmy Hill at Fulham secured the services of Kevin Keegan as Chief Operations Officer. Ray Wilkins was appointed as first team coach.

> # "I just hope I didn't bruise Nathan's hand with my face."
> PALLY AFTER HIS ALTERCATION WITH BOLTON'S NATHAN BLAKE

Another shock arrived when United were untied 1–0 by George Graham's well organised Leeds. A rare Leeds attack saw them claim the only goal from David Weatherall. Ferguson, though, attributed the goal to a rare error by keeper Schmeichel: "Peter knows he is at fault, he has held his hands up. The ball travelled 45 yards so he should have done better." United had to iron out these faults before their next game, the all-important Champions' League clash with Juventus. The Italians were the favourites but the bookies aren't always right, as the European golfers proved in their Ryder Cup triumph over the USA.

Could United possibly make it another great European triumph?

Candles in the wind

MANCHESTER UNITED 2
WEST HAM UNITED 1

HOME TEAM

		RATING
1.	Peter Schmeichel	7
2.	Gary Neville	7
12.	Phil Neville	6
6.	Gary Pallister	5
21.	Henning Berg	6
16.	Roy Keane	9
8.	Nicky Butt	8
7.	David Beckham	6
11.	Ryan Giggs	7
18.	Paul Scholes	7
9.	Andy Cole	6

SUBSTITUTES

		RATING
13.	Brian McClair Cole | 90 mins	6
15.	Karel Poborsky Giggs | 68 mins	7
3.	Denis Irwin	
32.	Michael Clegg	
17.	Rai Van Der Gouw	

SCORERS

Keane | 20 mins
Scholes | 75 mins

REFEREE

D Elleray | Middlesex

VISITORS

		RATING
1.	Ludek Miklosko	7
4.	Steve Potts	7
15.	Rio Ferdinand	8
6.	David Unsworth	7
2.	Tim Breacker	6
29.	Eyal Berkovic	7
16.	John Moncur	6
11.	Steve Lomas	6
24.	Michael Hughes	6
10.	John Hartson	7
9.	Paul Kitson	6

SUBSTITUTES

		RATING
21.	Les Sealey	
18.	Frank Lampard Moncur | 81 mins	6
14.	Iain Dowie	
13.	David Terrier	
12.	Keith Rowland	

SCORERS

Hartson | 14 mins

MATCH REPORT

The script for this game was decided when Harry Redknapp singled out his striker Paul Kitson before the game for special praise. "He makes the most of a chance when he gets it," said Harry. Kitson then spent most of the game proving his manager wrong.

The game started well for West Ham. They became the first team this season to breach United's defence when John Hartson opened the scoring. But Paul Kitson's persistent profligacy prevented the East Londoners from adding to their lead.

United got back into the game through a deflected shot from Roy Keane. The most entertaining aspect of this goal was the ensuing celebration when Gary Neville, David Beckham and Keane formed a trio of contorted faces and jaunted over to goad the West Ham fans who had been asking Beckham if his girlfriend indulged in what the *Star* later called "Sordid sexual practices." Paul Scholes snatched a win for United by heading home 14 minutes from the end.

"We expected a bigger difference between United and West Ham," said the Kosice director who was at Old Trafford on a spying mission. The only difference between the sides was the finishing.

Keane's goal... here

> "I thought we had the three best players on the pitch in Keane, Butt and Scholes."
>
> ALEX FERGUSON

Paul nuts in the winner

33

BOLTON WANDERERS 0
MANCHESTER UNITED 0

HOME TEAM

1.	Keith Brannagan	7
4.	Per Frandsen	9
5.	Gerry Taggart	8
7.	Jamie Pollock	7
8.	Scott Sellars	7
9.	Nathan Blake	6
10.	John McGinlay	6
11.	Alan Thompson	8
12.	Gudni Bergsson	7
21.	Mark Fish	7
22.	Mike Whitlow	7

SUBSTITUTES

13.	Peter Beardsley Sellars | 66 mins	6
14.	Michael Johansen	
16.	Gavin Ward	
17.	Andy Todd	
24.	Steve McAnespie	

REFEREE

P Durkin | Portland

VISITORS

		RATING
1.	Peter Schmeichel	7
2.	Gary Neville	8
3.	Denis Irwin	7
6.	Gary Pallister	6
21.	Henning Berg	8
15.	Karel Poborsky	6
7.	David Beckham	7
16.	Roy Keane	9
8.	Nicky Butt	8
18.	Paul Scholes	6
9.	Andy Cole	7

SUBSTITUTES

20.	Ole G Solskjaer Scholes | 55 mins	7
12.	Phil Neville Poborsky | 55 mins	6
13.	Brian McClair	
23.	Ben Thornley	
17.	Rai Van Der Gouw	

MATCH REPORT

"The manager told us to go out there and play with controlled aggression," revealed Bolton's John McGinlay. There was plenty of aggression from Bolton, but mercilessly little of it controlled.

Both Bolton and United played with little regard for FIFA's Fair Play day. Bolton, harbouring a grievance since they were beaten 6–0 by United, charged around looking to unsettle the Reds.

Gary Pallister was obviously chosen as a target. John McGinlay tried to jump to Pallister's height to headbutt him. Then Nathan Blake took to cleaning his studs on the back of Pallister's calf, an incident which flared up and saw the pair of them sent off. In the whole commotion the referee could be forgiven for thinking that Pallister did more, but it later transpired that all he did was stand there and allow Blake to slap him.

In between the fracas, some football was played. Jamie Pollock missed a chance to give Bolton the lead when Schmeichel dropped the ball at his feet and the closest United came to scoring was when Andy Cole hit the outside of the post.

So the Reebok Stadium had yet to witness a goal and, on this Saturday, it didn't see anything resembling a football match either.

Fergie greets Nathan Blake

Butt evades
Bolton's Fish

Life on
Planet
Reebok

MANCHESTER UNITED 2
CHELSEA 2

HOME TEAM

		RATING
1.	Peter Schmeichel	7
2.	Gary Neville	7
3.	Denis Irwin	7
21.	Henning Berg	6
6.	Gary Pallister	8
8.	Nicky Butt	6
16.	Roy Keane	7
18.	Paul Scholes	7
7.	David Beckham	7
15.	Karel Poborsky	7
9.	Andy Cole	6

SUBSTITUTES

		RATING
11.	Ryan Giggs	7
	G Neville	79 mins	
20.	Ole G Solskjaer	5
	Poborsky	66 mins	
10.	Teddy Sheringham	6
	Scholes	66 mins	
5.	Ronny Johnsen	
17.	Rai Van Der Gouw	

SCORERS

Scholes | 36 mins
Berg | 79 mins og
Solskjaer | 86 mins

REFEREE

G Willard | West Sussex

VISITORS

		RATING
1.	Ed De Goey	7
21.	Paul Hughes	6
5.	Frank Leboeuf	7
18.	Andy Myers	7
14.	Graeme Le Saux	7
8.	Gustavo Poyet	7
11.	Dennis Wise	6
7.	Bernie Lambourde	7
25.	Giafranco Zola	8
2.	Dan Petrescu	8
10.	Mark Hughes	9

SUBSTITUTES

19.	Tore Andre Flo	
	Zola	88 mins	
4.	Ruud Gullit	
9.	Gianluca Vialli	
13.	Kevin Hitchcock	
22.	Mark Nicholls	

SCORERS

Hughes| 68 mins

MATCH REPORT

Ole Gunnar Solskjaer's nonchalant grin did not reveal the importance of his match-saving goal. With just four minutes remaining, Manchester United were at risk of losing for the first time this season, before the Norwegian came off the bench to guide in the equaliser.

Solskjaer's wonderful finish was the one pleasing moment in a match overshadowed by managerial moaning and on-field indiscipline.

Chelsea continued their impressive record at United. They've only been beaten twice in their last 24 visits. The Londoners went ahead when Peter Schmeichel could only parry a shot from Le Saux on to Henning Berg which flew back over him. United drew level when Cole beat the off-side trap and slipped the ball forward for Paul Scholes to score.

Only days earlier Alex Ferguson had expressed his regret at prematurely losing Mark Hughes. The Welshman rubbed it in by giving Chelsea the lead. Then Ole Gunnar Solskjaer announced his return.

Guess who just scored an own goal

IN THE PAPERS

"You need a golden touch and a lion's heart to step into Mark Hughes shoes. To over shadow him on the night of his greatest triumph against his old club, you must be really special. Luckily for Manchester United, Ole Gunner Solskjaer is."
EXPRESS

"This was the type of robust, typically English game we were once assurred foreign players would not relish. But at Old Trafford last night, the imports were to be found in the thick of it all, taking to the blood-and-guts action like ducks to water."
GUARDIAN

"It was the sort of goal you expect of Brazilians. A looping right-footer that curled and kept curling. Ole Gunner Solskjaer is normally known as a tap-in merchant in these parts, the sort of goalscorer who finishes from close in. When he climbed off the bench for his second appearance of the season as a a late sub, the locals would have accepted one off his bottom. Instead they got a spectacular finish they remember from George Best and Bobby Charlton."
DAILY STAR

Scholes celebrates, Chelsea protest

Pure class: Solskjaer

LEEDS UNITED 1

MANCHESTER UNITED 0

HOME TEAM

1.	Nigel Martyn	9
18.	Gunnar Halle	7
6.	David Wetherall	8
5.	Lucas Radebe	7
3.	David Robertson	7
2.	Gary Kelly	7
12.	David Hopkin	7
10.	Bruno Ribeiro	6
4.	Alf-Inge Haaland	7
19.	Harry Kewell	7
8.	Rodney Wallace	7

SUBSTITUTES

30.	Robert Molenaar	6
	Hopkin	78 mins	
17.	Derek Lilley	
15.	Mark Beeney	
11.	Lee Bowyer	
9.	Jimmy Floyd Hasselbaink	

SCORERS

Wetherall | 34 mins

REFEREE

M Bodenham | East Looe

VISITORS   RATING

1.	Peter Schmeichel	6
2.	Gary Neville	6
3.	Denis Irwin	6
6.	Gary Pallister	7
21.	Henning Berg	6
7.	David Beckham	6
16.	Roy Keane	6
15.	Karel Poborsky	6
18.	Paul Scholes	6
10.	Teddy Sheringham	6
20.	Ole G Solskjaer	6

SUBSTITUTES

5.	Ronny Johnsen	6
	Scholes	54 mins	
12.	Phil Neville	6
	G Neville	72 mins	
23.	Ben Thornley	7
	Poborsky	72 mins	
17.	Rai Van Der Gouw	
13.	Brian McClair	

MATCH REPORT

Leeds manager George Graham was honest enough to admit that his team played like the away team. They went ahead through a David Wetherall header in the first half, then put 11 players behind the ball to defend their lead. It was not pretty, but it was effective.

Although the better team, Manchester United just did not have the nous to break Leeds down.

In the final third of the field, United seemed to lack ideas. Lofted crosses from Beckham and Gary Neville were merely swatted away by the towering Wetherall and Radebe. Solskjaer, so inspirational against Chelsea four days earlier, was anonymous and his inaugural pairing with Sheringham was forgettable.

Leeds' keeper Nigel Martyn must have impressed England's goalkeeping coach Ray Clemence who was there to watch him. Two outstanding saves from Martyn were responsible for Leeds' win. He managed to hold on to a Teddy Sheringham header bound for the top corner and then, in the dying seconds, stuck a hand out to deny a close-range header from Gary Pallister.

Peter Schmeichel's jaunt up from goal to attempt an overhead kick in injury time just about summed up United's desperation. But it was not enough to save the Reds' unbeaten record.

Done in the neck

IN THE PAPERS

"The better side lost this game, and that's no disrespect to Leeds, who battled throughout. It's been a bad week for the Champions; one point from six is a sad statistic that will be over shadowed by the antics of Roy Keane and one or two others."
DAILY STAR

"For one reason, and one reason only, Fergie looks effectively to have lost half a team with Roy Keane leaving the stadium on crutches. The Irishman's buccaneering week, full of anger and aggro, ended in one fall and submission amid a tangle of legs."
SUN

"Roy Keane needed a pair of crutches to make a pain-wrecked exit from Elland Road. Listen to Aalf Inge Haaland for a couple of minutes you can't help but feel a straightjacket would have been more appropriate."
DAILY MIRROR

"Schmeichel looked to be coming out for the decisive left-wing free-kick from Leeds midfield man Kelly late in the first half. But he fatally changed his mind, threw his defence into chaos and presented home defender Wetherall with the chance to soar above Pallister and power home the decisive header."
PEOPLE

Weatherall clinches the win for Leeds

September STATS

PLAYER RECORDS

home | away
- PREMIERSHIP
- COCA-COLA CUP ■ FA CUP

		FULL APPEARANCES	SUB APPEARANCES	GOALS
1.	Peter Schmeichel	9	0	0
2.	Gary Neville	7	0	0
3.	Denis Irwin	7	1	0
4.	David May	0	0	0
5.	Ronny Johnsen	2	1	0
6.	Gary Pallister	9	0	0
7.	David Beckham	7	2	2
8.	Nicky Butt	8	0	1
9.	Andy Cole	4	1	1
10.	Teddy Sheringham	6	1	1
11.	Ryan Giggs	6	1	0
12.	Phil Neville	4	2	0
13.	Brian McClair	0	1	0
14.	Jordi Cruyff	3	0	0
15.	Karel Poborsky	4	2	1
16.	Roy Keane	9	0	2
17.	Rai Van Der Gouw	0	0	0
18.	Paul Scholes	7	1	2
20.	Ole Gunnar Solskjaer	1	2	1
21.	Henning Berg	7	0	0
22.	Erik Nevland	0	0	0
23.	Ben Thornley	0	1	0
24.	John O'Kane	0	0	0
25.	Kevin Pilkington	0	0	0
26.	Chris Casper	0	0	0
27.	Terry Cooke	0	0	0
28.	Phil Mulryne	0	0	0
30.	Ronnie Wallwork	0	0	0
31.	John Curtis	0	0	0
32.	Michael Clegg	0	0	0

Key:
- FULL APPEARANCE / CAME ON AS SUB
- FULL APPEARANCE / GAME ON AS SUB
- SCORER / SCORED AS SUB

PLAYER OF THE MONTH

Roy Keane

AVERAGE PERFORMANCE RATING: 7.8

FA CARLING PREMIERSHIP

as at 27 September 1997

	Pld	W	D	L	F	A	Pts	GD
▲ Arsenal	9	5	4	0	22	10	19	12
■ Manchester United	9	5	3	1	12	4	18	8
▲ Leicester City	9	5	3	1	13	6	18	7
■ Chelsea	8	5	1	2	22	10	16	12
▼ Blackburn Rovers	8	4	3	1	19	9	15	10
▲ Leeds United	9	4	1	4	11	11	13	0
▼ West Ham United	9	4	1	4	12	14	13	-1
▲ Derby County	7	4	0	3	14	7	12	7
▲ Liverpool	8	3	3	2	12	8	12	14
▼ Newcastle United	6	4	0	2	6	5	12	1
▼ Crystal Palace	9	3	2	4	9	11	11	-2
■ Coventry City	8	2	4	2	8	11	10	-3
▼ Tottenham Hotspur	9	2	4	3	6	10	10	-4
▲ Aston Villa	9	3	1	5	10	15	10	-5
▲ Wimbledon	8	2	3	3	10	10	9	0
▼ Bolton Wanderers	8	1	5	2	8	11	8	-3
■ Everton	8	2	2	4	10	13	8	-3
▼ Sheffield Wednesday	9	1	3	5	11	22	8	-11
▼ Barnsley	9	2	0	7	7	23	6	-16
▼ Southampton	9	1	1	7	5	17	4	-12

OCTOBER

1 | 2 | 3 | 4 | 5 | 6 | 7 | 8 | 9 | 10 | 11 | 12 | 13 | 14 | 15 | 16 | 17 | 18 | 19 | 20 | 21 | 22 | 23 | 24 | 25 | 26 | 27 | 28 | 29 | 30 | 31

OCTOBER

THE MONTH AHEAD

October got off to a bad start as it was revealed skipper Roy Keane would be out for the rest of the season. A challenge on Leeds' Alf-Inge Haalalnd left Keane with serious cruciate ligament damage to his right knee.

Better news for fans came on the commercial front. Linking with Sky and Granada, United confirmed they would be the first club to launch its own TV channel. From the beginning of 1998/99, fans will be able to see up to six hours of coverage a day – if their partners allow it.

To get the month off to a flying start, United played host to Juventus in the Champions' League. The Old Lady of Turin quickly silenced the home support with a strike from Del Piero after just 19 seconds. United reacted with maturity and style. Goals by Sheringham, Scholes and a scorcher from Ryan Giggs completed mission impossible. Zinedine Zidane's last minute free-kick made a few hearts flutter, but United held on for one of their most memorable victories ever.

Injured Diana bodyguard Trevor Rees-Jones was released from a Paris hospital. With his left arm in plaster, he cut a more popular figure on his arrival in England than Andrew Morton. The biographer of *Diana: Her True Story* whipped up a storm of controversy when he chose to release a new edition just weeks after her death. Chris Evans, on the other hand, gave the whole of his £200,000 salary for his breakfast show to the Memorial Fund set up in her name.

United resumed their defence of the League title with a 2–0 win over Crystal Palace. It was all over by half-time with a Sheringham strike and an own goal from Hreiderson, Palace's new recruit from Iceland – the country, not the shop. Nothing, it seemed, could keep United out of the news. Posh Spice and David Beckham's relationship pitched camp in the front pages of the tabloids. The singer revealed that she had no plans to join David in Manchester on the grounds that there were "Not many nice shops in Manchester, no Prada or Gucci." She was instantly re-named "Snobby Spice".

England flew over for the vital clash with Italy in Rome. Hoddle's boys needed to avoid defeat to qualify automatically, whilst Italy required all three points. Captained by former United idol Paul "Guinness" Ince, England did the nation proud. But not without some scares. Following an Ian Wright shot deep into injury time that hit the post, Italy surged forward and, when Del Piero planted a

Rome glory boys

Juve destroyed

Is this the end of United's season?

cross on the head of Vieri, they looked certain to score. His header went past the post and consigned Italy to the play-offs.

The victory brought the nation together, but unemployed Man United fan Kevin Morgan wasn't so lucky. His wife Emma divorced him because of his obsession with the Reds. Typical behaviour included watching repeats of United games up to 20 hours a day. Another marriage was also in trouble. Family man Glenn Hoddle revealed his separation from wife Anne after 18 years. Much to the embarrassment of *Shredded Wheat*.

The Coca-Cola Cup had lost its fizz for Alex Ferguson. Fielding a "weakened" team away to Ipswich, the FA threatened to kick the Reds out of the competition. In the end it wasn't necessary, as a plucky Ipswich side did the damage with goals from Alex Mathie and Mauricio Taricco.

In the Premiership, United, outclassed away to high-flying Derby County, were saved by the late introduction of supersub Andy Cole. County went two up by half-time through the Italian Baiano and leggy Costa Rican Paulo Wanchope. Sheringham's goal made up for another missed penalty and Cole's late strike saved the day.

The Champions' League took centre

"I wish people would get it into their heads that Juventus are not invincible."

JUVENTUS COACH MARCELLO LIPPI

stage again at Old Trafford. A wonderfully improvised strike from Paul "Goals" Scholes and a confident penalty from Denis Irwin saw United come through. A late goal from Henk Vos, though, created a nervy end to the night.

Back in the Premiership, Andy Cole silenced the cynics with a hat-trick against struggling Barnsley in a 7–0 win. Ryan Giggs too weighed in with an electric performance and two goals.

Off the field, the month ended with a shock life jail sentence for 19-year-old Cheshire nanny Louise Woodward. An American jury found her guilty of the murder of a boy in her care. Immediately her defence team launched an appeal as supporters protested her innocence.

MANCHESTER UNITED 2
CRYSTAL PALACE 0

HOME TEAM

	RATING
1. Peter Schmeichel	9
2. Gary Neville	7
21. Henning Berg	6
6. Gary Palister	7
12. Phil Neville	7
7. David Beckham	7
19. Ronny Johnsen	7
8. Nicky Butt	7
18. Paul Scholes	7
10. Teddy Sheringham	7
11. Ryan Giggs	8

SUBSTITUTES

3. Denis Irwin P. Neville | 84 mins	6
15. Karel Poborsky Johnsen | 70 mins	5
4. David May	
13. Brian McClair	
17. Rai Van Der Gouw	

SCORERS

Sheringham | 17 mins
Hreiderson | og 30 mins

REFEREE

S Lodge | Barnsley

VISITORS

1. Kevin Miller	6
2. Marc Edworthy	6
6. Andy Linighan	6
4. Andy Roberts	6
22. Herman Hreiderson	7
3. Dean Gordon	7
7. Atillo Lombardo	7
26. Jamie Fullarton	6
14. Simon Rodger	6
18. George Ndah	7
8. Paul Warhurst	6

SUBSTITUTES

11. Dougie Freedman Linighan | 70 mins	6
27. Itzik Zoher Lombardo | 84 mins	6
9. Neil Shipperley	
17. Kevin Muscat	
25. Gareth Ormshaw	

MATCH REPORT

Three days earlier United had dismissed a whole *team* of Italians, so Palace's solitary one was never going to be a problem as United secured victory with a mediocre performance.

"You're bound to get a falling-off period at some stage after a night like we had on Wednesday," observed Alex Ferguson. "Palace might have had a couple in the second half, but I think if they had got one, we'd have put our foot back on the pedal."

The inevitable hangover from Juventus and Roy Keane's season-ending injury made for a strange, diluted atmosphere at Old Trafford. Teddy Sheringham's first Premiership goal at Old Trafford, an impressive volley from close range, briefly livened up proceedings before Hreiderson poked in David Beckham's over-hit cross to kill the game as a spectacle.

United's post-Europe lethargy was in evidence when they failed to build on their lead. Giggs and then Beckham contrived to miss the target with only the goalkeeper to beat.

Peter Schmeichel clearly enjoyed his new role as captain, stopping Palace on three occasions after they had beaten the offside trap.

IN THE PAPERS

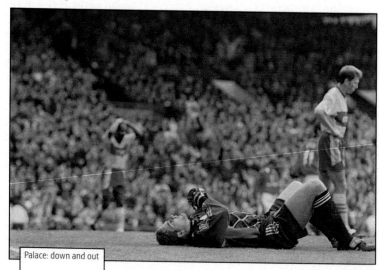

Palace: down and out

The first of many

Giggs stopped in his tracks

IPSWICH TOWN 2
MANCHESTER UNITED 0

HOME TEAM

1.	Richard Wright	7
2.	Mick Stockwell	7
3.	Mauricio Taricco	8
4.	Geraint Williams	6
5.	Tony Mowbray	7
6.	Jason Cundy	7
7.	Kieron Dyer	8
8.	Matt Holland	7
9.	Alex Mathie	8
10.	Jason Dozzell	8
11.	Bobby Petta	8

SUBSTITUTES

12.	Mark Stein	7
	Williams	84 mins	
13.	Lee Bracey	
14.	Simon Milton	7
	Petta	73 mins	

SCORERS

Mathie | 14 mins
Taricco | 45 mins

REFEREE

P Alcock | Redhill, Surrey

VISITORS

		RATING
1.	Rai Van Der Gouw	7
2.	John Curtis	8
3.	Phil Neville	6
4.	David May	7
5.	Brian McClair	6
6.	Ronny Johnsen	6
7.	Karel Poborsky	6
8.	Phil Mulryne	6
9.	Andy Cole	6
10.	Jordi Cruyff	6
11.	Ben Thornley	6

SUBSTITUTES

12.	Denis Irwin	6
	Johnsen	74 mins	
13.	Erik Nevland	7
	Mulryne	74 mins	
14.	Paul Scholes	7
	Thornley	65 mins	

MATCH REPORT

Threatened with expulsion from the competition by the Football League, Manchester United did a good job of expelling themselves at Portman Road.

Alex Ferguson was far from distraught at the loss. Tiring trips to East Anglia are not what he needs when he would rather conquer Turin and Madrid.

United's weakened team was not an acceptable excuse for this defeat. Brimming with internationals and yet more promising youngsters, they should have done better. While John Curtis and Phillip Mulryne impressed on their debuts, Poborsky and Cruyff failed to take the opportunity to impose themselves against lesser opponents.

Ipswich swept into a two-goal lead by half-time. Alex Mathie stroked in Jason Dozzell's pass past Van Der Gouw after 13 minutes and then the Argentinian Mauricio Taricco produced a stunning shot from 25 yards just before half-time.

United improved in the second half and had an Andy Cole goal cancelled out for offside, but seemingly didn't have the desire to overhaul Ipswich's lead.

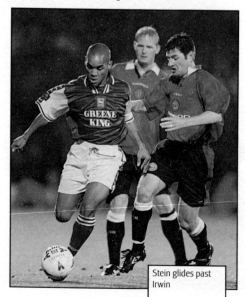

Stein glides past Irwin

IN THE PAPERS

"Manchester United payed the price for their undisguised contempt for the Coca-Cola Cup. They decided they could do without seven key players, including World Cup heroes David Beckham and Teddy Sheringham, as well as Ryan Giggs. Boss Alex Ferguson could still boast nine internationals at Portman Road."
SUN

"Alex Feguson can pick any team he likes, whenever he likes – but this was no Manchester United team he sent out last night. The only similarities between this side and that of the Premiership Champions of England is that they played in the same colour shirts."
DAILY STAR

"Any tears from Alex Ferguson, who normally hates defeat with a vengeance, would have been of the crocodile variety last night. The United manager has made no secret that the League Cup comes a lowly fourth on his list of priorities and the indifference was reflected in the shadow of his side's performance."
TELEGRAPH

"United had little excuse for defensive naivety, given that their backline included May, Johnsen and Phil Neville, but they were caught in disarray when Dozzell received possession on the edge of the penalty area. Twice tackles were missed, and the former Spurs player was able to square the ball to the unmarked Mathie near the penalty spot for a simple, side-footed finish."
TIMES

Phil Mulryne in full flight

Mathie makes

DERBY COUNTY 2
MANCHESTER UNITED 2

HOME TEAM
RATING

21.	Mart Poom	8
2.	Gary Rowett	7
22.	Christian Dailly	7
16.	Jacob Laursen	7
4.	Darryl Powell	7
7.	Robin Van Der Laan	6
18.	Lee Carsley	7
15.	Paul Trollope	7
8.	Dean Sturridge	6
27.	Francesco Baiano	8
9.	Paulo Wanchope	9

SUBSTITUTES

24.	Deon Burton	6
	Baiano	68 mins	
26.	Jonathan Hunt	6
	Van Der Laan	78 mins	
23.	Mauricio Polis	
25.	Robert Kozluk	
1.	Russell Hoult	

SCORERS

Baiano | 24 mins
Wanchope | 39 mins

REFEREE

Graeme Poll | Tring

VISITORS
RATING

1.	Peter Schmeichel	6
2.	Gary Neville	7
21.	Henning Berg	6
6.	Gary Pallister	7
3.	Denis Irwin	6
7.	David Beckham	6
8.	Nicky Butt	8
18.	Paul Scholes	6
11.	Ryan Giggs	8
10.	Teddy Sheringham	6
20.	Ole G Solskjaer	6

SUBSTITUTES

5.	Ronny Johnsen	8
	Butt	45 mins	
9.	Andy Cole	7
	Scholes	71 mins	
12.	Phil Neville	6
	Irwin	88 mins	
13.	Brian McClair	
17.	Rai Van Der Gouw	

SCORERS

Sheringham | 51 mins
Cole | 84 mins

MATCH REPORT

After skipping through the entire United defence on his Premiership debut at Old Trafford, Paulo Wanchope came up with the perfect encore: doing it again.

A simple tap-in is not good enough for Wanchope; when he scores, he has to humiliate his opponents. After Baiano had given Derby the lead, Wanchope set off on another stunning run. He shrugged off Gary Neville and slipped the ball through Henning Berg's legs before slotting it past Schmeichel.

United's first-half display was quite appalling. Passes were over-hit, tackles were lost and, to top it all, Teddy Sheringham missed another penalty.

United were transformed for the second half. Only six minutes into it, Gary Neville sent over a cross for Sheringham to glance in and, Cole, on as a substitute, came on and promptly delivered the equaliser with just five minutes remaining.

Rams raiding

IN THE PAPERS

MANCHESTER UNITED 7
BARNSLEY 0

HOME TEAM

1.	Peter Schmeichel	7
2.	Gary Neville	6
6.	Gary Pallister	7
12.	Phil Neville	7
31.	John Curtis	8
8.	Nicky Butt	7
7.	David Beckham	6
11.	Ryan Giggs	9
18.	Paul Scholes	8
20.	Ole G Solskjaer	7
9.	Andy Cole	9

SUBSTITUTES

10.	Teddy Sheringham	
14.	Jordi Cruyff	6
	Scholes	68 mins	
15.	Karel Poborsky	8
	Beckham	56 mins	
30.	Ronnie Wallwork	7
	Pallister	63 mins	
13.	Brian McClair	

SCORERS

Cole | 17/19/45 mins
Giggs | 43/57 mins
Scholes | 59 mins
Poborsky | 80 mins

REFEREE

A Riley | Leeds

VISITORS   RATING

1.	David Watson	5
2.	Nicky Eaden	6
4.	Darren Sheridan	5
6.	Arjan De Zeeuw	6
8.	Neil Redfearn	7
11.	Neil Thompson	5
14.	Martin Bullock	7
22.	Georgi Hristov	5
23.	Ales Krizan	6
24.	Darren Barnard	5
25.	Ashley Ward	6

SUBSTITUTES

5.	Arian Moses	6
	Krizan	58 mins	
7.	John Hendrie	6
	Hristov	58 mins	
10.	Clint Marcelle	
13.	Lars Leese	
15.	Jovo Bosancic	5
	Thompson	69 mins	

MATCH REPORT

Too often during his time at Old Trafford, Andy Cole has welcomed his goals with a look of sheer relief, but after every goal of his hat-trick against Barnsley he celebrated with his old arrogance. This was his day. He clenched his fist, asked the crowd to read the name on his shirt and delighted in the acclaim.

His hat-trick was an example of clinical finishing. For his first, he latched on to a poor back pass, rounded a defender and fired the ball past Watson. A minute later, he scored with a low first-time shot from the edge of the area and then, just before half-time, he ran on to a through ball from Giggs and placed the ball past the unfortunate Watson.

Hat-trick scorers are rarely upstaged, but Ryan Giggs nearly managed it. He complimented his running with two exquisite goals from the kind of finishing that too frequently eludes him. Paul Scholes and Karel Poborsky got in the act with fine goals of their own.

But Barnsley manager Danny Wilson found time to smile, "There was nothing between the teams, except seven goals!" he said, ruefully.

IN THE PAPERS

Nice one, Ryan

Cole scores
the second

57 minutes:
time stands still

October STATS

PLAYER RECORDS

■ PREMIERSHIP
■ COCA COLA CUP ■ FA CUP

home | away

FULL APPEARANCE
CAME ON AS SUB

SCORER
SCORED AS SUB

Match columns (left to right): Tottenham Hotspur, Southampton, Leicester City, Everton, West Ham United, Bolton Wanderers, Chelsea, Leeds United, Crystal Palace, Ipswich Town, Derby County, Barnsley, Sheffield Wednesday, Arsenal, Wimbledon, Blackburn Rovers, Liverpool, Aston Villa, Newcastle United, Coventry City, Tottenham Hotspur, Southampton, Walsall, Leicester City, Chelsea, Bolton Wanderers, West Ham United, FA Cup Round Five, Derby County, Chelsea, Sheffield Wednesday, Arsenal, Wimbledon, Blackburn Rovers, FA Cup Round Six, Liverpool, FA Cup Semi Final, Newcastle United, Aston Villa, Crystal Palace, Leeds United, Barnsley, FA Cup Final

	FULL APPEARANCES	SUB APPEARANCES	GOALS
1. Peter Schmeichel	13	0	0
2. Gary Neville	10	0	0
3. Denis Irwin	8	3	0
4. David May	1	0	0
5. Ronny Johnsen	4	2	0
6. Gary Pallister	12	0	0
7. David Beckham	10	2	2
8. Nicky Butt	11	0	1
9. Andy Cole	6	2	5
10. Teddy Sheringham	8	1	3
11. Ryan Giggs	9	1	2
12. Phil Neville	7	2	0
13. Brian McClair	1	1	0
14. Jordi Cruyff	4	1	0
15. Karel Poborsky	5	4	2
16. Roy Keane	9	0	2
17. Rai Van Der Gouw	0	0	0
18. Paul Scholes	10	2	3
20. Ole Gunnar Solskjaer	3	2	1
21. Henning Berg	9	0	0
22. Erik Nevland	0	1	0
23. Ben Thornley	1	1	0
24. John O'Kane	0	0	0
25. Kevin Pilkington	0	0	0
26. Chris Casper	0	0	0
27. Terry Cooke	0	0	0
28. Phil Mulryne	1	0	0
30. Ronnie Wallwork	0	1	0
31. John Curtis	2	0	0
32. Michael Clegg	0	0	0

PLAYER OF THE MONTH

Nicky Butt

AVERAGE PERFORMANCE RATING: 7.5

FA CARLING PREMIERSHIP

as at 25 October 1997

	Pld	W	D	L	F	A	Pts	GD
▲ Manchester United	12	7	4	1	23	6	25	17
▼ Arsenal	11	6	5	0	27	10	23	17
▲ Blackburn Rovers	12	6	5	1	22	10	23	12
■ Chelsea	10	6	1	3	25	14	19	11
▲ Liverpool	11	5	3	3	20	12	18	8
▼ Leicester City	11	5	3	3	14	9	18	5
▲ Derby County	11	5	2	4	19	15	17	4
▼ Leeds United	12	5	2	5	15	13	17	2
▲ Wimbledon	12	4	4	4	14	13	16	1
■ Newcastle United	9	5	1	3	9	10	16	-1
▼ West Ham United	11	5	1	5	15	17	16	-2
▼ Crystal Palace	12	4	3	5	12	14	15	-2
▲ Aston Villa	11	4	1	6	12	17	13	-5
▼ Tottenham Hotspur	12	3	4	5	11	16	13	-5
▼ Coventry City	12	2	7	3	8	13	13	-5
▲ Everton	11	3	3	5	13	16	12	-3
▲ Southampton	12	3	1	8	11	20	10	-9
■ Sheffield Wednesday	12	2	3	7	17	29	9	-12
■ Barnsley	12	3	0	9	9	35	9	-26
▼ Bolton Wanderers	10	1	5	4	8	15	8	-7

NOVEMBER

1 | 2 | 3 | 4 | 5 | 6 | 7 | 8 | 9 | 10 | 11 | 12 | 13 | 14 | 15 | 16 | 17 | 18 | 19 | 20 | 21 | 22 | 23 | 24 | 25 | 26 | 27 | 28 | 29 | 30

NOVEMBER

THE MONTH AHEAD

United started the month off with a top v bottom clash against David Pleat's Sheffield Wednesday, and literally hit the Yorkshiremen for six. It was too much for the Wednesday board, who promptly sacked their manager. There were also fireworks at Maine Road as City fans went on the rampage after losing 3–2 at home to Port Vale... Port Vale!

In midweek, it was back to the Champions' League and it was good and bad news for United. They beat Feyenoord 3–1 in Rotterdam with an Andy Cole hat-trick, but lost the services of Denis Irwin for two months after a horror tackle by Paul Bosvelt. Amazingly, reports to UEFA by match officials didn't even mention the incident. Meanwhile, strikerless Newcastle virtually went out of the competition after losing 2–0 at home to PSV Eindhoven.

November also saw Michael Schumacher in disgrace after attempting to ram Jacques Villeneuve off the track in the F1 showdown in Spain – only to go off himself and hand the Canadian the title. The FIA shamefully decided not to ban or fine the German, who had got away with similar behaviour two years

before against Damon Hill. Meanwhile, there was another casualty in the managerial merry-go-round: the Spice Girls' gaffer Simon Fuller who had broken Baby Spice's heart after a torrid affair... allegedly. United fans' hearts were broken too, as Arsenal beat them 3–2 with a late headed goal from David Platt.

With England playing the Cameroon at the weekend, there was a fortnight's break from domestic football in the middle of the month. But the newspapers had plenty to talk about. Judge Hiller Zobel freed Louise Woodward, the Brazilian Government refused to extradite Ronnie Biggs, 60 tourists, including 8 Brits, were slaughtered in the Luxor temple massacre in Egypt, INXS singer Michael Hutchence mysteriously hanged himself

Bosvelt shame

> ## "Everyone is talking about United as if they are the only team in the country."
>
> ARSENE WENGER

in a Sydney hotel room and Gary Glitter found himself in hot water after taking his PC to be mended.

On the soccer front, former United boss Ron "Bojangles" Atkinson was appointed manager of Sheffield Wednesday.

In the international friendly, England beat Cameroon with two goals in a minute just before half-time. The first was a cheeky chip over the onrushing keeper by Scholes, making it three goals in five international appearances. Bobby Charlton's 49-goal record already looks under threat. Meanwhile Italy beat Russia in the play-offs to qualify for France '98 alongside Croatia, Yugoslavia and Belgium, who edged out a Keane-less, Irwin-less Eire.

There was another team of world-beaters in the country. The New Zealand Rugby Union team defeated England 25–8 at Twickers, despite Richard Cockerill's disruption of the pre-match Haka. Another Antipodean team, El Tel's Australian Socceroos, were looking good for the World Cup after a 1–1 draw in Iran.

Earl Spencer found the press biting back when they learnt he was accused of being a serial adulterer, having allegedly slept with 12 women in five months while his wife was in a clinic fighting alcoholism.

Meanwhile, United clinched Champions' League qualification by beating Kosice 3–0, having racked up £7.2 million on the way.

Down under, El Tel was in despair after Australia went out of the World Cup in the cruellest fashion – on away goals. Fergie was a much happier manager the next day: United thrashed their nearest rivals Blackburn 4–0. Roll on December.

Big Ron back in management

Serves him right

MANCHESTER UNITED 6
SHEFFIELD WEDNESDAY 1

HOME TEAM

1.	Peter Schmeichel	7
2.	Gary Neville	8
3.	Denis Irwin	8
6.	Gary Pallister	8
21.	Henning Berg	7
7.	David Beckham	8
8.	Nicky Butt	8
9.	Andy Cole	9
10.	Teddy Sheringham	7
20.	Ole G Solskjaer	9
18.	Paul Scholes	7

SUBSTITUTES

15.	Karel Poborsky	7
	Scholes	55 mins	
31.	John Curtis	7
	Berg	75 mins	
13.	Brian McClair	7
	Butt	75 mins	

SCORERS

Newsome | og 20 mins
Cole | 38 mins
Sheringham | 13/63 mins
Solskjaer | 41/75 mins

REFEREE

Gerald Ashby | Worcester

VISITORS

		RATING
1.	Kevin Pressman	5
3.	Ian Nolan	5
4.	Mark Pembridge	5
5.	Jon Newsome	5
6.	Des Walker	6
7.	Guy Whittingham	6
8.	Benito Carbone	6
11.	Paolo Di Canio	6
20.	Wayne Collins	6
24.	Jim Magilton	6
25.	Petter Rudi	7

SUBSTITUTES

14.	Steve Nicol	6
	Carbone	45 mins	
16.	Ritchie Humphreys	6
	Di Canio	45 mins	
21.	Adem Poric	
	Collins	75 mins	

SCORERS

Whittingham | 69 mins

MATCH REPORT

Manchester United are a team in decline. After scoring seven a week earlier against Barnsley, they could only manage a mere six against Sheffield Wednesday. Afterwards, Wednesday keeper Kevin Pressman described the experience as "horrific" as he watched the goals fly past him as United recorded their biggest ever win over the Owls.

For the first time this season Ferguson started with his full compliment of strikers: Andy Cole, Ole Gunnar Solskjaer and Teddy Sheringham. It worked wonderfully. United went through the Wednesday defence with ease and each striker should have claimed a hat-trick.

Solskjaer's finishing was as clinical as ever, Cole's renewed confidence brought him his two goals and Sheringham took his chances well.

Gary Pallister was asked after the game if he could remember the last time so many goals flew in in consecutive matches, "Oh yes! Against Newcastle and Southampton last year." This time last autumn, Schmeichel watched as 11 goals whizzed past him in consecutive games. A year on, this performance showed United have emerged as a stronger, more mature outfit.

Cole heads in United's third

IN THE PAPERS

"Alex Ferguson watched his goal-hungry strikers mastermind this demolition of Sheffield Wednesday and then admitted, "It should have been NINE." The Manchester United manager is delighted the team, so often accused of being goal-shy, followed their 7–0 win over Barnsley with a six-goal win yesterday."
SUNDAY TIMES

"The message from Manchester United was clear – when you go to Old Trafford either batten down the hatches or prepare to be swept away."
EXPRESS

"Alex Ferguson is waltzing into Europe with a magnum of a bubbly and a team cascading with goals. The champagne, from winning the manager of the month award was surely uncorked last night to toast his magnificent champions."
SUNDAY MIRROR

"With 20 minutes on the clock, Wednesday were doomed. Again they were undone by an intricate one-two between Cole and Sheringham, and as Walker tried to clear, the ball rebounded off Pembridge, ricocheted off Cole, and squirmed into the net."
OBSERVER

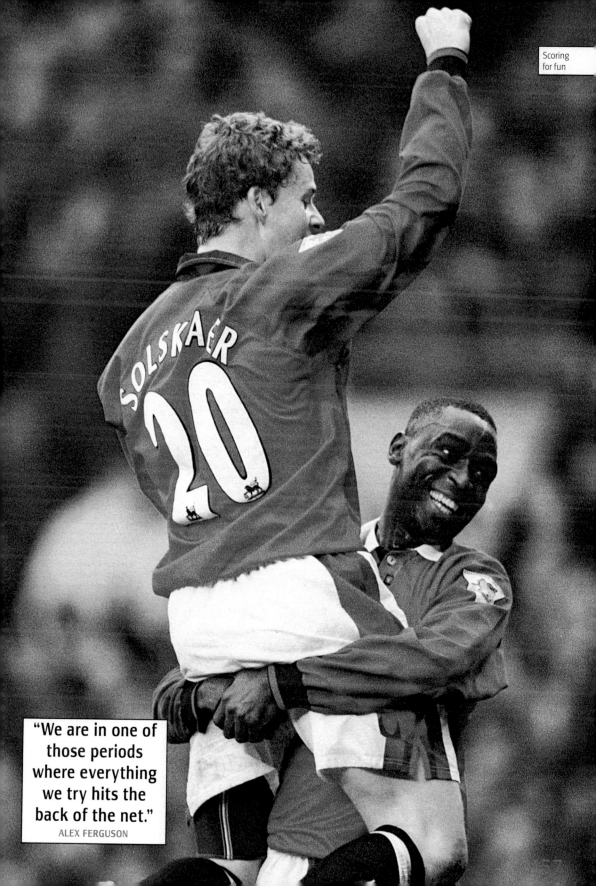

"We are in one of
those periods
where everything
we try hits the
back of the net."
ALEX FERGUSON

ARSENAL 3
MANCHESTER UNITED 2

HOME TEAM

1.	David Seaman	7
2.	Lee Dixon	7
3.	Nigel Winterburn	7
4.	Patrick Vieira	8
6.	Tony Adams	8
7.	David Platt	7
8.	Ian Wright	7
9.	Nicholas Anelka	7
11.	Marc Overmars	7
15.	Ray Parlour	8
18.	Gilles Grimandi	6

SUBSTITUTES

5.	Steve Bould	6
	Vieira I 45 mins	
12.	Christopher Wreh	
28.	Stephen Hughes	
	Anelka I 79 mins	
21.	Luis Boa Morte	
13.	Alex Manninger	

SCORERS

Anelka I 7 mins
Vieira I 27 mins
Platt I 83 mins

REFEREE

M Bodenham I West Sussex

VISITORS   RATING

1.	Peter Schmeichel	7
2.	Gary Neville	7
6.	Gary Pallister	6
12.	Phil Neville	6
21.	Henning Berg	7
8.	Nicky Butt	8
7.	David Beckham	7
11.	Ryan Giggs	7
18.	Paul Scholes	6
10.	Teddy Sheringham	8
9.	Andy Cole	7

SUBSTITUTES

5.	Ronny Johnsen	7
	Pallister I 39 mins	
20.	Ole G Solskjaer	6
	Giggs I 72 mins	
13.	Brian McClair	
15.	Karel Poborsky	
17.	Rai Van Der Gouw	

SCORERS

Sheringham I 33/41 mins

MATCH REPORT

The nation cheered United's defeat at Highbury. Threatening to run away with the title, United were dragged back by Arsenal with a late winner from former United apprentice David Platt.

Arsenal's win was all the more remarkable because they achieved it without the suspended Bergkamp and Petit. It was left to Anelka and Viera to give Arsenal a two-goal lead with fine strikes in the first half-hour.

But they failed to stay out in front for long. Teddy Sheringham, keen to respond to the abuse he received for his Tottenham past, brought United level with two goals in the space of eight minutes. The first was a well-taken header, the second was a wonderful volley on the turn that was in before Seaman had moved.

Half-time saved Arsenal from going further behind, but the Londoners regrouped and emerged as the better team in the second half. The introduction of Bould shored up the defence and Arsenal attacked with greater confidence. Wreh went close before Platt's looping header pinched the points.

Johnsen plays Parlour games

IN THE PAPERS

"With 16 goals in the previous three games – while the Gunners have been goalless – United seemed unstoppable, and it was an amazing turnabout for Wenger to mastermind Arsenal's first win against United in 14 games."
MIRROR

"The forgotten David Platt transformed the Premiership from a procession into a genuine title race with a glorious header that used to be his trademark."
SUN

"Ferguson's visitors looked so composed, so confident on the ball but were unable to turn possession into penetration. Arsenal made more out of less. Within nine minutes they were ahead, Nicholas Anelka exploiting the carnage created by a Marc Overmars run with a crisp drive that beat the mightly Peter Schmeichel at the near post."
TELEGRAPH

"Arsenal injected hope into themselves and the top half of the Premiership yesterday when they grabbed hold of Manchester United's reins and gave them a severe tug. Talk of runaway leaders and one-horse races have been silenced temporarily."
INDEPENDENT

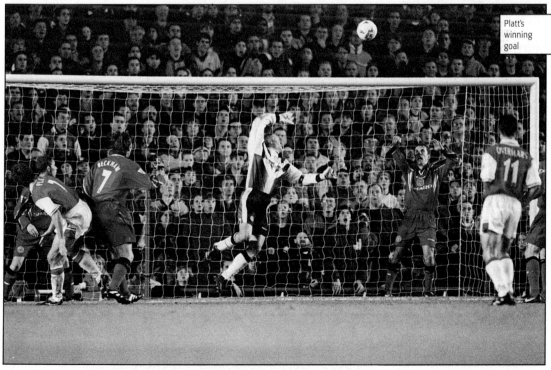

WIMBLEDON 2
MANCHESTER UNITED 5

HOME TEAM

1.	Neil Sullivan	6
2.	Kenny Cunningham	6
4.	Vinny Jones	7
5.	Dean Blackwell	7
6.	Ben Thatcher	6
7.	Ceri Hughes	6
11.	Marcus Gayle	7
12.	Chris Perry	6
16.	Michael Hughes	7
18.	Neil Ardley	6
26.	Carl Cort	7

SUBSTITUTES

8.	Robbie Earle	6
	Jones	85 mins	
22.	Andy Clarke	6
	Hughes	85 mins	
10.	Stale Solbakken	6
	Ardley	85 mins	
3.	Alan Kimble	
13.	Paul Heald	

SCORERS

Neil Ardley | 68 mins
Michael Hughes | 70 mins

REFEREE

P Durkin | Dorset

VISITORS

RATING

1.	Peter Schmeichel	7
2.	Gary Neville	6
21.	Henning Berg	6
6.	Gary Pallister	6
12.	Phil Neville	6
8.	Nicky Butt	7
5.	Ronny Johnsen	7
11.	Ryan Giggs	8
18.	Paul Scholes	9
10.	Teddy Sheringham	7
9.	Andy Cole	8

SUBSTITUTES

7.	David Beckham	8
	Gary Neville	66 mins	
20.	Ole G Solskjaer	
15.	Karel Poborsky	
31.	John Curtis	
17.	Rai Van Der Gouw	

SCORERS

Nicky Butt | 48 mins
David Beckham | 67/75 mins
Paul Scholes | 82 mins
Andy Cole | 86 mins

MATCH REPORT

Manchester United's visits to Selhurst Park always guarantee entertainment. In the last four years, United have clinched the title there, hosted a celebration party, seen Eric Cantona leap in to the crowd and witnessed David Beckham's 57-yard goal. On this occasion, they shared seven goals in a flattering 5–2 win over Joe Kinnear's Wimbledon fighters.

This win took United's goal tally to 23 in their last 5 matches, but the scoreless first half gave no clue to what lay ahead. "At half-time, it was 0–0 and we were jubilant," said Wimbledon's captain Vinnie Jones. "Then, bang, they score. Just when you think you've got them, they turn it on and score goals from everywhere."

Nicky Butt opened the scoring three minutes after the break; Beckham tapped in the second. Wimbledon responded with two goals in a minute from Ardley and Hughes to draw level, but it was a false revival and United regained the lead through Beckham's deflected shot. Scholes gained the goal his performance deserved, as did Cole when his left-footed drive beat Sullivan at the near post.

IN THE PAPERS

"The golden touch which David Beckham brings to Selhurst Park kept United surging on towards another title. Fifteen months ago he scored the 50-yard wonder goal which dominated the build-up chat for this eagerly awaited clash, only for Alex Ferguson to relegate him to the subs bench."
DAILY MAIL

"Beckham's second came 14 minutes from time but it was the late contributions of Paul Scholes and Andy Cole which Wimbledon found hard to stomach and unfairly implied United had romped to victory."
OBSERVER

"I love you, man"

Cole fires
number five

"Give us a
hug"

MANCHESTER UNITED 4
BLACKBURN ROVERS 0

HOME TEAM

		RATING
1.	Peter Schmeichel	7
2.	Gary Neville	8
6.	Gary Pallister	8
21.	Henning Berg	8
12.	Phil Neville	7
8.	Nicky Butt	8
7.	David Beckham	7
11.	Ryan Giggs	8
10.	Teddy Sheringham	8
20.	Ole G Solskjaer	9
9.	Andy Cole	8

SUBSTITUTES

15.	Karel Poborsky Pallister	69 mins	7
19.	Ronny Johnsen Butt	65 mins	7
13.	Brian McClair Beckham	75 mins	8
17.	Rai Van Der Gouw	
32.	Michael Clegg	

SCORERS

Solskjaer | 17/52 mins
Henchoz | og 59 mins
Kenna | og 84 mins

REFEREE

A Wilkie | Chester-le-Street

VISITORS

1.	Tim Flowers	5
3.	Jeff Kenna	6
4.	Tim Sherwood	5
6.	Tore Pedersen	6
7.	Stuart Ripley	7
5.	Chris Sutton	5
11.	Jason Wilcox	7
15.	Gary Flitcroft	5
17.	Billy McKinlay	6
20.	Gary Croft	5
24.	Stephane Henchoz	6

SUBSTITUTES

12.	Lars Bohinen Ripley	61 mins	7
8.	Kevin Gallacher McKinlay	74 mins	5
25.	Damien Duff Wilcox	59 mins	5
33.	Alan Fettis	
26.	Marlon Broomes	

MATCH REPORT

The tactical knowledge Roy Hodgson picked up on his managerial tour of the Continent has benefitted Blackburn this season, but at Old Trafford it hindered them. The Blackburn manager played five in midfield and just Chris Sutton up front to stop United's forays down the wing. But it backfired by nullifying their own attacking impulse which had brought them 27 goals so far this season.

To drop free-scoring Kevin Gallacher was gross over-caution. Deprived of his partner, Chris Sutton's frustration at his isolation up front boiled over and he was sent off.

United's response to Blackburn's tactics was simple: if they could not go down the flanks they would go down the centre. Twice Sheringham released Solskjaer down the middle and the Norwegian beat Tim Flowers with low shots. Kenna and Henchoz's own goals inflated the score, but reflected United's dominance.

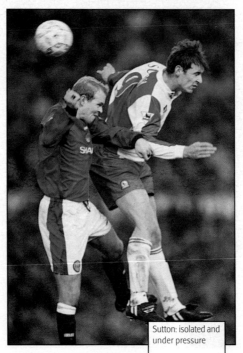

Sutton: isolated and under pressure

IN THE PAPERS

"He who dared, won. It seems there is no challenge too great for Alex Ferguson's young side this season. Faced with their most formidable Premiership rivals yesterday, Ferguson refused to lay out a safety net and was rewarded with a display of daring and ingenuity."
STAR

"It was billed as a heavyweight clash of the title contenders. Champion favourites against a side worthy of a flutter. But it was much, much more than that. This was a battle of two of the sharpest brains in the world of soccer. And quite frankly, Manchester United boss Alex Ferguson was the easy winner, not just on points, but by a bloody knockout in terms of tactics."
MIRROR

"Manchester United's potential centurians are steaming toward a Premiership goalscoring record. The ton-up target is being eaten away by the goal-hungry Reds who registered their 40th goal in just 16 games in the 4–0 destruction of Blackburn."
MANCHESTER EVENING NEWS

"Ryan Giggs and David Beckham provided the fantasy alongside Nicky Butt's more earthbound talents in midfield and they overwhelmed the pretenders, reducing them to nervous wrecks who put the ball through their own net twice."
EXPRESS

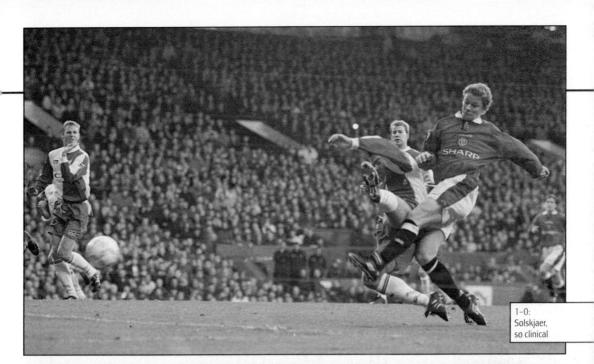

1–0: Solskjaer, so clinical

Keep yer tongue out

November STATS

PLAYER RECORDS

			FULL APPEARANCES	SUB APPEARANCES	GOALS
	1.	Peter Schmeichel	17	0	0
	2.	Gary Neville	14	0	0
	3.	Denis Irwin	8	3	0
	4.	David May	1	0	0
	5.	Ronny Johnsen	5	4	0
	6.	Gary Pallister	16	0	0
	7.	David Beckham	13	3	4
	8.	Nicky Butt	15	0	1
	9.	Andy Cole	10	2	7
	10.	Teddy Sheringham	12	1	7
	11.	Ryan Giggs	12	1	2
	12.	Phil Neville	11	2	0
	13.	Brian McClair	1	3	0
	14.	Jordi Cruyff	4	1	0
	15.	Karel Poborsky	5	6	2
	16.	Roy Keane	9	0	2
	17.	Rai Van Der Gouw	0	0	0
	18.	Paul Scholes	13	2	4
	20.	Ole Gunnar Solskjaer	5	3	5
	21.	Henning Berg	14	0	0
	22.	Erik Nevland	0	1	0
	23.	Ben Thornley	1	1	0
	24.	John O'Kane	0	0	0
	25.	Kevin Pilkington	0	0	0
	26.	Chris Casper	0	0	0
	27.	Terry Cooke	0	0	0
	28.	Phil Mulryne	1	0	0
	30.	Ronnie Wallwork	0	1	0
	31.	John Curtis	2	1	0
	32.	Michael Clegg	0	0	0

Key: home | away — ■ PREMIERSHIP, ■ COCA-COLA CUP, ■ FA CUP. ■ FULL APPEARANCE, ■ CAME ON AS SUB, ■ SCORER, ■ SCORED AS SUB

PLAYER OF THE MONTH

Andy Cole

AVERAGE PERFORMANCE RATING: 8

FA CARLING PREMIERSHIP

as at 1 December 1997

	Pld	W	D	L	F	A	Pts	GD
■ Manchester United	16	10	4	2	40	12	34	28
▲ Chelsea	16	10	1	5	35	17	31	18
■ Blackburn Rovers	16	8	6	2	27	17	30	10
▲ Leeds United	16	9	2	5	26	19	29	7
▼ Arsenal	16	7	6	3	30	18	27	12
■ Leicester City	16	7	5	4	21	14	26	7
▼ Liverpool	15	7	4	4	26	14	25	12
▲ Newcastle United	13	7	4	3	18	17	24	1
▼ Derby County	15	7	2	6	28	24	23	4
▲ Crystal Palace	15	5	4	6	15	17	19	-2
▼ Wimbledon	16	5	4	7	18	21	19	-3
▼ West Ham United	15	6	1	8	20	25	19	-5
■ Aston Villa	16	5	3	8	16	23	18	-7
▲ Sheffield Wednesday	16	5	3	8	28	37	18	-9
■ Coventry City	16	3	8	5	13	21	17	-8
▲ Southampton	16	5	1	10	20	26	16	-6
▼ Tottenham Hotspur	16	4	4	8	13	22	16	-9
▲ Bolton Wanderers	15	3	7	5	11	21	16	-10
■ Barnsley	16	4	1	11	14	43	13	-29
▼ Everton	16	3	3	10	16	27	12	-11

DECEMBER

1 | 2 | 3 | 4 | 5 | 6 | 7 | 8 | 9 | 10 | 11 | 12 | 13 | 14 | 15 | 16 | 17 | 18 | 19 | 20 | 21 | 22 | 23 | 24 | 25 | 26 | 27 | 28 | 29 | 30 | 31

DECEMBER

THE MONTH AHEAD

The month started badly for Earl Spencer, who, sick of all the newspaper stories emanating from the evidence in his divorce settlement with wife Victoria, agreed to call it a day and pay her £2 million.

Glenn Hoddle was none too happy, either, when the World Cup draw turned out to be more like a lottery, pitting England against Tunisia, Columbia and Romania. With all three in the top 20 of FIFA's rankings, it was easily the toughest group of the lot. Still, the country had something to cheer about when England's Rugby Union team looked for so long like beating the mighty All Blacks. In the end they settled for a 26-all draw and salvaged some of that lost pride.

There was a lot of lost pride on Merseyside as Liverpool kicked the month off with a 3–1 defeat to... United. Playing in their all-white strip, United took the lead through Cole and, although Liverpool equalised through a Fowler penalty, a stunning Beckham freekick put Ferguson's men back in front and Cole wrapped it up with 15 minutes to go. It was United's second 3–1 victory of the year at Anfield and, with Liverpool 15 points behind, looked like the second time that United had put paid to the Scousers' title challenge.

The sad death of former Leeds and Scotland skipper Billy Bremner, aged 54, overshadowed any other soccer news the following week. Meanwhile, the FA Cup Third round draw was announced with United getting the toughest tie possible – away to Chelsea. United were too busy preparing for their Champions' League match with Juventus in Turin to worry too much about it. Another Englishman abroad was Richard Branson, whose round-the-world balloon trip was slightly disrupted when the balloon set off without him, leaving the red-faced tycoon stuck in the Moroccan desert.

United took to the field in the Stadio Delle Alpi with a depleted team (no Butt or Scholes; Giggs, Schmeichel and Cole on the bench) but still held firm until the 84th minute when Inzaghi scored from a Zidane chip across the six-yard box. With Norwegian team Rosenborg leading Olympiakos 2–1, this wasn't enough to put the Italians through to the quarter finals... until the Greek team equalised in the last minute. Ferguson's 100 percent record was over, but United had still walked the group.

Tony Blair's Labour honeymoon looked to be nearing it's end too, though this time Europe wasn't the problem. 47 of his backbenchers revolted against him in the House on the question of benefit cuts. Two days later, the Blair administration was again in the news, with the-once-public-enemy-number-one Gerry Adams

The Prince of New York

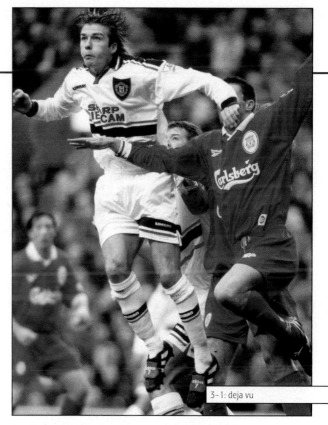

3-1: deja vu

popping into Number 10 for peace talks.

United got a good result in the draw for the European quarter finals. Fans started booking their tickets to Monte Carlo straight away. Any complacency about victorious Brits performing abroad was dispelled when, two days later, Prince Naseem faced his toughest opponent yet, American Kevin Kelley in Madison Square Gardens. Naz was knocked down twice but still managed to KO his man in the fourth round.

Back to reality and a tough trip to the windy North East to face Newcastle. Dalglish's men were in good form, and without a couple of outrageous Schmeichel saves the Reds might have come home empty-handed. But a second-half header from former Toon idol Andy Cole took the points back to Manchester and put the ghost of last season's 5–0 defeat to sleep.

Tottenham Hotspur director Alan Sugar ate humble pie the next day, giving Spurs fans the Christmas present they wanted: Jurgen Klinsmann.

Meanwhile, the *Sun* thought that David Beckham's pressie to Posh Spice – a £13,000 diamond-encrusted cross – was

such important news that they made it their front-page headline.

The month ended for United with a 2–0 win over Everton and a seemingly breezy tie with Coventry City. United were 2–1 up with time ticking away when Huckerby struck, first being brought down by young John Curtis for a penalty converted by former United man Dion Dublin, then hitting in a last-gasp winner.

Jurgen's back

Reds play their way to Monaco

The late, great Billy Bremner

LIVERPOOL 1
MANCHESTER UNITED 3

HOME TEAM

1.	David James	6
4.	Jason McAteer	6
3.	Bjorn Tore Kvarme	5
21.	Dominic Matteo	7
20.	Stig Inge Bjornebye	6
23.	Jamie Carragher	6
8.	Oyvind Leonhardsen	6
11.	Jamie Redknapp	5
7.	Steve McManaman	7
18.	Michael Owen	6
9.	Robbie Fowler	7

SUBSTITUTES

6.	Phil Babb	
13.	Karlheinz Riedle	6
	Bjornebye	71 mins	
12.	Steve Harkness	
26.	Jorgen Nielsen	
15.	Patrik Berger	5
	Kvarme	51 mins	

SCORERS

Fowler | 59 mins pen

REFEREE

D. Elleray | Harrow-on-the-hill

VISITORS   RATING

1.	Peter Schmeichel	7
2.	Gary Neville	7
6.	Gary Pallister	8
21.	Henning Berg	7
5.	Ronny Johnsen	7
12.	Phil Neville	7
8.	Nicky Butt	8
7.	David Beckham	7
11.	Ryan Giggs	7
10.	Teddy Sheringham	8
9.	Andy Cole	9

SUBSTITUTES

13.	Brian McClair	
15.	Karel Poborsky	
20.	Ole G Solskjaer	
17.	Rai Van Der Gouw	
28.	Phil Mulryne	

SCORERS

Beckham | 69 mins
Cole | 50/73 mins

MATCH REPORT

"Outclassed by the Champions," United's support gloated for the last 20 minutes of this game. There could not be a more succint summary of this game after United had humiliated their bitterest rivals at Anfield for the second time in six months.

In a game eerily similar to their last encounter in April, United produced a performance of direct attacking that exposed Liverpool's woeful defence.

Liverpool were the latest team to get in the way of Andy Cole's renaissance. Six minutes in to the second half, Cole pounced on a mistake by Kvarme, swerved past Matteo and shot low across David James.

Liverpool, who failed to test Schmeichel all afternoon, only looked like they were going to score from a penalty. That duly arrived after Nicky Butt and Phil Neville combined to bring down Michael Owen.

David Beckham's outstanding free-kick regained the lead for United, before Andy Cole tapped in Sheringham's flick from a corner for his 15th goal of the season.

"I'll probably be getting the sack again next week," Roy Evans joked. But he does have his supporters. "Evans must stay," demanded United's travelling support.

"Watch me dance"

IN THE PAPERS

Nothing we didn't already know was displayed at Anfield on Saturday. And yet, while being utterly predictable, there was something quite unnerving about the way United toyed with their former rivals before disposing of them like a Joe Pesci character in a Martin Scorcese film."

EXPRESS

"Liverpool are not a bad side, certainly not bad enough to be lying in eigth place in the Premiership, but they have got to a stage now where, with their hopes of the Championship fading with every week, their only hope of salvaging some pride comes from the chance of beating United. On Saturday, they found out just how far short of that goal they were."

TIMES

"The game was superb in many aspects, not least the way in which the furious tempo barely affected the skills which were on show – first-time control, penalty-box tackling, team organisation and ruthless finishing."

DAILY MAIL

Can he
free-kick it? Yes, he can

> "We looked the better side and I'm delighted by the win. You always get it hard at Anfield – we had to really perform today."
>
> ALEX FERGUSON

MANCHESTER UNITED 1
ASTON VILLA 0

HOME TEAM

		RATING
1.	Peter Schmeichel	7
2.	Gary Neville	7
5.	Ronny Johnsen	7
6.	Gary Pallister	7
12.	Phil Neville	6
7.	David Beckham	7
8.	Nicky Butt	7
11.	Ryan Giggs	8
10.	Teddy Sheringham	6
9.	Andy Cole	7
20.	Ole G Solskjaer	6

SUBSTITUTES

13.	Brian McClair	8
	Solskjaer | 84 mins	
4.	David May	
17.	Rai Van Der Gouw	
21.	Henning Berg	
31.	John Curtis	

SCORERS

Giggs | 52 mins

REFEREE

Paul Durkin | Portland

VISITORS

13.	Michael Oakes	8
2.	Gary Charles	6
5.	Ugo Ehiogu	7
3.	Steve Staunton	7
4.	Gareth Southgate	6
14.	Alan Wright	7
8.	Mark Draper	7
7.	Ian Taylor	6
16.	Simon Grayson	7
11.	Stan Collymore	6
9.	Savo Milosevic	6

SUBSTITUTES

17.	Lee Hendrie	6
	Grayson | 68 mins	
12.	Julian Joachim	6
	Milosevic | 68 mins	
15.	Fernando Nelson	
20.	Riccardo Scimeca	
21.	Matthew Ghent	

MATCH REPORT

For the first time since August 1995, Manchester United managed to breach Aston Villa's defence. Ryan Giggs' superb second-half winner gave United their first win over the Midlanders for nearly three years.

Aston Villa were never going to be another victim of United's autumn goal glut. Brian Little seems to have mastered the impossible: how to stop United scoring. Ryan Giggs' winner was only the third goal Villa have allowed the Reds to score in their last six matches.

It was a fine move that opened up Villa: Teddy Sheringham flicked on Peter Schmeichel's clearance to Andy Cole. He lifted it over Eghiou in to the path of Giggs, who volleyed in through Oakes' legs. End to end in under ten seconds.

It could be said that Giggs owed United a goal after shooting weakly at an open goal and allowing Ehiogu to clear in the first half. Sheringham and Solskjaer also spurned good opportunities.

Teddy Sheringham continued his 100% penalty record: three taken, three missed. This time, he missed the target altogether after Savo Milosevic had handled in the area.

"As far as penalties are concerned, he's put himself in the dole queue now," laughed Alex Ferguson afterwards.

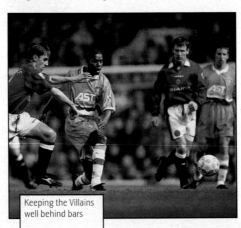

Keeping the Villains well behind bars

IN THE PAPERS

Ronny has Colly in his pocket

NEWCASTLE UNITED 0
MANCHESTER UNITED 1

HOME TEAM

15.	Shaka Hislop	8
19.	Steve Watson	7
5.	Darren Peacock	6
12.	Stuart Pearce	7
27.	Philippe Albert	6
23.	Alessandro Pistone	7
3.	John Beresford	7
4.	David Batty	8
18.	Keith Gillespie	7
10.	John Barnes	8
11.	Faustino Asprilla	7

SUBSTITUTES

2.	Warren Barton Albert | 32 mins	7
14.	Temuri Ketsbaia Beresford | 75 mins	6
1.	Shay Given	
8.	Ian Rush	
16.	Jon Dahl Tomasson	

REFEREE

P Jones | Loughborough

VISITORS   RATING

1.	Peter Schmeichel	9
2.	Gary Neville	7
6.	Gary Pallister	9
12.	Phil Neville	7
5.	Ronny Johnsen	7
18.	Paul Scholes	7
8.	Nicky Butt	7
7.	David Beckham	8
11.	Ryan Giggs	8
10.	Teddy Sheringham	6
9.	Andy Cole	8

SUBSTITUTES

13.	Brian McClair Sheringham | 84 mins	6
21.	Henning Berg	
20.	Ole G Solskjaer Scholes | 72 mins	6
25.	Kevin Pilkington	
31.	John Curtis	

SCORERS

Cole | 66 mins

MATCH REPORT

Desperate to prove a point to the Tyneside public, Peter Schmeichel and Andy Cole guided United to a valuable win at St James' Park.

Schmeichel had not forgotten the humiliation of conceding five goals on his last visit to Newcastle and Cole, booed with every touch, wanted to disprove the Geordie belief that they had seen the best of him and off-loaded used goods.

Schmeichel pulled off two extraordinary saves from John Barnes and Stuart Pearce. He contemptuously batted away their headers, the type that would beat most goalkeepers. Such performances make a compelling case for Schmeichel being named Footballer of the Year at long last.

United's goal was an example of counter-attacking football at its best. With just four passes, United swept down the length of the pitch before Andy Cole headed David Beckham's cross firmly past Shaka Hislop. End to end in 20 seconds. Cole's jaunt back down the pitch to celebrate with United's fans showed how much it meant to him.

But such individual performances couldn't mask a poor team display by United and, but for Schmeichel, Newcastle would have taken something from this game.

IN THE PAPERS

"Andy Cole's 16th goal of the season settled in the net and Fergie's men moved a step closer to becoming a dwindling dot on the horizon at the top of the Premiership."
EXPRESS

"The ground, a bedlam of noise up till then, fell silent for a moment as Cole ran the length of the pitch to take the acclaim of United's travelling support. It was a goal worthy of winning any match and it duly settled this bruising battle."
MIRROR

"Not since receiving a North London roasting from Arsenal have Manchester United been given a stiffer examination of their championship credentials, but the fact that they have a top-class goalscorer enabled them to leave Tyneside four points clear at the top of the table."
DAILY MAIL

Tackling Tino

Definitely the best goalkeeper in the world

Cole stoops to score

MANCHESTER UNITED 2
EVERTON 0

HOME TEAM

		RATING
1.	Kevin Pilkington	7
2.	Gary Neville	7
21.	Henning Berg	7
6.	Gary Pallister	7
12.	Phil Neville	7
7.	David Beckham	8
5.	Ronny Johnsen	8
18.	Paul Scholes	8
8.	Nicky Butt	7
20.	Ole Gunnar Solskjaer	7
9.	Andy Cole	9

SUBSTITUTES

15.	Karel Poborsky	6
	Beckham | 66 mins	
13.	Brian McClair	7
	Pallister | 75 mins	
31.	John Curtis	6
	P Neville | 84 mins	
10.	Teddy Sheringham	
11.	Ryan Giggs	

SCORERS

Berg | 14 mins
Cole | 35 mins

REFEREE

Uriah Rennie |

VISITORS

31.	Thomas Myhre	6
2.	Earl Barrett	6
3.	Andy Hinchcliffe	5
12.	Craig Short	6
5.	Dave Watson	5
23.	Carl Tiler	6
19.	John Oster	6
25.	Michael Ball	5
17.	Gareth Farrelly	6
29.	Danny Cadamateri	5
8.	Nick Barmby	6

SUBSTITUTES

31.	Paul Gerrard	
26.	Graham Allen	5
	Barrett | 65 mins	
15.	Claus Thomsen	5
	Ball | 79 mins	
34.	Francis Jeffers	6
	Watson | 45 mins	
20.	Tony Thomas	

MATCH REPORT

You know Andy Cole's revival is complete when he begins to be compared to Eric Cantona. Cole produced an exquisite chip Cantona would have been proud of as United strolled to victory against Everton.

"Andy's goal was the highlight of the game. It was absolutely brilliant," said Alex Ferguson, "and reminscent of a chip Eric Cantona scored for us against Sunderland a year ago."

United could afford to rest Giggs and Sheringham and still win with ease. They relentlessly battered Everton in the first half, gained a comfortable lead and then sat back and coasted the rest of the game.

Henning Berg headed his first League goal for United to put them ahead after 13 minutes. The contest was over after United's second: Butt put Cole through and he measured his chip perfectly over Myhre from 30 yards out.

Everton failed to exploit Peter Schmeichel's absence. In fact, they didn't test United's third-choice keeper Kevin Pilkington until the 56th minute, and then only with a tame long-range effort from Gareth Farrelly.

"Men against boys," is how Everton manager Howard Kendall saw it. "United have had two days off this week – Christmas Day *and* Boxing Day. It was a long, long 90 minutes for us."

IN THE PAPERS

"From the first to last it was a stroll, it was an exercise in over-elaboration, at others it was careless, even sloppy. But there was a great beauty amid the indolence, too, enough for Manchester United to make this Carling Premiership match against Everton look like an uneven battle between men and boys. The first half of the season over, they are in the home stretch and coasting."
TIMES

"Six points clear going into the second half of the season, Manchester United look unstoppable in their quest to secure a fifth Championship in six years before they concentrate their minds again on the overwhelming priorty of bringing the European Cup back to Old Trafford."
EXPRESS

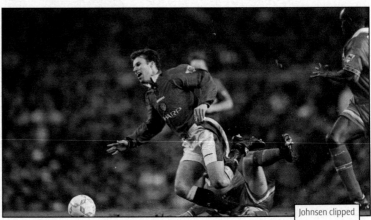

Johnsen clipped

Myre chipped

COVENTRY CITY 3
MANCHESTER UNITED 2

HOME TEAM

13.	Magnus Hedman	7
23.	Roland Nilsson	7
2.	Richard Shaw	7
4.	Paul Williams	7
3.	David Burrows	7
12.	Paul Telfer	7
16.	George Boateng	7
8.	Noel Whelan	8
18.	Marcus Hall	7
9.	Dion Dublin	8
7.	Darren Huckerby	9

SUBSTITUTES

1.	Steve Ogrizovic	
17.	Willie Boland	6
	Boateng | 64 mins	
14.	Tronde Soltvedt	6
	Hall | 77 mins	
15.	Kyle Lightbourne	
6.	Kevin Richardson	
37.	Sam Shilton	

SCORERS

Whelan | 13 mins
Dublin | 86 mins (pen)
Huckerby | 88 mins

REFEREE

Neale Barry | Scunthorpe

VISITORS

		RATING
25.	Kevin Pilkington	6
2.	Gary Neville	7
6.	Gary Pallister	7
21.	Henning Berg	6
5.	Ronny Johnsen	7
7.	David Beckham	6
18.	Paul Scholes	6
11.	Ryan Giggs	7
20.	Ole G Solskjaer	8
10.	Teddy Sheringham	7
9.	Andy Cole	6

SUBSTITUTES

13.	Brian McClair	
8.	Nicky Butt	5
	Solskjaer | 63 mins	
31.	John Curtis	5
	Johnsen | 71 mins	
28.	Phil Mulryne	
33.	Nick Culkin	

SCORERS

Solskjaer | 31 mins
Sheringham | 47 mins

MATCH REPORT

"We got what we deserved... nothing," said United's manager Alex Ferguson, after he had watched his side carelessly squander all three points in an enthralling game at Highfield Road.

At 2–1 with only five minutes remaining, United were coasting to another victory, but a penalty from Dion Dublin and a wonderful individual goal from Darren Huckerby saw Coventry complete a stunning comeback.

Call it cockiness or arrogance, but United seemed more interested in practising their training ground tricks than killing Coventry off. Even Alex Ferguson offered a guarded criticism, "Sometimes you can be over-confident and try little flicks and back-heels that you wouldn't normally do. There was too much of that."

Coventry took the lead through Noel Whelan in the first half, but goals from Solskjaer and Sheringham saw United reassert their expected superiority.

Coventry refused to be intimidated by United's showboating and were rewarded in the last five minutes. Darren Huckerby first forced Berg to concede a penalty which Dublin converted and then set off on a run which saw him dance past three defenders before scoring past Pilkington.

IN THE PAPERS

"Coventry City gave the Champions a timely reminder yesterday that despite their frightening lead at the top of the table, complacency comes before a fall."
GUARDIAN

"Darren Huckerby blew open the Championship race with a shock winner to give Coventry their first victory over United in nine years. United, who have now lost three League games this season, looked to be coasting to victory against the Premiership strugglers."
SUN

"It is a very small roll of honour, the teams that have beaten Manchester United this season, but Darren Huckerby's once-in-a-lifetime goal gave Coventry their place on it. Leeds at Elland Road and Arsenal at Highbury were the only teams to have beaten United. And now Coventry – an entry that sticks out like a sore thumb."
EXPRESS

"United can justifiably claim they threw this game away by allowing two goals in the last four minutes, but Coventry did not deserve to lose."
TELEGRAPH

Teddy takes a tumble

Through
the legs...

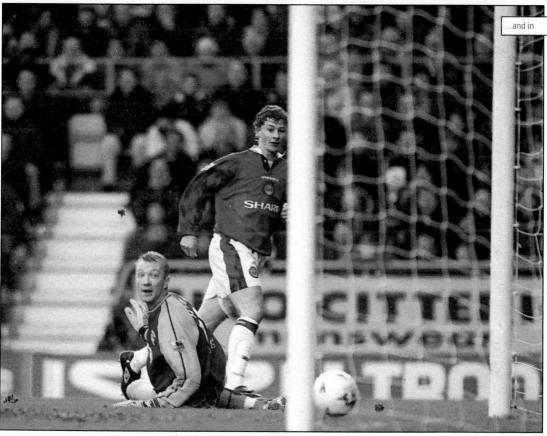

...and in

December **STATS**

PLAYER RECORDS

- ■ PREMIERSHIP
- ■ COCA-COLA CUP ■ FA CUP

home | away

■■ FULL APPEARANCE / CAME ON AS SUB

■■ SCORER / SCORED AS SUB

#	Player	FULL APPEARANCES	SUB APPEARANCES	GOALS
1.	Peter Schmeichel	20	0	0
2.	Gary Neville	19	0	0
3.	Denis Irwin	8	3	0
4.	David May	1	0	0
5.	Ronny Johnsen	10	4	0
6.	Gary Pallister	21	0	0
7.	David Beckham	18	3	5
8.	Nicky Butt	19	1	1
9.	Andy Cole	15	2	11
10.	Teddy Sheringham	16	1	8
11.	Ryan Giggs	16	1	3
12.	Phil Neville	15	2	0
13.	Brian McClair	1	6	0
14.	Jordi Cruyff	4	1	0
15.	Karel Poborsky	5	7	2
16.	Roy Keane	9	0	2
17.	Rai Van Der Gouw	0	0	0
18.	Paul Scholes	16	2	4
20.	Ole Gunnar Solskjaer	8	4	6
21.	Henning Berg	17	0	1
22.	Erik Nevland	0	1	0
23.	Ben Thornley	1	1	0
24.	John O'Kane	0	0	0
25.	Kevin Pilkington	2	0	0
26.	Chris Casper	0	0	0
27.	Terry Cooke	0	0	0
28.	Phil Mulryne	1	0	0
30.	Ronnie Wallwork	0	1	0
31.	John Curtis	2	3	0
32.	Michael Clegg	0	0	0

PLAYER OF THE MONTH

Andy Cole

AVERAGE PERFORMANCE RATING: 7.8

FA CARLING PREMIERSHIP

as at 29 December 1997

	Pld	W	D	L	F	A	Pts	GD
■ Manchester United	21	14	4	3	49	16	46	33
▲ Blackburn Rovers	21	11	8	2	38	21	41	17
▼ Chelsea	20	12	3	5	46	20	39	26
▲ Liverpool	20	11	4	5	36	19	37	17
▼ Leeds United	21	10	5	6	30	23	35	7
▼ Arsenal	20	9	7	4	35	23	34	12
▲ Derby County	21	9	5	7	34	28	32	6
▲ West Ham United	21	10	1	10	28	32	31	-4
▼ Leicester City	21	7	7	7	25	21	28	4
▲ Aston Villa	21	7	5	9	25	27	26	-2
▼ Newcastle United	20	7	5	8	21	25	26	-4
▼ Wimbledon	20	6	6	8	21	24	24	-3
▲ Coventry City	21	5	8	8	20	28	23	-8
▲ Crystal Palace	21	5	8	8	20	28	33	-8
▼ Sheffield Wednesday	21	6	5	10	32	44	23	-12
■ Southampton	20	6	3	11	24	30	21	-6
▲ Bolton Wanderers	21	4	9	8	19	33	21	-14
▲ Everton	21	5	5	11	20	31	20	-11
▼ Tottenham Hotspur	21	5	5	11	19	37	20	-19
▼ Barnsley	21	5	3	13	19	51	18	-32

JANUARY

1 | 2 | 3 | 4 | 5 | 6 | 7 | 8 | 9 | 10 | 11 | 12 | 13 | 14 | 15 | 16 | 17 | 18 | 19 | 20 | 21 | 22 | 23 | 24 | 25 | 26 | 27 | 28 | 29 | 30 | 31

JANUARY

THE MONTH AHEAD

January was to be the beginning of a period of mixed fortunes for the Reds, who started the month playing their best football for some time and ended it struggling for form.

It wasn't a great month for US President Bill Clinton, either, as allegations of his sexual liaisons with 24-year-old Monica Lewinsky in the corridors of power swept across the world. Nearer to home Tony Blair unveiled a blueprint for peace in Northern Ireland, although the euphoria at this announcement was tempered by continued tit-for-tat shootings in the troubled province.

Elsewhere in sport, rugby legend Will Carling finally hung up his boots and Frank Bruno admitted that his wife had once stabbed him during a blazing row. In football, Kenny Dalglish 'celebrated' his anniversary at Newcastle. Yes, it had only taken him a year to turn Newcastle from arguably the most entertaining team in the land to the most boring.

Pick of the bunch: Will Carling retires

If anyone had said that United would be celebrating five goals at Stamford Bridge in the plum tie of the FA Cup Third Round, they'd have been certified. First v third in the Premiership, a match with 1–0 written all over it... well, it was 1–0 to United after 22 minutes, 2–0 after 27 and 3–0 on half-time. When Teddy Sheringham made it 5–0 after 73 minutes United were in the midst of one of their best performances in months. In the last 20 minutes United must have felt sorry for the Londoners because they gifted them a late Christmas present of three consolation goals.

Seven days later, at home to Christian Gross's relegation-threatened Tottenham, featuring 'veteran' Eurostars Klinsmann and Berti, the Reds spluttered to a 2–0 win. Christian Gross had previously told reporters that he wanted to organise a team social outing to the circus for his Spurs side, but a video replay of one of their recent matches would have served the same purpose.

Next it was on to the Dell, and we all know what happens there. This time it was only a 1–0 defeat (it's better than 6–3), courtesy of a Nicky Butt slip which let in Kevin Davies for a third minute goal, a host of missed chances, desperated defending and some brilliant saves by Saints keeper Paul Jones.

It was back to the FA Cup the following week, and while Newcastle struggled against non-league Stevenage Borough, United eased past Second Division Walsall, 5–2. In fact, the Midlanders played with style and adventure and it was their admirable willingness to come

Joyful and triumphant:
Stevenage force a replay

to Old Trafford to play football which ultimately earned them a thrashing.

Talking of thrashings, England's cricket tour of the West Indies began in earnest with the first test in Jamaica. Billed as our first chance to win a test series against a major cricketing nation for 12 years, our boys were 17 for three when the match was sensationally abandoned due to the dangerous state of the pitch.

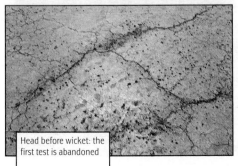

Head before wicket: the first test is abandoned

"I hope my goal costs United their title. There is a lot of arrogance surrounding them."

TONY COTTEE OVERESTIMATES HIS OWN IMPORTANCE

If only United could have called off their game at home to Leicester. Martin O'Neill's hard battling side came to Old Trafford to shut up shop and try and sneak a goal, and their gameplan worked a treat. For once there seemed to be a lack of fight, a lack of commitment in the first half and a lack of inspiration against a brick wall defence in the second.

Yet despite a couple of hiccups United went into February four points clear of Chelsea at the top of the league, at home to Premiership strugglers Barnsley in the FA Cup and with the European Cup quarter final against Monaco to look forward to. The good ship United, it seemed, was still firmly on course of another glorious season.

CHELSEA 3
MANCHESTER UNITED 5

HOME TEAM

		RATING
1.	Ed De Goey	6
5.	Frank Leboeuf	6
6.	Steve Clarke	7
2.	Dan Petrescu	8
14.	Graham Le Saux	8
12.	Michael Duberry	6
16.	Roberto Di Matteo	6
22.	Mark Nicholls	6
19.	Tore Andre Flo	7
25.	Gianfranco Zola	7
10.	Mark Hughes	6

SUBSTITUTES

9.	Gianluca Vialli	8
	Andre Flo	60 mins	
18.	Andy Myers	6
	Nicholls	45 mins	
13.	Kevin Hitchcock	
7.	Bernard Lambourde	
21.	Paul Hughes	

SCORERS

Le Saux | 77 mins
Vialli | 83/87 mins

REFEREE

Steve Lodge | Barnsley

VISITORS

1.	Peter Schmeichel	8
2.	Gary Neville	8
6.	Gary Pallister	7
5.	Ronny Johnsen	8
3.	Denis Irwin	8
7.	David Beckham	7
8.	Nicky Butt	9
18.	Paul Scholes	7
11.	Ryan Giggs	8
10.	Teddy Sheringham	8
9.	Andy Cole	9

SUBSTITUTES

13.	Brian McClair	
20.	Ole G Solskjaer	7
	Scholes	71 mins	
21.	Henning Berg	
25.	Kevin Pilkington	
32.	Michael Clegg	

SCORERS

Beckham | 22/27 mins
Cole | 45/65 mins
Sheringham | 73 mins

MATCH REPORT

For the first 75 minutes of this extraordinary game Manchester United played some of the finest football of Alex Ferguson's 11-year reign to humiliate and dethrone FA Cup holders Chelsea.

United were awesome, systematically taking apart Chelsea. It proved what United are capable of when the talents of Giggs, Butt, Cole, Beckham and co peak in the same game. Chelsea's Gianluca Vialli was in no doubt: "This United team is one of the finest Europe has ever seen," said the gracious Italian.

Chelsea's destruction undermined any claim they had to be serious rivals to United. Their three goals only came in the last 12 minutes when United had taken their foot off the pedal.

Beckham scored United's opening two, the first a tap-in, the second a sumptuous free-kick and, just when Chelsea thought they might survive further damage before the interval, Andy Cole raced from the half-way line before chipping De Goey.

United were in no mood to merely protect their lead and returned for the second half as hungry as ever; Cole scored the fourth after great work from Butt and Giggs before Sheringham headed the fifth from a Beckham cross.

IN THE PAPERS

"There was something cold and ominous about Alex Ferguson as he was urged to sift through the debris of Manchester United's 5–3 demolition of Chelsea yesterday. Some of his words and their humour brought hoots of laughter from his listeners, but his message only underlined the relentless ruthlessness of his side's charge toward an unprecedented Treble this season."
TIMES

"If Chelsea are the second best team in the land right now, then God help the rest. Cosmopolitan Chelsea took 27 years to win the Cup again and 27 minutes to throw it away. The only consolation for the remainder of the country is that Glenn Hoddle can field half of this formidable United team in the World Cup 1998."
MIRROR

"After 90 traumatic minutes at Stamford Bridge yesterday, Gullit was just another scalp on Ferguson's belt. As the FA Cup was ripped from his grasp, Gullit could only reflect on who was the boss and still is."
SUN

Cole makes it three at half-time

> "This United team is one of the finest Europe has ever seen."
>
> Gianluca Vialli

Can you hear the Chelsea sing?

MANCHESTER UNITED 2
TOTTENHAM HOTSPUR 0

HOME TEAM

		RATING
1.	Peter Schmeichel	7
2.	Gary Neville	7
5.	Ronny Johnsen	8
6.	Gary Pallister	8
12.	Phil Neville	7
7.	David Beckham	7
18.	Paul Scholes	8
11.	Ryan Giggs	9
10.	Teddy Sheringham	7
20.	Ole G Solskjaer	7
9.	Andy Cole	8

SUBSTITUTES

25. Kevin Pilkington
13. Brian McClair
8. Nicky Butt
21. Henning Berg
32. Michael Clegg

SCORERS

Giggs | 44/67 mins

REFEREE

Paul Alcock | Kent

VISITORS

13.	Espen Baardsen	7
12.	Stephen Carr	6
23.	Sol Campbell	8
15.	Ramon Vega	7
16.	Clive Wilson	6
7.	Ruel Fox	6
5.	Colin Calderwood	6
35.	Nicola Berti	6
25.	Stephen Clemence	6
20.	Jose Dominguez	7
33.	Jurgen Klinsmann	6

SUBSTITUTES

31.	Simon Brown	
6.	Gary Mabbutt	
30.	Paul Mahorn	
32.	Garry Brady	6
	Fox	77 mins	
22.	Andy Sinton	6
	Clemence	55 mins	

MATCH REPORT

"There has always been something very special about matches against Spurs," proclaimed United's programme before this game. But this refers to the days of Greaves and Charlton when the clubs were equals. Today, these games represent just another three points to United. This was United's fifth consecutive League victory over the North London side.

Since the opening day of the season when United triumphed at White Hart Lane, Tottenham have changed their manager and welcomed back Jurgen Klinnsman. But they showed little sign of improvement. Frankly, they were poor and displayed little heart for their battle against relegation. For heaven's sake, they allowed Ryan Giggs to score with a header!

United were well below their best. Six days earlier they had raised their game at Stamford Bridge to humiliate Chelsea, but they knew they could take it easy against Tottenham, and the result was never in doubt. United strolled around, safe in the knowledge that they would get the chances to win; it was merely a matter of converting them. Ryan Giggs did the job for them, driving home a volley and treating United's faithful to sight of a rare headed goal to finish off a very sorry-looking Tottenham.

Rare bird: Ryan's header flies in

SOUTHAMPTON 1
MANCHESTER UNITED 0

HOME TEAM

1.	Paul Jones	9
2.	Jason Dodd	7
5.	Ken Monkou	7
6.	Claus Lundekvam	7
15.	Frances Benali	7
8.	Matthew Oakley	7
4.	Carlton Palmer	8
7.	Matthew Le Tissier	7
18.	Kevin Richardson	7
16.	Kevin Davies	8
27.	David Hirst	7

SUBSTITUTES

22.	Duncan Spedding Richardson	87 mins	6
10.	Egil Ostenstad Davies	19 mins	7
11.	Robbie Slater Le Tissier	80 mins	6
19.	Richard Dryden	
13.	Neil Moss	

SCORERS

Davies | 3 mins

REFEREE

M Riley | Leeds

VISITORS

		RATING
1.	Peter Schmeichel	7
2.	Gary Neville	7
3.	Denis Irwin	7
6.	Gary Pallister	8
5.	Ronny Johnsen	7
10.	David Beckham	6
8.	Nicky Butt	6
11.	Ryan Giggs	6
18.	Paul Scholes	7
20.	Ole G Solskjaer	5
9.	Andy Cole	6

SUBSTITUTES

12.	Phil Neville	6
12.	Henning Berg	8
13.	Brian McClair Butt	80 mins	6
22.	Erik Nevland G Neville	85 mins	6
25.	Kevin Pilkington	

MATCH REPORT

Those wishing to stop Manchester United dominating English football should find a way to force them to play all their games at the Dell. For the third successive season, United were beaten on the south coast. "Somebody tell me how to pick up three points here!" pleaded Alex Ferguson afterwards.

Southampton displayed none of the flair that had seen them score six on United's last visit to the Dell, but their football was just as effective. After Kevin Davies had glanced a third-minute header past Schmeichel, Southampton formed an 11-man defence and hoofed away the ball like a Sunday park team. Survival football in January!

The Dell's narrow pitch did not suit United. It was a night where Teddy Sheringham's absence through injury was crucial. You sense his craft would have broken down Southampton's resistance. United's attacks lacked subtlety — too often high balls were aimlessly hit into the area.

Southampton triumphed because they denied United space in midfield and up front. Palmer and Richardson harried Scholes and Butt, while Ken Monkou smothered Cole and Solskjaer. When United did manage to get through, Paul Jones thwarted them with fine saves.

Keeping up with the Jones

IN THE PAPERS

"Manchester United never want to see this little Premiership ground again. The Dell has a jinx on them, the Champions simply cannot win here. Oh, how they must hate it after three shock defeats in successive seasons. But let us not talk only of a jinx and a hoodoo. Southampton surely produced their bravest 87 minutes of the season after Kevin Davies' early goal."
SUN

"Kevin Davies threw Manchester United's title rivals the slenderest of lifelines as they notched up an astonishing hat-trick of giant-killings over the Champions. The defeat is a huge encouragement to Liverpool, who can cut the gap down to just six points with victory over Newcastle United tonight."
DAILY STAR

"Southampton last night gave the rest of the Premiership hope that the title race is not a lost cause. Alex Ferguson called it "The christian thing to do." Unfortuanately for Chelsea, Liverpool and Blackburn, United only play at the Dell once a season. The setback to the Champions seemingly relentless march toward a fifth title in six years was not wholly unexpected. This was their third consecutive defeat in this fixture."
INDEPENDENT

"Kevin Davies, one of the finds of the season, condemned Manchester United to another night of hell at the Dell and left Alex Ferguson bemused. The United boss, beaten at Southampton for the third consecutive year after 20-year-old Davies scored with a third-minute header, asked: "Can someone tell me how we lost that game.""
DAILY MAIL

"Somebody
please tell me
how to pick up
three points at
the Dell!"

ALEX FERGUSON

What are
they doing?

MANCHESTER UNITED 5
WALSALL 1

HOME TEAM

		RATING
1.	Peter Schmeichel	7
3.	Denis Irwin	7
21.	Henning Berg	7
5.	Ronny Johnsen	8
12.	Phil Neville	7
13.	Brian McClair	7
7.	David Beckham	7
18.	Paul Scholes	9
23.	Ben Thornley	7
20.	Ole G Solskjaer	8
9.	Andy Cole	8

SUBSTITUTES

32.	Michael Clegg	7
	Irwin	24 mins	
22.	Erik Nevland	8
	Thornley	64 mins	
28.	Phil Mulryne	7
	Scholes	69 mins	
11.	Ryan Giggs	
25.	Kevin Pilkington	

SCORERS

Cole | 10/65 mins
Solskjaer | 39/69 mins
Johnsen | 74 mins

REFEREE

Paul Durkin | Dorset

VISITORS

1.	James Walker	6
2.	Wayne Evans	6
3.	Chris Marsh	6
4.	Adrian Viveash	6
5.	Derek Mountfield	6
6.	Jean Francois Peron	6
7.	Roger Boli	6
8.	Gary Porter	6
9.	Dean Keates	6
10.	Andrew Watson	6
11.	John Hodge	6

SUBSTITUTES

12.	Mark Blake	
	Peron	88 mins	
13.	Daniel Naisbitt	
14.	Ian Roper	
15.	Clive Platt	
16.	Michael Ricketts	

SCORERS

Boli | 65 mins

MATCH REPORT

When Walsall's greatest ambition was to come away from Old Trafford with a signed programme, Manchester United's progress to the fifth round of the FA Cup was never in danger.

Walsall came to enjoy their day out and play open, attacking football. The problem was this allowed United to do the same; only they are rather better at it. Walsall's French striker, Roger Boli, a friend of Eric Cantona, was impressed: "I'll tell Eric that even without him, his team is beautiful."

Ferguson rested four first-team players, but United still displayed the appetite they had shown at Chelsea. Andy Cole opened the scoring after ten minutes with a low shot from just inside the penalty box before Solskjaer made it two six minutes before the interval.

In the second half, Erik Nevland nearly marked his first appearance at Old Trafford with a goal. The young Norwegian ran onto a McClair through ball and went around the keeper, but Andy Cole enforced his seniority and brushed him aside to take advantage of the empty net. Solskjaer and Johnsen's goals turned the result into a thrashing, but Boli still managed a memorable consolation goal.

IN THE PAPERS

Boli's champagne moment

Hair-raising:
Don King
congratulates
goal-king Cole

MANCHESTER UNITED 0
LEICESTER CITY 1

HOME TEAM

1.	Peter Schmeichel	7
2.	Gary Neville	8
3.	Denis Irwin	7
5.	Ronny Johnsen	5
6.	Gary Pallister	7
7.	David Beckham	6
8.	Nicky Butt	7
9.	Andy Cole	7
11.	Ryan Giggs	7
18.	Paul Scholes	8
20.	Ole G Solskjaer	7

SUBSTITUTES

10.	Teddy Sheringham Berg | 55 mins	6
12.	Phil Neville Scholes | 83 mins	
13.	Brian McClair	
21.	Henning Berg Johnsen | 6 mins	6
25.	Kevin Pilkington	

REFEREE

Gerald Ashby | Worcester

VISITORS

		RATING
1.	Kasey Keller	8
14.	Rob Savage	8
24.	Steve Guppy	7
15.	Pontus Kaamark	7
18.	Matt Elliott	
5.	Steve Walsh	7
6.	Mustafa Izzet	7
7.	Neil Lennon	7
10.	Garry Parker	8
27.	Tony Cottee	8
11.	Emile Heskey	7

SUBSTITUTES

22.	Pegguy Arphexad	
21.	Graham Fenton	
17.	Spencer Prior Walsh | 34 mins	6
25.	Stuart Wilson Cottee | 88 mins	
16.	Stuart Campbell Parker | 65 mins	6

SCORERS

Cottee | 34 mins

MATCH REPORT

Only a month ago, teams who had beaten United were inducted in to an "elite" group. After Leicester condemned United to their third League defeat in four games, the elite is becoming somewhat overcrowded.

Leicester won courtesy of a Tony Cottee goal. Back from a spell in Malaysia, he showed the type of finishing that once made him Britain's most expensive player to condemn United to their first defeat at Old Trafford this season. Cottee pounced when the ball bounced over Henning Berg, giving him the time to volley past Schmeichel.

Martin O'Neill's side fully deserved their first Premiership win in two months. They worked hard and took their opening, while United started the game lethargically and were terribly profligate in front of goal. Teddy Sheringham was presented with a clear chance right at the death, but completely missed the target.

"We suffered because we didn't have the same work ethic as them. So we can't complain," said Alex Ferguson. "But we will work hard for the rest of the season. You can bet your lives on that!"

IN THE PAPERS

"Beaten 3–0 away by Crystal Palace a week ago – Palace who can barely beat an egg at home – Leicester were thought to be in no fit state to take on the wonder team. Yet United were anything but. They were, at first, over confident, arrogant and sloppy; later petulant, tetchy and edgy; finally, just desperate, panicking. Human frailties were being laid bare."
TIMES

"Manchester United showed the kind of world weariness which was unprofessional, unattractive and could even cost them their coveted Premiership. It may be too early to question their pedigree. After all, they ooze quality. But attitude... now, that is a different matter."
MIRROR

"Fergie had witnessed his title favourites outfought by a side who possess the attributes of an army of ants. Few sides toil harder or are better disciplined than Martin O'Neill's willing workers, every one of them a soldier ant on a mission."
DAILY MAIL

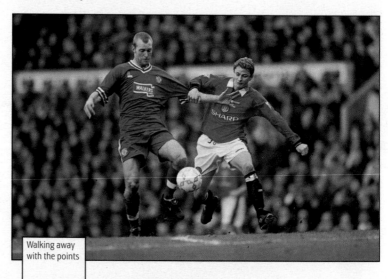

Walking away with the points

Cottee shocker: where did he come from?

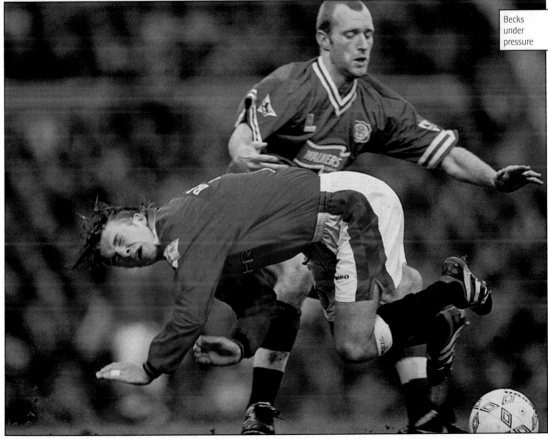

Becks under pressure

January STATS

PLAYER RECORDS

■ PREMIERSHIP
■ COCA-COLA CUP ■ FA CUP

home | away

■ ■ FULL APPEARANCE / CAME ON AS SUB

■ ■ SCORER / SCORED AS SUB

Column headers (opponents): Tottenham Hotspur, Southampton, Leicester City, Everton, Coventry City, West Ham United, Bolton Wanderers, Chelsea, Leeds United, Crystal Palace, Ipswich Town, Derby County, Barnsley, Sheffield Wednesday, Arsenal, Wimbledon, Blackburn Rovers, Liverpool, Aston Villa, Newcastle United, Coventry City, Chelsea, Tottenham Hotspur, Southampton, Walsall, Leicester City, Bolton Wanderers, West Ham United, FA Cup Round Five, Derby County, Chelsea, Sheffield Wednesday, FA Cup Round Six, Arsenal, Wimbledon, Blackburn Rovers, FA Cup Semi Final, Liverpool, Aston Villa, Newcastle United, Crystal Palace, Leeds United, Barnsley, FA Cup Final

	FULL APPEARANCES	SUB APPEARANCES	GOALS
1. Peter Schmeichel	25	0	0
2. Gary Neville	23	0	0
3. Denis Irwin	12	3	0
4. David May	1	0	0
5. Ronny Johnsen	15	4	0
6. Gary Pallister	25	0	0
7. David Beckham	23	3	7
8. Nicky Butt	22	1	1
9. Andy Cole	20	2	15
10. Teddy Sheringham	18	2	9
11. Ryan Giggs	20	1	5
12. Phil Neville	17	3	0
13. Brian McClair	2	7	0
14. Jordi Cruyff	4	1	0
15. Karel Poborsky	5	7	2
16. Roy Keane	9	0	2
17. Rai Van Der Gouw	0	0	0
18. Paul Scholes	21	2	4
20. Ole Gunnar Solskjaer	12	5	8
21. Henning Berg	18	1	1
22. Erik Nevland	0	3	0
23. Ben Thornley	1	1	0
24. John O'Kane	0	0	0
25. Kevin Pilkington	2	0	0
26. Chris Casper	0	0	0
27. Terry Cooke	0	0	0
28. Phil Mulryne	1	1	0
30. Ronnie Wallwork	0	1	0
31. John Curtis	2	3	0
32. Michael Clegg	0	1	0

PLAYER OF THE MONTH

Paul Scholes

AVERAGE PERFORMANCE RATING: 7.6

FA CARLING PREMIERSHIP

as at 1 February 1998

	Pld	W	D	L	F	A	Pts	GD
■ Manchester United	24	15	4	5	51	18	49	33
▲ Chelsea	24	14	3	7	52	25	45	27
▼ Blackburn Rovers	24	12	9	3	44	24	45	20
■ Liverpool	24	13	6	5	39	19	45	20
▲ Arsenal	23	11	8	4	42	26	41	16
▲ Derby County	24	11	6	7	39	30	39	9
▼ Leeds United	24	11	5	8	34	27	38	7
■ West Ham United	24	11	3	11	36	35	35	1
■ Leicester City	24	8	9	7	27	22	33	5
▲ Sheffield Wednesday	24	8	6	10	37	47	30	-10
■ Newcastle United	23	8	5	10	24	29	29	-5
■ Southampton	24	8	4	12	26	33	28	-7
■ Coventry City	24	6	9	9	28	34	27	-6
▲ Everton	24	7	6	11	28	35	27	-7
▼ Aston Villa	23	7	6	10	26	33	27	-7
▼ Wimbledon	23	6	8	9	22	27	26	-5
▼ Crystal Palace	24	5	8	11	21	34	23	-13
▲ Tottenham Hotspur	24	6	5	13	21	41	23	-20
▼ Bolton Wanderers	24	4	10	10	21	40	22	-19
■ Barnsley	24	6	3	15	20	59	21	-39

FEBRUARY

1 | 2 | 3 | 4 | 5 | 6 | 7 | 8 | 9 | 10 | 11 | 12 | 13 | 14 | 15 | 16 | 17 | 18 | 19 | 20 | 21 | 22 | 23 | 24 | 25 | 26 | 27 | 28

FEBRUARY

THE MONTH AHEAD

The month which marked the 40th anniversary of the Munich Air Disaster was a time when everyone connected with Manchester United, and football in general, was poignantly reminded that there are times when what happens on the football pitch is an irrelevance.

In a mark of tribute to those that died in the tragedy on 6 February 1958, a moving memorial service was held the day before United's Premiership match with Bolton at Manchester Cathedral. The following day the teams came onto the pitch at Old Trafford at 3.04 pm, the exact time of the disaster. Survivors from the crash were presented to the crowd and wreaths were laid on the pitch before an impeccably observed minute's silence.

Alex Ferguson had urged his players to follow the pre-match ceremony with a performance the occasion deserved. But clearly the emotion of the day had affected the team and only a late Andy Cole equaliser prevented the match ending with defeat, a goal greeted with jubilation by the crowd which included survivors

of the Munich disaster like Ray Wood and Albert Scanlon.

Elsewhere in the world, crisis was looming again in the Gulf, with American and British troops sent to the region in a bid to put pressure on Iraqi leader Saddam Hussein.

For United, the next battle was at home to Barnsley in the FA Cup. The game was notable for Schmeichel's horrendously sliced kick which allowed John Hendrie to nick in and slip the ball home, and Gary Neville's tackle on Andy Lidell which even Alex Ferguson admitted was a clear penalty. In between, Teddy Sheringham had equalised. The match went to a replay and so United had a tough match at Oakwell to add to their already demanding schedule.

In the meantime, all manner of sparks had been flying down in London where Chelsea manager Ruud Gullit had been sensationally sacked and replaced as boss by Gianluca Vialli. The sacking took the football world by storm. Gullit claimed he had been stabbed in the back and Chelsea claimed he had wanted too much money – all of which probably had Alex Ferguson (who had claimed the Blues were his team's biggest title rivals) rubbing his hands with glee.

He might not be rubbing his hands with the same glee when he considers the prospect of facing Brian Laudrup in a Chelsea shirt next season. Just after Vialli's appointment, the Rangers star, who was once a target for United, agreed a transfer to the London club and the highest wage in the Premiership, reputed

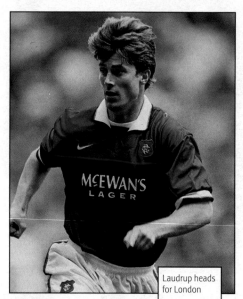

Laudrup heads for London

Ruud's a shadow of his former self

"That minute at Old Trafford was the quietest I have ever witnessed"

PETER SCHMEICHEL ON THE PERFECTLY-OBSERVED SILENCE BEFORE THE BOLTON MATCH

to be £75,000 a week. No wonder they couldn't afford Gullit!

Back on the pitch, United's next game after two 1–1 draws was away to Villa. A night of frustration was turned into a night of jubilation with goals from David Beckham and a late strike from Ryan Giggs earning a welcome 2–0 win in the last ten minutes.

But jubilation was turned to agony in the next game, at home to Derby County. United ran out 2–0 winners, but Ryan Giggs – Man of the Match and in the form of his life – limped off with a hamstring injury. And just as you think it can't get any worse, you have to go and play a resurgent Barnsley in an FA Cup replay at Oakwell. So it was goodbye to the FA Cup.

In the build-up to the Monaco away game, United faced Chelsea at Stamford Bridge and Ferguson sent his team out to

play Vialli's side as if playing an away leg in Europe, getting men behind the ball and breaking swiftly and incisively. It worked and Phil Neville scored his first senior goal for the club

Six days later, the strangely sculptured Louis II Stadium was packed with United fans who'd come for a day out in the millionaire's playground. The bank balances of the Monaco fans (yes, both of them) might be full, but the scoresheet remained empty at full time after a scrappy match on a potato patch of a pitch. Alex Ferguson professed himself happy with the 0–0 result but United were soon to learn, to their cost, that scoring a goal away from home is crucial in Europe...

Munich remembered

MANCHESTER UNITED 1
BOLTON WANDERERS 1

HOME TEAM

1.	Peter Schmeichel	7
2.	Gary Neville	8
3.	Denis Irwin	6
6.	Gary Pallister	6
12.	Phil Neville	5
18.	Paul Scholes	7
7.	David Beckham	5
20.	Ole G Solskjaer	6
10.	Teddy Sheringham	6
11.	Ryan Giggs	6
9.	Andy Cole	9

SUBSTITUTES

21.	Henning Berg	6
	Sheringham	68 mins	
13.	Brian McClair	
31.	John Curtis	
34.	Michael Twiss	
17.	Rai Van Der Gouw	

SCORERS

Cole | 85 mins

REFEREE

Stephen Lodge | Barnsley

VISITORS

		RATING
1.	Keith Branagan	8
2.	Gudni Bergsson	7
6.	Chris Fairclough	6
2.	Neil Cox	6
17.	Andy Todd	6
7.	Jamie Pollock	7
8.	Scott Sellars	7
4.	Per Frandsen	8
11.	Alan Thompson	7
9.	Nathan Blake	6
33.	Bob Taylor	7

SUBSTITUTES

16.	Gavin Ward	
14.	Michael Johansen	
15.	John Sheridan	
28.	Hasney Aljofree	
23.	Dean Holdsworth	6
	Taylor	82 mins	

SCORERS

Taylor | 60 mins

MATCH REPORT

The blip is back. Alex Ferguson revived that dreaded word to explain United's failure to win a third consecutive League match.

It was a shame this blip continued on the day United marked the 40th anniversary of the Munich air disaster. They were hoping to put on a performance to honour the Babes, but were grateful to finish with a point.

United were led out by Bobby Charlton at 3:04 pm, the exact time 40 years and a day earlier the aeroplane carrying the Babes had crashed. The current team, survivors and the victim's families stood on the pitch for a minute's silence. Perhaps the emotion of the day overwhelmed United for they appeared jaded and off the pace in the first half.

Bolton looked anything but a team facing relegation. They went ahead through Bob Taylor, on loan from West Brom. It was his first goal in the top division and, as he returned to the Hawthorns after this game, possibly his last.

Bolton's goal infused United with the spirit they'd been lacking. They spent the last 20 minutes bombarding Bolton's area and were rewarded when Andy Cole headed an equaliser with five minutes remaining.

IN THE PAPERS

"Putting your finger on what's gone wrong for United in the bleak mid-winter is as hard a brain teaser as the one facing young Neville. The commitment is there. So is the pride and passion. But once you're in a rut it's so difficult to claw your way out. Somehow the ball isn't being moved about the way it should. Movement up front isn't as free flowing. And at the back there's a hesitancy that leaves boss Alex Ferguson shaking his head on the bench."
MIRROR

Their famous shirts might have bulged with legends on such an emotionally gripped day.Instead they were mostly filled with mere shadows. No, not of the Busby Babes. Simply of themselves.Because this was surely the closet Manchester United have ever got to a title trauma".
SUN

"The tragic heritage that has helped to make United one of the best supported teams in the world was paraded in front of 55,000 fans and turned it into an uplifting celebration of everything that is good and noble in the game."
TIMES

Gary rues his last-minute miss

United in mourning

Cole, the Saviour

MANCHESTER UNITED 1
BARNSLEY 1

HOME TEAM

1.	Peter Schmeichel	6
3.	Denis Irwin	7
21.	Henning Berg	7
6.	Gary Pallister	8
32.	Michael Clegg	8
12.	Phil Neville	5
5.	Ronny Johnsen	7
13.	Brian McClair	7
11.	Ryan Giggs	7
10.	Teddy Sheringham	6
22.	Erik Nevland	6

SUBSTITUTES

7.	David Beckham	7
	Johnsen | 45 mins	
14.	Jordi Cruyff	7
	Nevland | 58 mins	
20.	Gary Neville	8
	McClair | 79 mins	
17.	Van Der Gouw	
26.	Chris Casper	

SCORERS

Sheringham | 42 mins

REFEREE

Mike Riley | Leeds

VISITORS   RATING

1.	David Watson	9
2.	Nicky Eaden	7
6.	Arjan De Zeeuw	6
5.	Adrian Moses	7
27.	Chris Morgan	7
23.	Ales Krizan	7
8.	Neil Redfearn	8
15.	Jovo Bosancic	7
14.	Martin Bullock	7
7.	John Hendrie	7
25.	Ashley Ward	6

SUBSTITUTES

13.	Lars Leese	
21.	Eric Tinkler	
3.	Matty Appleby	6
	De Zeeuw | 24 mins	
10.	Clint Marcelle	
12.	Andy Liddell	6
	Hendrie | 81 mins	

SCORERS

Hendrie | 30 mins

MATCH REPORT

Alex Ferguson gambled and lost. He had hoped to sneak past Barnsley by fielding a weakened team, but the Tykes were having none of it and were disappointed to finish with just a replay.

Barnsley should have been making plans for a sixth-round tie at Newcastle rather than a rematch at Oakwell after being refused a blatant penalty with time running out. Gary Neville felled Andy Liddel with a waist-high tackle, but referee Steve Riley inexpicably ignored Barnsley's appeals. "Everyone in the ground apart from the ref thought it was a penalty," said Barnsley manager Danny Wilson.

Chastened by a 7–0 defeat on their last visit to Old Trafford, Barnsley were not going to be overawed again and took the game to United early on. They went in front when Schmeichel sliced a back pass from Pallister into the path of John Hendrie who tapped it in to the empty net. For once the Dane could not blame anyone but himself.

But United responded almost immediately when Ryan Giggs brilliantly back-heeled the ball in to Teddy Sheringham's path who took it in to his stride and placed the ball past Watson.

IN THE PAPERS

"Barnsley, who scored first through John Hendrie after a shocking error by Peter Schmeichel, were swiftly pegged back by Teddy Sheringham. But they left with mixed emotions: delighted to have drawn, but despairing of referee Mike Riley, who refused them a late penalty which even the United manager admitted was blatant."
INDEPENDENT

"Peter Schmeichel was spared some embarrassment because at least United remain in the Cup. But Alex Ferguson will not thank his Danish keeper for the fifth round replay at Barnsley. The Old Trafford manager needs another game in the run up to to United's all-important trip to Monaco on 4 March like he needs a kick in the teeth."
EXPRESS

"Peter Schmeichel would be the number one goalkeeper in most people's world team. In one cringing, horror-filled second yesterday he looked more like a fugitive from the Nag's Head second team."
SUN

The incident

Oh, Teddy,
Teddy...

ASTON VILLA 0
MANCHESTER UNITED 2

HOME TEAM

1.	Mark Bosnich	8
20.	Riccardo Scimeca	6
5.	Ugo Ehiogu	8
4.	Gareth Southgate	8
14.	Alan Wright	7
12.	Julian Joachim	7
7.	Ian Taylor	7
16.	Simon Grayson	7
15.	Fernando Nelson	6
11.	Stan Collymore	7
9.	Savo Milosovic	7

SUBSTITUTES

17. Lee Hendrie
21. Lee Collins
25. Darren Byfield
13. Michael Oakes
27. Richard Walker

REFEREE

Martin Bodenham | Sussex

VISITORS   RATING

1.	Peter Schmeichel	8
2.	Gary Neville	6
21.	Henning Berg	6
6.	Gary Pallister	7
3.	Denis Irwin	6
7.	David Beckham	8
13.	Brian McClair	6
8.	Nicky Butt	6
11.	Ryan Giggs	6
10.	Teddy Sheringham	6
9.	Andy Cole	6

SUBSTITUTES

12.	Phil Neville	6
	McClair | 47 mins	
17.	Rai Van Der Gouw	
14.	Jordi Cruyff	
22.	Erik Nevland	
32.	Michael Clegg	

SCORERS

Beckham | 82 mins
Giggs | 89 mins

MATCH REPORT

Two late goals from David Beckham and Ryan Giggs saw United eagerly grasp their first League win for six weeks.

United triumphed because they remained composed as time ran out, rather than allowing themselves to be gripped by the same blind panic that had failed them against Southampton, Leicester and Bolton.

Early on, United struggled to overcome their recent malaise and it was Villa who created the better chances; Collymore intially showed interest in the game with a couple of menacing runs and Savo Milosevic tried hard to win over – rather than spit over – the Villa faithful.

"Up until the last 20 minutes it was a very even match," said Alex Ferguson. "Then we started to express ourselves with our passing. We went back to what we are good at and deserved to win."

Cole and Sheringham had threatened Villa's goal, before Beckham strode on to a Sheringham pass, skipped past a defender and slammed a left-footed shot through Bosnich's hands.

Three minutes later, Beckham turned provider when he whipped a ball across the goal mouth which Giggs converted at the far post.

IN THE PAPERS

"The chasing pack have had their fingers crossed that Alex Ferguson's thoroughbreds might run out of steam in their bid for a fifth title in six years. Even struggling Aston Villa, more concerned with what's happening at the other end of the table, carried illusions that they could lower United's colours for most of this match. But Beckham had different ideas and, when the England midfielder struck, it was over in a flash."
MIRROR

"There is a large amount of daylight between United and the rest and, on the horizon, stands the silhouette of the Premiership trophy. It was far from vintage United, but they stuck at it and got their reward. They showed they had grit, even when the stingiest tide is turning against them."
SUN

"It is not the first time recently that United have moved away from the chasing pack despite a diffident performance, as the likes of Blackburn, Liverpool, Arsenal and Chelsea have failed to capitalize on United's slip-ups."
GUARDIAN

Gatecrashing the party

Becks breaks the deadlock

Giggsy sees them off

MANCHESTER UNITED 2
DERBY COUNTY 0

HOME TEAM

		RATING
1.	Peter Schmeichel	7
2.	Gary Neville	7
21.	Henning Berg	7
6.	Gary Pallister	7
3.	Denis Irwin	7
7.	David Beckham	8
12.	Phil Neville	7
8.	Nicky Butt	7
11.	Ryan Giggs	8
10.	Teddy Sheringham	6
9.	Andy Cole	7

SUBSTITUTES

13.	Brian McClair	6
	Giggs	79 mins	
14.	Jordi Cruyff	6
	Cole	75 mins	
17.	Rai Van Der Gouw	
26.	Chris Casper	
32.	Michael Clegg	7
	Irwin	75 mins	

SCORERS

Giggs | 18 mins
Irwin | 70 mins (pen)

REFEREE

Mike Reed | Birmingham

VISITORS

21.	Mart Poom	6
2.	Gary Rowett	7
6.	Igor Stimac	6
22.	Christian Dailly	7
10.	Rory Delap	7
20.	Stefano Eranio	6
18.	Lee Carsley	6
3.	Chris Powell	6
27.	Francesco Baiano	6
9.	Paulo Wanchope	6
8.	Dean Sturridge	6

SUBSTITUTES

11.	Ron Willems	6
	Delap| 87 mins	
4.	Darryl Powell	
19.	Steve Elliott	
25.	Robert Kozluk	
1.	Russell Hoult	

MATCH REPORT

Ryan Giggs dominated this game. He scored a wonderful opener, was fouled for United's game-clinching penalty and then limped off ten minutes from the end with a pulled hamstring that ruled him out of United's trip to Monaco. So inventive and attacking had Giggs been, some thought United's European ambitions would now be mortally wounded by his absence.

Giggs' injury overshadowed a comfortable win for United. Derby were disappointing and never looked like maintaining their position as the only team to remain unbeaten against United since the Premiership began. Their front line of Baiano, Wanchope and Sturridge all failed to live up to their billing. Wanchope wasted Derby's only real chance when he broke free in the first half, but scuffed a shot which rolled safely into Schmeichel's hands.

After 18 minutes, Giggs stroked the ball to Cole who, spotting the Welshman's dash in to the area, curled the ball to his feet for him to finish first time beyond Poom. Cole should have scored when Giggs returned the favour minutes later.

United killed the game after 70 minutes. Cole nodded the ball down to Giggs who ran past Poom but was barged over by Delap. Irwin made no mistake with the penalty.

Giggs limps to the exit

IN THE PAPERS

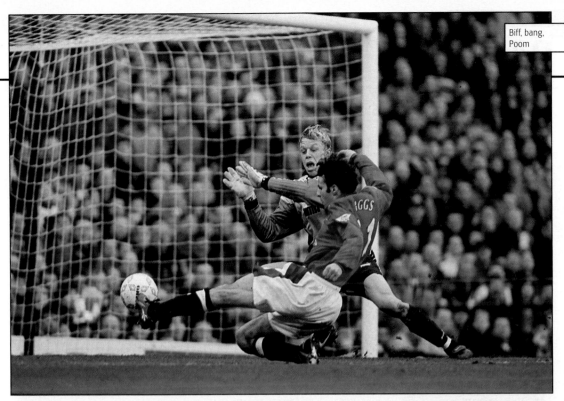

Biff, bang, Poom

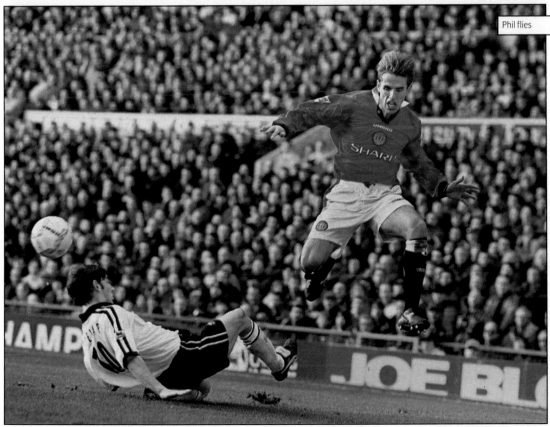

Phil flies

BARNSLEY 3
MANCHESTER UNITED 2

HOME TEAM

1.	David Watson	8
29.	Peter Markstedt	7
18.	Scott Jones	8
5.	Adrian Moses	7
3.	Matty Appleby	6
14.	Martin Bullock	7
8.	Neil Redfearn	8
15.	Jovo Bosancic	7
24.	Darren Barnard	7
7.	John Hendrie	7
25.	Ashley Ward	7

SUBSTITUTES

4.	Darren Sheridan	6
	Appleby | 65 mins	
21.	Eric Tinkler	
22.	Georgi Hristov	
10.	Clint Marcelle	6
	Bullock | 73 mins	
12.	Andy Liddell	6
	Hendrie | 46 mins	

SCORERS

Hendrie | 9 mins
Jones | 45/65 mins

REFEREE

Mike Riley | Leeds

VISITORS   RATING

1.	Peter Schmeichel	6
2.	Gary Neville	7
4.	David May	7
6.	Gary Pallister	7
32.	Michael Clegg	7
12.	Phil Neville	6
13.	Brian McClair	6
7.	David Beckham	6
23.	Ben Thornley	6
22.	Erik Nevland	6
9.	Andy Cole	8

SUBSTITUTES

10.	Teddy Sheringham	7
	Nevland | 34 mins	
3.	Denis Irwin	7
	McClair | 48 mins	
34.	Michael Twiss	7
	Clegg | 78 mins	
26.	Chris Casper	
17.	Rai Van Der Gouw	

SCORERS

Sheringhan | 55 mins
Cole | 81 mins

MATCH REPORT

Voted the best town in England only days earlier, living conditions improved for Barnsley natives after they knocked United out of the FA Cup on a night Barnsley's manager Danny Wilson called, "One of the greatest in the club's history."

While there was unconfined joy on the award-winning streets of Barnsley, no mass suicides were reported in Manchester. Ejection from the FA Cup will surely help United's two main priorities of the Premiership and the European Cup. Indeed, the presence of Sheringham and Irwin on the bench illustrated Ferguson's limited desire for this competition.

Fired up by the penalty they should have had and Ferguson's "disrespectful" team selection, Barnsley flew into a two-goal lead by half-time through John Hendrie and Scott Jones. Faced with defeat, Ferguson was unable to contain his innate competitive spirit and threw on Irwin and Sheringham.

Sheringham got a goal back, but Jones, who nearly left Oakwell for Mansfield a month earlier, re-established Barnsley's two-goal lead by heading in unmarked at the far post. Cole gave United late hope, but Barnsley held out to progress to the quarter finals for the first time in 13 years.

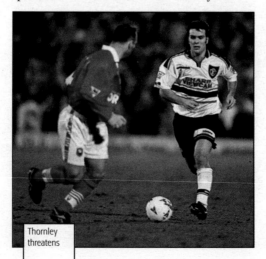

Thornley
threatens

IN THE PAPERS

Hendrie's opener

Andy makes a late bid to save face

CHELSEA 0
MANCHESTER UNITED 1

HOME TEAM

21.	Dmitri Kharine	7
2.	Dan Petrescu	6
5.	Frank Leboeuf	5
6.	Steve Clarke	7
9.	Gianluca Vialli	5
10.	Mark Hughes	6
11.	Denis Wise	6
12.	Michael Duberry	6
14.	Graeme Le Saux	5
16.	Roberto Di Matteo	6
25.	Gianfranco Zola	6

SUBSTITUTES

7.	Bernard Lambourde	
13.	Kevin Hitchcock	
19.	Tore Andre Flo	5
	Vialli | 78 mins	
22.	Mark Nicholls	
24.	Eddie Newton	

REFEREE

Stephen Dunn \| Bristol

VISITORS   RATING

1.	Peter Schmeichel	7
2.	Gary Neville	7
3.	Denis Irwin	7
6.	Gary Pallister	6
5.	Ronny Johnsen	9
7.	David Beckham	7
12.	Phil Neville	7
8.	Nicky Butt	7
18.	Paul Scholes	7
10.	Teddy Sheringham	7
9.	Andy Cole	7

SUBSTITUTES

13.	Brian McClair	
20.	Ole G Solskjaer	
17.	Rai Van Der Gouw	
21.	Henning Berg	7
	Pallister | 28 mins	
27.	Ben Thornley	

SCORERS

P Neville \| 31 mins

MATCH REPORT

Previously known as 'Jigsaw' for his propensity to fall to pieces in front of goal, Phil Neville requires a new nickname after his first senior goal secured a lunchtime victory against Chelsea at Stamford Bridge. The win put United 11 points clear at the top of the table.

Victory was secured with none of the flair United had used to humiliate Chelsea 5–3 in the FA Cup two months earlier. It was based on the solid defence of Johnsen and Berg who restricted Chelsea to just a long-range effort from Dan Petrescu. Johnsen's performance proved that he is, "One of the most outstanding centre halfs around," said Alex Ferguson.

Chelsea's new manager Gianluca Vialli's call to end the vendettas between the clubs went unheeded as seven yellow cards were handed out, taking the total of cautions to 25 in the four games played between the sides this season. Dennis Wise and Nicky Butt staged their own private bout throughout the game.

The game was won in the first half when Phil Neville ran on to Sheringham's through ball and crisply finished in off the post. "I didn't know what to do or how to celebrate," he said. "It was all a new experience."

IN THE PAPERS

"What's Dicky Attenborough doing here?"

> "Now we're 14 points ahead of Chelsea, who I saw as our main rivals this season."
>
> ALEX FERGUSON

The final piece of the jigsaw

February STATS

PLAYER RECORDS

■ PREMIERSHIP
■ COCA-COLA CUP ■ FA CUP

home | away

■ FULL APPEARANCE
CAME ON AS SUB

■ SCORER
SCORED AS SUB

	Player	FULL APPEARANCES	SUB APPEARANCES	GOALS
1.	Peter Schmeichel	31	0	0
2.	Gary Neville	28	1	0
3.	Denis Irwin	17	4	1
4.	David May	2	0	0
5.	Ronny Johnsen	16	4	0
6.	Gary Pallister	31	0	0
7.	David Beckham	28	4	8
8.	Nicky Butt	25	1	1
9.	Andy Cole	25	2	16
10.	Teddy Sheringham	23	3	11
11.	Ryan Giggs	24	1	7
12.	Phil Neville	22	4	1
13.	Brian McClair	5	8	0
14.	Jordi Cruyff	4	3	0
15.	Karel Poborsky	5	7	2
16.	Roy Keane	9	0	2
17.	Rai Van Der Gouw	0	0	0
18.	Paul Scholes	23	2	4
20.	Ole Gunnar Solskjaer	14	5	8
21.	Henning Berg	21	3	1
22.	Erik Nevland	2	3	0
23.	Ben Thornley	2	1	0
24.	John O'Kane	0	0	0
25.	Kevin Pilkington	2	0	0
26.	Chris Casper	0	0	0
27.	Terry Cooke	0	0	0
28.	Phil Mulryne	1	1	0
30.	Ronnie Wallwork	0	1	0
31.	John Curtis	2	3	0
32.	Michael Clegg	2	2	0
34.	Michael Twiss	0	1	0

PLAYER OF THE MONTH

Gary Neville

AVERAGE PERFORMANCE RATING: 7.2

FA CARLING PREMIERSHIP

as at 2 March 1998

	Pld	W	D	L	F	A	Pts	GD
■ Manchester United	28	18	5	5	57	19	59	38
▲ Blackburn Rovers	27	13	9	5	49	33	48	16
▼ Arsenal	25	13	8	4	45	26	47	19
▲ Liverpool	28	13	8	7	46	28	47	18
▲ Chelsea	27	14	3	10	55	30	45	22
▲ Derby County	28	13	6	9	44	34	45	10
▼ Leicester City	28	10	10	8	44	28	40	6
■ Leeds United	27	11	6	10	35	30	39	5
■ West Ham United	26	12	3	11	38	36	39	2
▲ Coventry City	28	10	9	9	35	35	39	0
■ Southampton	28	11	4	13	34	37	37	-3
▲ Newcastle United	27	9	7	11	26	31	34	-5
■ Sheffield Wednesday	28	9	7	12	41	54	34	-13
▲ Aston Villa	28	9	6	13	30	39	33	-9
▼ Wimbledon	26	8	8	10	28	30	31	-2
▼ Everton	28	7	9	12	32	40	30	-8
▼ Tottenham Hotspur	27	7	6	14	25	43	27	-18
▲ Barnsley	27	7	4	16	24	60	25	-39
▼ Bolton Wanderers	26	4	12	10	23	42	24	-19
■ Crystal Palace	27	5	8	14	21	41	23	-20

MARCH

1 | 2 | 3 | 4 | 5 | 6 | 7 | 8 | 9 | 10 | 11 | 12 | 13 | 14 | 15 | 16 | 17 | 18 | 19 | 20 | 21 | 22 | 23 | 24 | 25 | 26 | 27 | 28 | 29 | 30 | 31

MARCH

THE MONTH AHEAD

March 1998 was to be the crunch month for Manchester United. Alex Ferguson had made no secret of the fact that the European Cup was the club's priority this season, and the first leg of the quarter final at Monaco was looming large.

In the end it was the failure to score in the first game in the luxury Louis II Stadium that cost United a place in the semis. On a pitch more reminiscent of Hackney Marshes than the French Riviera – some patches were so bare the dry mud was painted green to make it look like grass – there was little chance of a game of flowing football and United settled for keeping the opposition out. They did so fairly comfortably, but in two weeks time that 0–0 wouldn't look quite the great result many had thought.

If the pitch at Monaco was a farce, how about the first Grand Prix of the season? A contrived win for McLaren's Mika Hakinen made the sport a laughing stock,

Chelsea guzzle up the Coca-Cola Cup

just like the England cricket team out in the West Indies. And United didn't fare much better in their next game away to Sheffield Wednesday, going down to two goals from Peter Atherton and Paolo Di Canio.

Things improved slightly with a 1–1 draw at West Ham with Paul Scholes equalising Trevor Sinclair's goal for the Hammers late on. But perhaps Caesar's warning to "Beware the Ides of March" should have been delivered to Alex Ferguson. It was turning into a shocker, and next up were Arsenal.

Arsene Wenger's team had been slowly but surely creeping back up the table, and the Old Trafford showdown was being billed as the title decider. United were on a downer, plagued by injuries to key players like Giggs, Pallister, Butt, Scholes and Johnsen, while Arsenal were on a roll... so when it finished 1–0 to Arsenal, no one was that surprised.

Not exactly the best preparation for the even bigger one three days later, the eagerly-anticipated second leg quarter final with Monaco. Everyone knew it was going to be tough, but that didn't prepare Old Trafford for the disappointment of going out of the Cup in the 30th anniversary year of the club's only European Cup win.

It was David Treseguet's stunning fifth-minute strike which did the damage, and it was a goal fit to decide any tie. No matter how much United huffed and puffed, they just couldn't find their form. By keeping possession and frustrating their opponents, Monaco took the sting

Good on ya, mate:
Mika Hakinen wins his first
Grand Prix in Australia

out of the crowd, and the match. Even after Solskjaer had brought the scores level on 53 minutes, there was a sense that this wasn't going to be United's night.

All of a sudden the world didn't seem such a bright place. In the next few days England lost the test series in the West Indies and Mike Atherton resigned as skipper. England drew 1–1 with Switzerland in a match Glenn Hoddle admitted they could have lost 3–0. That was nothing to events at Newcastle United, however, when a Sunday newspaper carried a story on directors Freddie Shepherd and Douglas Hall claiming that they frequented a Marbella brothel, joked about how they were ripping the fans off with £50 replica shirts and described Geordie girls as 'dogs'.

Away from sport it was also a dreadful end to the month. There were fears that

Saddam Hussein was plotting an anthrax attack on Britain, putting the lethal chemical weapon spores in duty free goods like perfume. Then on 25 March in Jonesboro, Arkansas, two schoolboys, aged 11 and 13, shot dead their teacher and four classmates.

> ## "In Europe, the team that makes the least errors will go through. It's less entertaining, but it works"
>
> JOHN COLLINS' FORMULA FOR EUROPEAN SUCCESS

It had been an awful month all round, and United had to wait 10 days to play again and record their only win of a dismal 31 days. Even the 2–0 victory against Wimbledon was fortunate, with TV replays showing both late goals from Johnsen and Scholes were offside.

The following day Chelsea beat Middlesbrough 2–0 in the Coca-Cola Cup Final, but all eyes were on what was hotting up to be one of the tightest title finishes in years.

A polite message to
Newcastle's directors

SHEFFIELD WEDNESDAY 2
MANCHESTER UNITED 0

HOME TEAM

1.	Kevin Pressman	7
27.	Earl Barrett	7
5.	Jon Newsome	8
6.	Des Walker	7
20.	Andy Hinchcliffe	7
8.	Benito Carbone	8
2.	Peter Atherton	8
18.	Dejan Stefanovic	7
4.	Mark Pembridge	7
11.	Paolo Di Canio	8
10.	Andy Booth	7

SUBSTITUTES

13.	Matt Clarke	
14.	Steve Nicol	
15.	Christian Mayrleb	
19.	Scott Oakes	6
	De Canio	89 mins	
7.	Guy Whittingham	7
	Pembridge	49 mins	

SCORERS

Atherton | 26 mins
De Canio | 88 mins

REFEREE

Peter Jones | Loughborough

VISITORS
RATING

17.	Rai Van Der Gouw	7
2.	Gary Neville	7
4.	David May	8
5.	Ronny Johnsen	6
21.	Henning Berg	6
7.	David Beckham	6
12.	Phil Neville	6
8.	Nicky Butt	6
20.	Ole G Solskjaer	6
10.	Teddy Sheringham	6
9.	Andy Cole	6

SUBSTITUTES

25.	Kevin Pilkington	
31.	John Curtis	7
	P Neville	59 mins	
18.	Paul Scholes	7
	Johnsen	45 mins	
23.	Ben Thornley	
13.	Brian McClair	6
	Cole	77 mins	

MATCH REPORT

Sacked by United 12 years ago, Ron Atkinson has reaped plenty of revenge on his former club. He's had two Cup final victories and he's now stealing more precious points from their title run-in.

After being humbled 6–1 by United in November, Wednesday were not lacking sources of motivation. As Wednesday's keeper Kevin Pressman said, "After losing so heavily, we had something to prove." Their determination was further stoked by a 3–0 defeat to Derby earlier in the week.

Alex Ferguson's decision to allow his side to remain in France for an extra day after their Champions' League match with Monaco to relax and enjoy the sunshine failed to have the desired effect. Monaco's pitch had evidently taken its toll, and against Wednesday, United appeared tired.

After Peter Atherton headed Wednesday into the lead after 26 minutes when he met a Carbone corner at the back post, United looked like they'd never get back into the game.

Paolo Di Canio had troubled United all afternoon, so it was fitting he should wrap up the game for Wednesday with an overhead kick that crossed the line before May could clear it.

IN THE PAPERS

"Not your best work, Laddie"

Atherton opens the scoring

Heels over head

WEST HAM UNITED 1

MANCHESTER UNITED 1

HOME TEAM

32.	Bernand Lama	7
20.	Andy Impey	7
4.	Steve Potts	7
15.	Rio Ferdinand	7
19.	Stuart Pearce	7
17.	Stan Lazaridis	8
18.	Frank Lampard	8
29.	Eyal Berkovic	7
11.	Steve Lomas	8
24.	Samassi Abou	7
8.	Trevor Sinclair	8

SUBSTITUTES

22.	Craig Forest	
25.	Lee Hodges	
7.	Ian Bishop	
28.	Chris Coyne	
23.	Scott Mean	

SCORERS

Sinclair | 6 mins

REFEREE

Gary Willard | West Sussex

VISITORS

		RATING
1.	Peter Schmeichel	8
2.	Gary Neville	7
21.	Henning Berg	7
4.	David May	7
3.	Denis Irwin	7
7.	David Beckham	6
8.	Nicky Butt	6
13.	Brian McClair	7
18.	Paul Scholes	8
10.	Teddy Sheringham	8
9.	Andy Cole	7

SUBSTITUTES

17.	Rai Van Der Gouw	
26.	Chris Casper	
23.	Ben Thornley	6
	McClair | 45 mins	
31.	John Curtis	6
	Butt | 55 mins	
20.	Ole G Solskjaer	6
	Cole | 78 mins	

SCORERS

Scholes | 66 mins

MATCH REPORT

The Manchester bookmaker who declared United Champions and paid out £50,000 in winnings looked rather foolish after they dropped more points at Upton Park.

The result left United nervously looking over their shoulder at Arsenal, whose win at Wimbledon put them theoretically level with United; nine points behind, but with three games in hand.

In the first half, West Ham looked the livelier team and swept through United's ill-suited 4-3-3 formation. They took the lead after only six minutes when Berkovic glided through the centre of United's defence and rounded Schmeichel, only to hit May on the line. Trevor Sinclair was on hand to force in the rebound.

Only a breathtaking save from Schmeichel – he tipped a Frank Lampard shot on to the post – prevented the Hammers taking an even bigger lead before half-time.

Ben Thornley replaced Brian McClair in the second half and, though the young winger' distribution was inconsistent, he gave United some extra width.

Scholes grabbed United's equaliser when he lifted a shot over Lama. Though United had chances to win, it was West Ham's Samassi Abou who spurned the best opening when he fired over from a yard out.

IN THE PAPERS

"The dismantling of Manchester United's Championship ambition has almost become tradition at Upton Park in recent years. And while a look at the League table this morning would indicate the red malaise is only temporary, with the visit of challengers Arsenal on Saturday, United have Paul Scholes to thank for ensuring the damage report is not altogether more worrying."
EXPRESS

"Twice in recent seasons this has been a graveyard ground, Man United arriving in search of silverware and leaving with nothing. Again they failed to win at Upton Park last night, but the single point United earned to add to their leading total did not represent failure. That they clawed their way back into this Premiership struggle and came away undefeated is another indication the trophy is going back to Old Trafford."
STAR

Denis in
Sinc-opation

Get in there: Scholes equalises

MANCHESTER UNITED 0
ARSENAL 1

HOME TEAM

1.	Peter Schmiechel	7
2.	Gary Neville	8
21.	Hennig Berg	6
3.	Denis Irwin	6
31.	John Curtis	6
7.	David Beckham	6
18.	Paul Scholes	7
12.	Phil Neville	7
5.	Ronny Johnsen	7
10.	Teddy Sheringham	6
9.	Andy Cole	6

SUBSTITUTES

20.	Ole G Solskjaer P Neville	77 mins	6
4.	David May Johnsen	79 mins	6
23.	Ben Thornley Curtis	52 mins	7
13.	Brian McClair	
17.	Rai Van Der Gouw	

REFEREE

Stephen Dunn | Bristol

VISITORS   RATING

13.	Alex Manninger	8
2.	Lee Dixon	7
6.	Tony Adams	7
14.	Martin Keown	8
3.	Nigel Winterburn	7
15.	Ray Parlour	7
17.	Emmanuel Petit	9
4.	Patrik Viera	7
10.	Dennis Bergkamp	6
11.	Marc Overmars	9
12.	Christopher Wreh	7

SUBSTITUTES

9.	Nicolas Anelka Wreh	66 mins	7
19.	Remi Garde Parlour	70 mins	7
18.	Gilles Grimandi	
24.	John Lukic	
28.	Stephen Hughes	

SCORERS

Overmars | 70 mins

MATCH REPORT

Arsenal blew the title race wide open with a powerful performance at Old Trafford against a jaded United side whose season, increasingly ravaged by injuries, is threatening to burn out.

The pre-match feeling that United would raise themselves for the big game proved a false assumption. They looked tired and lacked their usual belief.

Arsenal's central midfield partnership of Petit and Viera were superb, outmuscling United and forcing Ferguson to concede, "We did not have the strength to beat Arsenal." Rarely has this United side been so humbled.

Overmars was the main beneficiary of Arsenal's midfield dominance. The Dutch winger terrified United's defence all afternoon with his pace and directness and could have had a hat-trick. He scored Arsenal's winner in the 79th minute when he ran on to a nod down from Anelka and calmly placed the ball through Schmeichel's legs.

As United's desperation grew Schmeichel went upfield for a corner in the last minute but, as he attempted to tackle Bergkamp, tore his hamstring.

At the final whistle, Arsenal danced beneath their travelling support while United and Schmeichel limped to the exit.

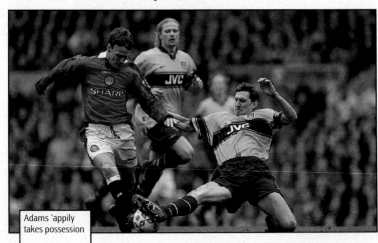

Adams 'appily takes possession

IN THE PAPERS

"United had their blood-red heart ripped out of them in cruel twists of fate that have left Fergies multi-million-pound squad in tatters. Cruel luck mingled unmercifully with a strangely subdued performance that left you with no other impression than that these are weary warriors feeling the strain of just one win in the past four Premiership games."
MIRROR

"They cannot claim we didn't warn them. The eggs are well and truly scrambled all right and most of the mixture can be found on Manchester United's faces this morning. Now they are treading on discarded shells as their panic-stricken army of supporters chorus the hysterical question: what happens next? All of them dreading the answer could be the surrender of their Premiership crown and the failure to nail that glorious obsession, the winning of the European Cup."
SUN

Over-run by
Overmars

That's
torn it

MANCHESTER UNITED 2
WIMBLEDON 0

HOME TEAM

		RATING
17.	Rai Van Der Gouw	7
2.	Gary Neville	7
21.	Henning Berg	6
4.	David May	7
3.	Denis Irwin	7
7.	David Beckham	8
18.	Paul Scholes	7
5.	Ronny Johnsen	7
12.	Phil Neville	7
20.	Ole G Solskjaer	6
9.	Andy Cole	8

SUBSTITUTES

23. Ben Thornley
Solskjaer | 81 mins

13. Brian McClair
Cole | 89 mins

25. Kevin Pilkington

26. Chris Casper

31. John Curtis

SCORERS

Johnsen | 83 mins
Scholes | 90 mins

REFEREE

Dermot Gallagher | Banbury

VISITORS

1.	Neil Sullivan	7
2.	Kenny Cunningham	7
6.	Ben Thatcher	8
12.	Chris Perry	7
3.	Alan Kimble	6
16.	Michael Hughes	7
18.	Neal Ardley	7
10.	Andy Roberts	7
8.	Robbie Earle	6
29.	Carl Leaburn	6
11.	Marcus Gayle	6

SUBSTITUTES

13. Paul Heald

15. Alan Reeves

23. Jason Euell — 6
Gayle | 60 mins

24. Peter Fear

27. Damien Francis

MATCH REPORT

Ronny Johnsen's decisive goal seven minutes from time precipitated scenes of jubilant relief not seen at Old Trafford since Steve Bruce rescued United five years before with his late goals against Sheffield Wednesday.

It was a huge relief for the biggest Premiership crowd of the season. It provided United with their first win for a month and lifted the malaise that had recently engulfed the whole club after their Champions' League exit to Monaco.

For 83 minutes it appeared United were about to lose further ground to Arsenal. They played with plenty of spirit, but precious little composure. Johnsen was an unlikely source of a goal, this being his first after two seasons in the Premiership. He volleyed past Sullivan – with a technique Mark Hughes would be envious of – after Wimbledon failed to clear from a corner.

Ben Thornley's replacement of Solskjaer led directly to United's second goal. Thornley played wide on the left and in the last minute, set free by Philip Neville, sprinted from the halfway line, jinked past Perry and cut back a cross for Beckham whose header was nodded in on the line by Paul Scholes.

IN THE PAPERS

Ronny runs into Red bliss

Pressure
released, joy
unconfined

119

March STATS

PLAYER RECORDS

Legend:
- home | away
- ■ PREMIERSHIP
- ■ COCA-COLA CUP ■ FA CUP
- ■ FULL APPEARANCE
- ■ CAME ON AS SUB
- ■ SCORER
- ■ SCORED AS SUB

#	Player	Full Appearances	Sub Appearances	Goals
1.	Peter Schmeichel	33	0	0
2.	Gary Neville	32	1	0
3.	Denis Irwin	20	4	1
4.	David May	5	1	0
5.	Ronny Johnsen	19	4	1
6.	Gary Pallister	31	0	0
7.	David Beckham	32	4	8
8.	Nicky Butt	27	1	1
9.	Andy Cole	29	2	16
10.	Teddy Sheringham	26	3	11
11.	Ryan Giggs	24	1	7
12.	Phil Neville	25	4	1
13.	Brian McClair	6	10	0
14.	Jordi Cruyff	4	3	0
15.	Karel Poborsky	5	7	2
16.	Roy Keane	9	0	2
17.	Rai Van Der Gouw	2	0	0
18.	Paul Scholes	26	3	6
20.	Ole Gunnar Solskjaer	16	7	8
21.	Henning Berg	25	3	1
22.	Erik Nevland	2	3	0
23.	Ben Thornley	2	4	0
24.	John O'Kane	0	0	0
25.	Kevin Pilkington	2	0	0
26.	Chris Casper	0	0	0
27.	Terry Cooke	0	0	0
28.	Phil Mulryne	1	1	0
30.	Ronnie Wallwork	0	1	0
31.	John Curtis	3	5	0
32.	Michael Clegg	2	2	0
34.	Michael Twiss	0	1	0

PLAYER OF THE MONTH

Gary Neville

AVERAGE PERFORMANCE RATING: 7.3

FA CARLING PREMIERSHIP

as at 29 March 1998

	Pld	W	D	L	F	A	Pts	GD
Manchester United	32	19	6	7	60	23	63	37
Arsenal	29	16	9	4	48	26	57	22
Liverpool	31	15	9	7	54	34	54	20
Chelsea	30	15	3	12	59	35	48	24
Leeds United	30	14	6	10	45	30	48	15
Blackburn Rovers	29	13	9	7	49	38	48	11
Derby County	30	13	6	11	44	40	45	4
West Ham United	29	13	5	11	41	38	44	3
Coventry City	29	11	10	9	36	35	43	1
Southampton	31	13	4	14	41	43	43	-2
Aston Villa	32	12	6	14	38	42	42	-4
Leicester City	30	10	10	10	35	32	40	3
Sheffield Wednesday	31	10	7	14	45	58	37	-13
Wimbledon	29	9	8	12	30	34	35	-4
Newcastle United	30	9	8	13	28	35	35	-7
Tottenham Hotspur	31	9	7	15	32	48	34	-16
Everton	31	8	9	14	35	46	33	-11
Barnsley	30	9	4	17	31	60	31	-38
Bolton Wanderers	30	6	12	12	29	47	30	-18
Crystal Palace	31	6	8	17	27	54	26	-27

APRIL

1 | 2 | 3 | 4 | 5 | 6 | 7 | 8 | 9 | 10 | 11 | 12 | 13 | 14 | 15 | 16 | 17 | 18 | 19 | 20 | 21 | 22 | 23 | 24 | 25 | 26 | 27 | 28 | 29 | 30

APRIL

THE MONTH AHEAD

April Fools' Day came and went. Thousands of *Sun* readers were fooled into believing Paul Ince had radar football boots and a Portuguese radio station convinced its listeners that they *were* going to the World Cup after all.

Events in the Premiership, however, were no joke for United. On 2 April at Bolton, Arsenal recorded their fourth 1–0 win in a row, closing the gap to three points with two games in hand. Things looked to be getting even worse when Blackburn took the lead at Ewood Park in the Lancashire derby but United crawled back and eventually won 3–1. This was getting exciting.

Obviously, the title race was overshadowing all world events, although the small matter of a peace deal for Northern Ireland did make the news. Other items included the dreaded Arsenal also making it to the FA Cup Final by beating Wolves, er, 1–0, and Newcastle beating Sheffield United by the same score to join them.

The Premiership action resumed for the Easter programme with a Good Friday battle of the giants at Old Trafford between United and Liverpool. A crunch match if ever there was one. Despite Owen being sent off for a dreadful foul on Johnsen late in the first half, United couldn't break through and the 1–1 scoreline meant another two points lost.

At Highbury the following day, Arsenal at last conceded their first goal in eight games to fellow FA Cup finalists Newcastle, but then scored three goals at the other end. United's lead was four points but Arsenal had three games in hand. In the first of those they sensationally went 4–0 up against Blackburn in 15 minutes... Arsene Wenger's men were looking unstoppable.

United's chances of holding on to the Premiership title looked about as good as fans' chances of getting hold of a World Cup ticket. When an extra 115,000 tickets went on sale, the hotline received four million calls in the first hour and, unsurprisingly, few people got through.

In the European Cup Winners' Cup Chelsea beat Vicenza to go through to the final thanks to a late goal by Sparky Hughes. Arsenal keeper David Seaman crashed his Jaguar XK8 in a car park and the Spice Girls had afternoon tea with Prince Harry.

Back in the Premiership, Arsenal faced Wimbledon at Highbury and United faced Newcastle at Old Trafford in a crucial round of matches. It was during

Spoonhead

Faith in Hod?

United hopes
gunned down

this weekend that it really dawned on Alex Ferguson that he might not get his hands on a trophy this season, as Arsenal won 5–0 and United stuttered to a 1–1 draw. It was out of United's hands now.

The League programme was interrupted for England's international against Portugal. The week was taken up almost entirely with references to Glenn Hoddle's use of faith healer Eileen Drewery and, if some reports were to be believed, spoon bender Uri Geller, magician Paul Daniels, Mickey Mouse and Mystic Meg. For the record England won 3–0, so the stars must have been aligned well.

The news of Arsenal's 2–0 win at Barnsley a few days later – with Footballer of the Year Dennis Bergkamp scoring yet again – must have had Alex Ferguson looking to the heavens. In fact, the only piece of good news for United was that PSV Eindhoven had finally agreed to sell Dutch international defender Jaap Stam for £10 million.

Stam will join the Reds next season but, as far as the 1997/98 campaign was concerned, nothing less than victory against Crystal Palace would do to keep United's slim hopes alive. Palace Manager Atillo Lombardo picked an

"Jaap is the best defender around. Even Ronaldo didn't give him any problems"

JAAP'S FORMER PSV EINDHOVEN TEAM-MATE STAN VALCKX

ambitous side – himself, Brolin and Sasa Curcic in midfield – and paid the penalty when Scholes and Butt started running the show and United romped home 3–0 winners. Even so, Arsenal were a point ahead with two games in hand and Ferguson admitted it would take a complete collapse from a team that had won their last 10 games on the trot to retain the title.

Phil Neville, however, refused to throw in the towel: "Looking back and looking at the fixtures Arsenal have got, I still think we can win the title," he said. "And that is the attitude of a lot of players at United."

BLACKBURN ROVERS 1
MANCHESTER UNITED 3

HOME TEAM

33.	Alan Fettis	6
3.	Jeff Kenna	7
4.	Tim Sherwood	7
5.	Colin Hendry	8
8.	Kevin Gallacher	6
9.	Chris Sutton	7
11.	Jason Wilcox	7
15.	Garry Flitcroft	7
17.	Billy McKinlay	7
24.	Stephane Henchoz	7
25.	Damien Duff	8

SUBSTITUTES

2.	Callum Davidson
7.	Stuart Ripley
10.	Martin Dahlin
26.	Marlon Broomes
32.	Anthony Williams

SCORERS

Sutton | 32 mins (pen)

REFEREE

Gerald Ashby | Worcester

VISITORS

		RATING
1.	Peter Schmeichel	7
2.	Gary Neville	7
3.	Denis Irwin	7
5.	Ronny Johnsen	7
6.	Gary Pallister	7
7.	David Beckham	7
9.	Andy Cole	8
11.	Ryan Giggs	8
12.	Phil Neville	7
18.	Paul Scholes	8
20.	Ole G Solskjaer	7

SUBSTITUTES

4.	David May	
8.	Nicky Butt	8
	Solskjaer	45 mins	
10.	Teddy Sheringham	
23.	Ben Thornley	
17.	Rai Van Der Gouw	

SCORERS

Cole | 56 mins
Scholes | 73 mins
Beckham | 90 mins

MATCH REPORT

Down and out at half-time, Manchester United regrouped and fought back with a stirring second-half comeback to open up a six-point lead over Arsenal.

"We were out-thought, outfought, outrun and outplayed," admitted Alex Ferguson on United's woeful first half efforts. "I can't remember us being given that kind of doing in the last two years."

Sutton and Gallacher pulled United's back line all over the pitch and cut through them with relative ease. Sutton gave Blackburn the lead from the penalty spot after Gary Neville had sought to get a ride on the back of Damien Duff.

Andy Cole dragged United back into the game with a stunning goal early in the second half. Played down the wing by Beckham, Cole shook off Henchoz by cutting into the area and beat Fettis with a low, swerving shot inside the far post.

Beckham was the provider again when his early cross eluded Hendry and fortuitously went in of Scholes' hip. Blackburn were unfortunate not to draw level before Beckham ran onto a fine Giggs pass and beat Fettis to secure the win.

Three shots, three goals. If United keep up that strike rate, they will surely be Champions again.

IN THE PAPERS

1–1: Clinical Cole finish

2–1:
open wide

3–1:
Becks
finishes it

MANCHESTER UNITED 1
LIVERPOOL 1

HOME TEAM

1.	Peter Schmeichel	7
2.	Gary Neville	7
6.	Gary Pallister	6
5.	Ronny Johnsen	7
3.	Denis Irwin	7
8.	Nicky Butt	7
7.	David Beckham	7
18.	Paul Scholes	7
12.	Phil Neville	7
11.	Ryan Giggs	7
9.	Andy Cole	8

SUBSTITUTES

23.	Ben Thornley	6
	Giggs	38 mins	
4.	David May	6
	Johnsen	43 mins	
10.	Teddy Sheringham	5
	Neville	65 mins	
13.	Brian McClair	
17.	Rai Van Der Gouw	

SCORER

Johnsen | 12 mins

REFEREE

Graham Poll | Tring

VISITORS   RATING

29.	Brad Friedel	7
2.	Rob Jones	7
6.	Phil Babb	8
21.	Dominic Matteo	6
12.	Steve Harkness	6
8.	Oyvind Leonhardsen	6
7.	Steve McManaman	6
17.	Paul Ince	6
11.	Jamie Redknapp	6
24.	Danny Murphy	6
18.	Michael Owen	6

SUBSTITUTES

15.	Patrik Berger	6
	Murphy	75 mins	
1.	David James	
3.	Bjorn Tore Kvarme	
16.	Michael Thomas	
23.	Jamie Carragher	

SCORER

Owen | 36 mins

MATCH REPORT

"Arsenal can only throw it away," said Alex Ferguson after he had seen his team drop yet more points with a draw against Liverpool. This was immediately jumped upon as classic Fergie psychology, but, in truth, it was an honest assesment of the title race. United may be seven points ahead, but they have played four more games than Arsenal.

United started with gusto. Giggs burst thorugh the middle after a minute, only for Friedel to save his shot and Babb to clear Scholes' follow-up effort off the line. United took the lead after 12 minutes when Johnsen was left unmarked to head in a Beckham corner.

This should have given United the platform to display their title credentials, but Liverpool bucked the trend of recent encounters and responded with an uncharacteristically gritty performance.

Too gritty in Michael Owen's case. He was sent off after two disgraceful lunges; the second ended Ronny Johnsen's game.

But this was *after* he had claimed the equaliser, beating Pallister for pace before neatly chipping Schmeichel.

In the second half, United looked tired and desperate, snatching at what few chances they had while Liverpool were happy to play on the break and give a rare performance of defensive solidity.

IN THE PAPERS

"The Spice Girls were in the crowd, but the Spice Boys were nowhere to be seen. If Liverpool take any solace from another season of under-achievement, it is that with ten men at Old Trafford, they may just have wrested the title from the greedy hands of Manchester United. It will not reside in their own cabinet, but if Arsenal take their chances it will not remain at the home of their rivals a third year, either."
EXPRESS

"Michael Owen was Arsenal's title saviour, but still in public shame last night. His marvellous goal was a piece of Old Trafford plunder that United could hardly afford in the great Championship race. But his behaviour not many minutes later may have justified Glenn Hoddle's concerns about putting him in the England starting line-up."
SUN

"Peter Schmeichel sent title rivals Arsenal into their Easter programme today defiantly gripping on to Manchester United's Premiership trophy, declaring, 'It's not over yet!'"
MANCHESTER EVENING NEWS

Oh, bugger!

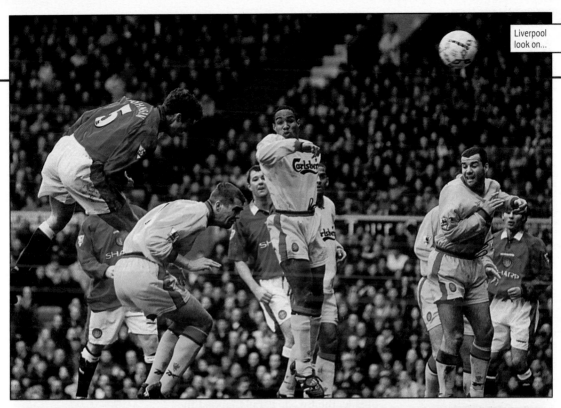

Liverpool look on...

...Johnsen scores

MANCHESTER UNITED 1
NEWCASTLE UNITED 1

HOME TEAM

1.	Peter Schmiechel	6
2.	Gary Neville	7
6.	Gary Pallister	7
4.	David May	7
3.	Denis Irwin	7
7.	David Beckham	7
8.	Nicky Butt	6
12.	Phil Neville	7
11.	Ryan Giggs	7
10.	Teddy Sheringham	6
9.	Andy Cole	7

SUBSTITUTES

20.	Ole G Solskjaer	6
	P Neville	78 mins	
18.	Paul Scholes	7
	Butt	40 mins	
17.	Rai Van Der Gouw	8
	Schmiechel	17 mins	
21.	Henning Berg	
32.	Michael Clegg	

SCORER

Beckham | 38 mins

REFEREE

Uriah Rennie | Sheffield

VISITORS   RATING

1.	Shay Given	8
3.	Nikolaos Dabizas	7
27.	Phillipe Albert	7
12.	Stuart Pearce	7
23.	Alessandro Pistone	7
7.	Robert Lee	6
4.	David Batty	6
11.	Gary Speed	6
2.	Warren Barton	7
9.	Alan Shearer	7
40.	Andreas Andersson	7

SUBSTITUTES

14.	Temuri Ketsbaia	6
	Andersson	66 mins	
21.	Pavel Srnicek	
16.	Jon Dahl Tomasson	
18.	Keith Gillespie	
19.	Steve Watson	

SCORER

Andersson | 11 mins

MATCH REPORT

At the end of this engrossing match, a few United players slumped to the ground. Mathematically the title is still possible, but their body language told the true story: United are mentally and physically vanquished. As if, to compound their grief, the tannoy brought news from Highbury. "Arsenal 5, Wimbledon 0."

Afterwards Alex Ferguson refused to surrender the title. But his belief, stated earlier in the week, that, "One more dropped point and the title is over," must now be true.

Newcastle took the lead after 11 minutes. Batty chipped over United's static defence for Speed to head down for Andersson. While United appealed for offside, the Swede calmly tapped the ball past Schmeichel.

United equalised in the 38th minute when David Beckham dived to head in a wonderful floated cross from Ryan Giggs.

Newcastle could have snatched victory in the last minute when Rob Lee raced from within his own half with only Van Der Gouw to beat, only to be cynically brought down by Solskjaer. The Norwegian left the field to great acclaim; shame it was for a Red card rather than a goal.

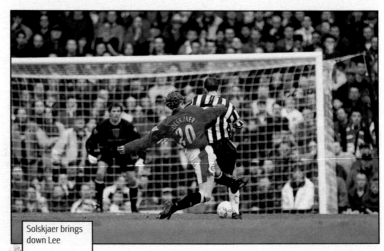

Solskjaer brings down Lee

IN THE PAPERS

"As the goals poured in at Highbury, Old Trafford became the theatre of broken dreams. Ole Gunnar Solskjaer's kamikaze stunt may yet have a bearing on the outcome of this season's title. But in reality, talk of United winning it for a third successive year is as reckless as the Norwegian's challenge."
MIRROR

"After 24 years in management, Alex Ferguson still cannot hide the wear and tear, the deep loss of faith he takes so personally when his team finishes anywhere but top. Ferguson on Saturday wore the baleful look of a man who had gone 15 rounds in vain."
TIMES

"'We're at the bottom of the hill ready to run up it,' Alex Ferguson said, brimming with defiance, but even he looked like a man going through the motions. Arsenal need only nine points to deny United their fifth Championship in six years and, the way the Gunners are finding their range, those could come in the next three matches."
INDEPENDENT

1–1: Beckham delivers hope

Cole and Sheringham look down

CRYSTAL PALACE 0
MANCHESTER UNITED 3

HOME TEAM
		RATING
1.	Kevin Miller	8
2.	Marc Edworthy	6
3.	Dean Gordon	6
4.	Sasa Curcic	7
7.	Atillo Lombardo	8
9.	Neil Shipperly	5
11.	Michele Padovano	5
12.	Thomas Brolin	5
16.	Marcus Bent	6
17.	Jamie Smith	6
18.	Valerien Ismael	7

SUBSTITUTES

22.	Herman Hreidarsson	
	Lombardo	87 mins	
10.	Bruce Dyer	6
	Padovano	75 mins	
26.	Jamie Fullarton	6
	Brolin	68 mins	
8.	Paul Warhurst	
13.	Carlo Nash	

REFEREE

P Jones | Loughborough

VISITORS
		RATING
1.	Peter Schmeichel	7
3.	Denis Irwin	7
4.	David May	7
6.	Gary Pallister	7
12.	Phil Neville	7
7.	David Beckham	8
8.	Nicky Butt	8
9.	Andy Cole	7
10.	Teddy Sheringham	7
11.	Ryan Giggs	7
18.	Paul Scholes	9

SUBSTITUTES

32.	Michael Clegg	7
	Irwin	76 mins	
24.	Ben Thornley	
17.	Rai Van Der Gouw	
21.	Henning Berg	
20.	Ole Gunnar Solskjaer	

SCORERS

Scholes | 5 mins
Butt | 21 mins
Cole | 84 mins

MATCH REPORT

A lone voice amongst Manchester United's travelling support tried to start up a chant of "Champions." He was roundly ignored. Though they watched their team comfortably defeat Crystal Palace to move to within a point of Arsenal, United's faithful realise their two-year tenure as Champions only has a week to run.

There was an end-of-term feeling at Selhurst Park. Manchester United played without the nerves that have undermined their title challenge in recent weeks while Palace seemed resigned to relegation which was confirmed with this defeat.

Palace were the most gracious of hosts, allowing United to attack at will in the first half. Paul Scholes and Nicky Butt, possibly spurred on by Fergie's assertion that United would not have let the title slip with a fit Keane in midfield, redis-covered their autumn form and gave United a two-goal lead within 21 minutes. Andy Cole scored United's third with a simple tap six minutes from time.

All three goals climaxed slick passing moves by United. A welcome change from the desperate high balls that have characterised so much of United's play in the last month.

IN THE PAPERS

"Alex Ferguson's players hardly raised an arm in celebration after last night's embarrassingly easy win at Selhurst Park. Palace seemed to be in better spirits on the night, and they were relegated! In this end-of-season pre-occupation with mystical powers, you would have to believe in fairies to put any money on United winning the title."
MIRROR

"Manchester United cruised to within one point of Arsenal at the top of the Premiership, whilst condemning Palace to relegation. It was, in the end, a painless execution and Ferguson strode off at the final whistle, mission accomplished. His team are still there, clinging to Arsenal's coat-tails just waiting for Arsene Wenger's side, perhaps, to show some Championship nerves."
DAILY MAIL

"'All that was settled last night was Palace's third relegation from the Premiership in six years. In the end, Crystal Palace went down with guns blazing, even if their aim was generally awry."
GUARDIAN

Superman

Scholes claims an early lead

Cole calmly strokes it in

April STATS

PLAYER RECORDS

■ PREMIERSHIP
■ COCA-COLA CUP ■ FA CUP

home | away

■ FULL APPEARANCE
■ CAME ON AS SUB

■ ■ SCORER
■ SCORED AS SUB

	Player	FULL APPEARANCES	SUB APPEARANCES	GOALS
1.	Peter Schmeichel	37	0	0
2.	Gary Neville	35	1	0
3.	Denis Irwin	24	4	1
4.	David May	7	2	0
5.	Ronny Johnsen	21	4	2
6.	Gary Pallister	35	0	0
7.	David Beckham	36	4	10
8.	Nicky Butt	30	2	2
9.	Andy Cole	33	2	18
10.	Teddy Sheringham	28	4	11
11.	Ryan Giggs	28	1	7
12.	Phil Neville	29	4	1
13.	Brian McClair	6	10	0
14.	Jordi Cruyff	4	3	0
15.	Karel Poborsky	5	7	2
16.	Roy Keane	9	0	2
17.	Rai Van Der Gouw	2	1	0
18.	Paul Scholes	29	4	8
20.	Ole Gunnar Solskjaer	17	8	8
21.	Henning Berg	25	3	1
22.	Erik Nevland	2	3	0
23.	Ben Thornley	2	5	0
24.	John O'Kane	0	0	0
25.	Kevin Pilkington	2	0	0
26.	Chris Casper	0	0	0
27.	Terry Cooke	0	0	0
28.	Phil Mulryne	1	1	0
30.	Ronnie Wallwork	0	1	0
31.	John Curtis	3	5	0
32.	Michael Clegg	2	3	0
34.	Michael Twiss	0	1	0

PLAYER OF THE MONTH

Andy Cole

AVERAGE PERFORMANCE RATING: 7.5

FA CARLING PREMIERSHIP

as at 28 April 1998

	Pld	W	D	L	F	A	Pts	GD
▲ Arsenal	34	21	9	4	63	28	72	35
▼ Man United	36	21	8	7	68	26	71	42
▲ Chelsea	35	19	3	13	68	39	60	29
▼ Liverpool	35	16	11	8	59	41	59	18
■ Leeds United	36	17	7	12	56	42	58	14
■ Blackburn Rovers	35	14	10	11	55	50	52	5
▲ West Ham United	35	15	7	13	49	46	52	3
▲ Aston Villa	36	15	6	15	45	47	51	-2
▲ Leicester City	35	12	13	10	47	37	49	10
▼ Derby County	35	14	7	14	49	48	49	1
▼ Coventry City	35	11	14	10	43	43	47	0
▼ Southampton	36	14	5	17	49	52	47	-3
■ Sheffield Wednesday	36	12	8	16	51	63	44	-12
■ Wimbledon	35	10	12	13	31	39	42	-8
■ Newcastle United	35	10	10	15	32	42	40	-10
■ Tottenham Hotspur	36	10	10	16	37	53	40	-16
▼ Everton	36	9	12	15	40	51	39	-11
▲ Bolton Wanderers	36	8	13	15	36	57	37	-21
▼ Barnsley	36	10	5	21	37	79	35	-42
■ Crystal Palace	35	7	8	20	31	63	29	-32

MAY

1 | 2 | 3 | 4 | 5 | 6 | 7 | 8 | 9 | 10 | 11 | 12 | 13 | 14 | 15 | 16 | 17 | 18 | 19 | 20 | 21 | 22 | 23 | 24 | 25 | 26 | 27 | 28 | 29 | 30 | 31

MAY

THE MONTH AHEAD

On 2 May, Arsenal thumped Everton 4–0 in ruthless fashion to clinch the Premiership title. An estimated crowd of 100,000 thronged the streets around Highbury to celebrate the first half of a possible Double

Back in Manchester, Alex Ferguson paid the Gunners a glowing tribute. "They deserve to win it after the way they've done the business," he said. "Any team that wins the League has to be congratulated because it's such a hard League to win."

But if United supporters were depressed by the loss of the Championship and an uncustomary trophyless season, it was nothing to how Manchester City fans were feeling. Despite winning 5–2 at Stoke, City were relegated to the Second Division for the first time in their history. At the other end of the Division One table, Middlesbrough bounced back into the top flight with a 4–1 win over Oxford. Away from football, actor Kevin Lloyd –

best known for his portrayal of Tosh Lines in *The Bill* – died after a five-day drinking binge. On top of that was the sad news that Justin Fashanu, the former England B international and Britain's first openly gay player, had hanged himself.

In the last Old Trafford appearance of the season, United beat Leeds 3–0, watched by our new £10.75-million signing Jaap Stam – the world's most expensive defender. Down in London, the Highbury party continued as Arsenal Ladies won the women's FA Cup Final, beating Croydon 3–2 at the Den. Meanwhile, there was a bizarre murder in the Vatican as the commander of the Swiss Papal Guard and his wife were killed by another guard, who then turned his gun on himself.

The next day, Foreign Secretary Robin Cook was rocked by allegations that weapons and arms were unlawfully supplied to Sierra Leone by Britain. Gary Glitter – charged with five sex attacks on two schoolgirls – was in even deeper trouble. It was a much better day for Alec Stewart, appointed England cricket captain following the resignation of United fan Mike Atherton. Stewart's Surrey team-mate Adam Hollioake, though, will remain skipper of the one-day international side. There was less good news for Juninho as the pint-sized midfielder was left out of Brazil's World Cup squad.

Definitely going to France in the summer, however, was England captain Alan Shearer, despite being told that he must appear before the FA to explain why he seemed to kick Leicester's Neil

Fashanu tragedy

Naughty, naughty

to go to the polls. Then, former United star Ray Wilkins was given his marching orders from Craven Cottage by his old mate Kevin Keegan, who promptly took over the running of Fulham's team affairs himself. His first match, a play-off clash with Grimsby, ended in a disappointing 1–1 draw.

The real excitement was saved for the following day's relegation deciders in the Premiership. At Stamford Bridge, Bolton went down rather meekly 2–0 to Chelsea.

"Our players will be up for it again next season"

ALEX FERGUSON LOOKS FORWARD

Lennon in the face during Newcastle's recent match at Filbert Street. Back on the pitch, a weakened Arsenal side were blitzed 4–0 at Liverpool, clinching third spot with this emphatic win. A more significant victory, though, was Inter Milan's 3–0 humbling of fellow Italians Lazio in the UEFA Cup Final.

The Capital took centre stage again as the first week of May drew to a close. First, Londoners decided they would like to elect a mayor with executive powers; at least that was the majority wish of the barely one in three voters who bothered

That result left Everton requiring a point to stay up. The Goodison side scrambled a 1–1 draw to preserve their 47-year run in the top flight.

United ended the season with a comfortable 2–0 victory against Barnsley. With Arsenal losing at Villa, the Reds finished just one point behind the Champions. Later that evening, Fergie presented the Carling Manager of the Year award to Arsene Wenger.

Next year, the roles will be reversed!

It's only on loan

MANCHESTER UNITED 3
LEEDS UNITED 0

HOME TEAM

		RATING
17.	Rai Van Der Gouw	7
2.	Gary Neville	9
3.	Denis Irwin	8
4.	David May	7
6.	Gary Pallister	7
7.	David Beckham	7
8.	Nicky Butt	7
18.	Paul Scholes	7
11.	Ryan Giggs	8
10.	Teddy Sheringham	7

SUBSTITUTES

12.	Phil Neville	7
	Irwin	45 mins	
33.	Wes Brown	8
	May	60 mins	
13.	Brian McClair	7
	Sheringham	60 mins	
21.	Henning Berg	

SCORERS

Giggs | 6 mins
Irwin | 31 mins (pen)
Beckham | 58 mins

REFEREE

Gary Willard | West Sussex

VISITORS

1.	Nigel Martyn	7
2.	Gary Kelly	6
4.	Alf-Inge Haaland	6
5.	Lucas Radebe	7
6.	David Wetherall	6
9.	Jimmy Hasselbaink	6
11.	Lee Bowyer	6
18.	Gunner Halle	6
19.	Harry Kewell	7
13.	Ian Harte	5
7.	Martin Hiden	6

SUBSTITUTES

12.	David Hopkin	6
	Hiden	60 mins	
15.	Mark Beeney	
3.	David Robertson	6
	Harte	73 mins	
8.	Rodney Wallace	
14.	Mark Jackson	

MATCH REPORT

So the Championship is gone. For only the second time in six seasons Manchester United finished their League campaign without a trophy procession around Old Trafford.

The morning papers were full of glowing Arsenal faces staging their own trophy procession. United were going to have to get used to being second best, for the next year at least.

United's intention to regain their League supremacy was demonstrated by the presence of Jaap Stam in the directors' box. Stam was in town to complete his £10.75 million signing from PSV Eindhoven. After witnessing Wes Brown's debut, the Dutchman might wonder about his place in the team next season – the 18-year-old central defender showed remarkable maturity.

Leeds must surely be a team of Europhobes. Needing only a point to qualify for Europe, they showed no interest in this game and were duly reprimanded by George Graham for their "worst performance of the season."

With the pressure lifted, United turned in a confident display. Giggs gave United the lead after only six minutes by heading in an impressive cross from Gary Neville. Irwin made it 2–0 with a penalty after Sheringham had been toppled by Harte. Beckham added the third in the second half with a powerful volley.

Giggs nods in United's opener

IN THE PAPERS

"Manchester United wasted no time mourning the loss of their Premiership crown. Sitting in the Old Trafford stands last night to watch the demolition job of Leeds was Jaap Stam, the first building block of Alex Ferguson's millennium vision. The £10.5 million talent immediate verdict was emphatic and full of thundering resolve. Without a flicker of doubt he said, 'It is a shame that we are not Champions this year, but we will be next season.'"
SUN

"United may have been desperately disappointed, but this was United's final game in front of their own fans, and they were determined to put on a show."
EXPRESS

"Champions no longer, but defiant to the end, Manchester United supported brave words from their manager with a typically competent victory over Leeds yesterday. Yet with all the ease with which they brushed aside the Yorkshire men their was something missing, not just a Premiership trophy which normally finds itself around Old Trafford this time of year. 'Eric, Eric Cantona' the United fans sang, taunting the Leeds faithful, but with a pleading hint in their collective voices."
TIMES

Penalty
demon
Denis
delivers
again

BARNSLEY 0

MANCHESTER UNITED 2

HOME TEAM

	RATING
1. David Watson	7
2. Matty Appleby	7
24. Darren Barnard	6
4. Darren Sheridan	6
5. Adie Moses	7
8. Neil Redfearn	7
14. Martin Bullock	8
18. Scott Jones	7
22. Georgi Hristov	6
25. Ashley Ward	6
27. Chris Morgan	6

SUBSTITUTES

	RATING
30. Jan–Aage Fjortoft	6
Hristov | 62 mins	
2. Nicky Eaden	6
Appleby | 46 mins	
10. Clint Marcelle	
12. Andy Liddell	
15. Jovo Bosancic	

REFEREE

P Durkin | Dorset

VISITORS

	RATING
17. Rai Van Der Gouw	7
32. Michael Clegg	6
4. David May	6
21. Henning Berg	7
35. Wes Brown	8
31. John Curtis	7
28. Phil Mulryne	7
6. Nicky Butt	8
9. Andy Cole	8
10. Teddy Sheringham	7
11. Ryan Giggs	8

SUBSTITUTES

	RATING
38. Danny Higginbotham	7
Clegg | 60 mins	
37. Jonathan Greening	
33. Nick Culkin	
36. Alex Notman	
34. Michael Twiss	

SCORERS

Cole | 5 mins
Sheringham | 76 mins

MATCH REPORT

With the Premiership trophy ensconsed at Highbury, Alex Ferguson gave his first batch of youngsters a free afternoon to prepare for the World Cup and paraded his next batch at Oakwell. Wes Brown and Phil Mulryne made their full Premiership debuts while United's bench consisted of five Premiership virgins.

Wes Brown was the most impressive of the new generation. In central defence the young Mancunian gave a performance reminiscent of Paul McGrath, smothering Barnsley's attacks and bringing the ball foward with confidence. With Brown as protection, Rai Van Der Gouw was not called on to make a save all afternoon.

At the start of the season this game was expected to decide the destiny of both teams, but with Barnsley already relegated and United already runners-up both sides went through the motions. United were just better at it.

Andy Cole opened the scoring after five minutes. The England striker took down a deflected cross from Sheringham, span round and volleyed past Watson. Fourteen minutes from the end of the season, Sheringham scored United's second with a low shot inside Watson's near post. It was his first Premiership goal of 1998.

Welcome, Wes

IN THE PAPERS

"Despite the pride and passion which has won Barnsley so many friends, although not many points, their glorious Premiership adventure fizzled out with a disappointing defeat by a hugely unfamiliar Manchester United side."

INDEPENDENT

"Andy Cole revealed a touch more compassion in helping apply the last rites for dear departed Barnsley. Back in October, he beat them up to such a degree that the side they suggest play like Brazil looked more like Ragbag Rovers. Yesterday, he contented himself with an important fifth-minute strike at more homely Oakwell, instead of the hat-trick amid the seven goals of Old Trafford's most savage humiliation of the campaign."

SUN

Cole finishes his season in style

Barnsley's battle is over

FOREVER RED!

Charity Shield shootout joy

We did win something!

Teddy stoops to conquer at Highbury

Cole flies in at Anfield

Giggs nut v Spurs

Ted destroys Juve

We're in this together

The Salford boy done good

Nice one, mate

Season STATS

PLAYER RECORDS

■ PREMIERSHIP
■ COCA-COLA CUP ■ FA CUP

home | away

■ ■ FULL APPEARANCE
CAME ON AS SUB

■ ■ SCORER
SCORED AS SUB

	Player	Full Appearances	Sub Appearances	Goals
1.	Peter Schmeichel	37	0	0
2.	Gary Neville	36	1	0
3.	Denis Irwin	25	4	2
4.	David May	9	2	0
5.	Ronny Johnsen	21	4	2
6.	Gary Pallister	36	0	0
7.	David Beckham	37	4	11
8.	Nicky Butt	32	2	2
9.	Andy Cole	35	2	19
10.	Teddy Sheringham	30	4	12
11.	Ryan Giggs	30	1	8
12.	Phil Neville	29	5	1
13.	Brian McClair	6	11	0
14.	Jordi Cruyff	4	3	0
15.	Karel Poborsky	5	7	2
16.	Roy Keane	9	0	2
17.	Rai Van Der Gouw	4	1	0
18.	Paul Scholes	30	4	8
20.	Ole Gunnar Solskjaer	17	8	8
21.	Henning Berg	26	3	1
22.	Erik Nevland	2	3	0
23.	Ben Thornley	2	5	0
24.	John O'Kane	0	0	0
25.	Kevin Pilkington	2	0	0
26.	Chris Casper	0	0	0
27.	Terry Cooke	0	0	0
28.	Phil Mulryne	2	1	0
30.	Ronnie Wallwork	0	1	0
31.	John Curtis	4	5	0
32.	Michael Clegg	3	3	0
34.	Michael Twiss	0	1	0

PLAYER OF THE MONTH

Ryan Giggs

AVERAGE PERFORMANCE RATING: 8

FA CARLING PREMIERSHIP

Final League table

	Pld	W	D	L	F	A	Pts	GD
■ Arsenal	38	23	9	6	68	33	78	35
■ Man United	38	23	8	7	73	26	77	47
▲ Liverpool	38	18	11	9	68	42	65	26
▼ Chelsea	38	20	3	15	71	43	63	28
■ Leeds United	38	17	8	13	57	46	59	11
■ Blackburn Rovers	38	16	10	12	57	52	58	5
▲ Aston Villa	38	17	6	15	49	48	57	1
▼ West Ham United	38	16	8	14	56	57	56	-1
▲ Derby County	38	17	7	15	52	49	55	3
▼ Leicester City	38	13	14	11	51	41	53	10
■ Coventry City	38	12	16	10	46	44	52	2
■ Southampton	38	14	6	18	50	55	48	-5
▲ Newcastle	38	11	11	16	35	44	44	-9
▲ Tottenham Hotspur	38	11	11	16	44	56	44	-12
▼ Wimbledon	38	10	14	14	34	46	44	-12
▼ Sheffield Wednesday	38	12	8	18	52	67	44	-15
■ Everton	38	9	13	16	41	56	40	-15
■ Bolton Wanderers R	38	9	13	16	41	61	40	-20
■ Barnsley R	38	10	5	23	37	82	35	-45
■ Crystal Palace R	38	8	9	21	37	71	33	-34

CHAMPIONS' LEAGUE

FC KOSICE 0

MANCHESTER UNITED 3

HOME TEAM

1.	Ladislav Molnar	7
2.	Marek Spilar	7
3.	Andras Telek	6
4.	Ivan Kozak	6
6.	Vladimir Janocko	6
7.	Ruslan Ljubarskij	6
9.	Jozef Kozlej	6
10.	Robert Semenik	7
11.	Vladislav Zvara	7
13.	Miroslav Sovic	6
17.	Radoslav Kral	6

SUBSTITUTES

12.	Branislav Benko	
14.	Lubomir Faktor	6
	Kozlej	77 mins	
15.	Marian Bochnovic	
18.	Albert Rusnak	6
	Ljubarskij	45 mins	
20.	Milan Cvirk	

REFEREE

Leif Sundell | Sweden

VISITORS

		RATING
1.	Peter Schmeichel	7
2.	Gary Neville	7
3.	Denis Irwin	8
6.	Gary Pallister	7
21.	Henning Berg	7
16.	Roy Keane	8
8.	Nicky Butt	7
7.	David Beckham	7
15.	Karel Poborsky	5
18.	Paul Scholes	7
9.	Andy Cole	7

SUBSTITUTES

13.	Brian McClair	7
	Beckham	75 mins	
17.	Rai Van Der Gouw	
10.	Teddy Sheringham	
12.	Phil Neville	
19.	Michael Clegg	

SCORERS

Irwin | 30 mins
Berg | 60 mins
Cole | 88 mins

MATCH REPORT

In their opening Champions' League game last season, Manchester United were humiliated by Juventus, like the playground bully finally given their comeuppence. A year on, better for the experience, it was United's turn to do the bullying.

The Champions' League came too early for Kosice. They were renovating their stadium in prepartion for these sort of nights and, caught out by their own progress, were forced to stage the match at the home of their lower league rivals, a ground that would look out of place in the English Third Division.

Andy Cole, doing a very good impression of Mark Hughes, held up the ball with his back to goal and laid the ball in to the path of Denis Irwin, who slotted it in under the goalkeeper. Henning Berg took adavntage of the defender's shooting practice that Kosice were offering by extending United's lead when the goalkeeper dropped the ball at his feet.

Andy Cole, guilty of a glaring miss earlier, made amends by neatly volleying home United's third goal.

Into the unknown and out again with three valuable Champions' League points.

IN THE PAPERS

"United's bruised Euro troops were on the back foot from day one and facing a monumental climb back up the European Cup mountain. To their credit, they scaled the group section despite one or two moments when they almost lost their footing altogether."
MANCHESTER EVENING NEWS

"Manchester United have made no secret of their intention to make the Champions' League their priority this season and last night they made a confident step in their chosen direction. Sure, not spectacular, they nullified Kosice, drew them in and comfortably beat them."
INDEPENDENT

"Manchster United nullified the Orange Tigers of Kosice last night without really needing to resort to a whip and a kitchen chair. The victory would have settled some nerves for some stiffer tests that lie ahead."
GUARDIAN

Keane: our man of the match

Cole makes it a cool three

MANCHESTER UNITED 3

JUVENTUS 2

HOME TEAM

		RATING
1.	Peter Schmeichel	7
2.	Gary Neville	9
3.	Denis Irwin	8
6.	Gary Pallister	9
21.	Henning Berg	8
7.	David Beckham	8
8.	Nicky Butt	8
5.	Ronny Johnsen	8
11.	Ryan Giggs	9
20.	Ole G Solskjaer	7
10.	Teddy Sheringham	8

SUBSTITUTES

12.	Phil Neville	7
	Solskjaer | 48 mins	
18.	Paul Scholes	9
	Butt | 37 mins	
13.	Brian McClair	
4.	David May	
32.	Michael Clegg	

SCORERS

Sheringham | 38 mins
Scholes | 69 mins
Giggs | 89 mins

REFEREE

Antonio Nieto | Spain

VISITORS

1.	Angelo Peruzzi	7
15.	Alessandro Birindelli	7
2.	Ciro Ferrara	8
4.	Paolo Montero	7
6.	Manuel Dimas	7
5.	Fabio Pecchia	8
4.	Didier Deschamps	7
20.	Alessio Tacchinardi	7
21.	Zinedine Zidane	5
9.	Filippo Inzaghi	7
10.	Alessandro Del Piero	7

SUBSTITUTES

16.	Nicola Amoruso	7
	Del Piero | 77 mins	
13.	Mark Luliano	7
	Pecchia | 68 mins	
22.	Gianluca Pessotto	7
	Tacchinardi | 19 mins	
12.	Michelangelo Rampulla	
11.	Michele Padovano	

SCORERS

Del Piero | 1 min
Zidane | 90 min

MATCH REPORT

" I wish peope would get it into their heads that Juventus are not invincible," said their coach Marcello Lippi after this game. He need not have worried as Manchester United had just spent the previous 90 minutes proving that to become the first English side to defeat Juventus for 18 years

Brushed aside twice by Juventus last season, United had learned their lessons. This time they were stronger, quicker and bereft of the fear that had allowed the Italians to dominate them.

Not even the momentary lapse that allowed Del Piero to give the Italians the lead after 19 seconds could dent their belief. United kept calm and were rewarded when Sheringham headed in Giggs' high cross at the far post.

Giggs was at his stunning best all evening, frightening the normally composed Italians with his pace and trickery.

Scholes gave United the lead when he found himself free of the Juve back line; he drew Peruzzi and slotted the ball in. It was then left to Giggs to race on to a pass from Sheringham and power the ball into the top corner before Zidane made the score respectable with a curling free-kick.

3–1: Giggs thunderbolt

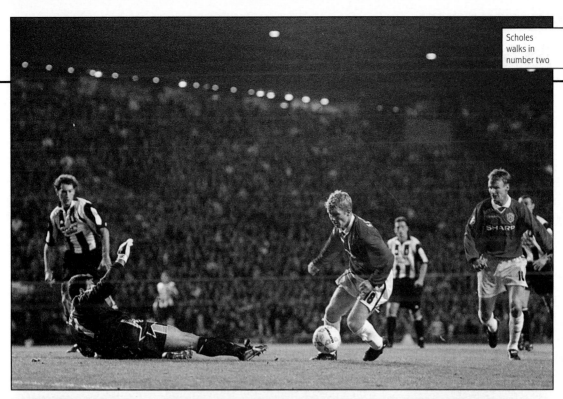

Scholes walks in number two

A night of celebration

MANCHESTER UNITED 2
FEYENOORD 1

HOME TEAM

		RATING
1.	Peter Schmeichel	7
2.	Gary Neville	9
3.	Denis Irwin	8
6.	Gary Pallister	8
12.	Phil Neville	7
7.	David Beckham	7
8.	Nicky Butt	8
18.	Paul Scholes	8
11.	Ryan Giggs	7
9.	Andy Cole	7
10.	Teddy Sheringham	7

SUBSTITUTES

20.	Ole G Solskjaer	6
	Cole	80 mins	
13.	Brian McClair	
14.	Jordi Cruyff	
15.	Karel Poborsky	
23.	Ben Thornley	

SCORERS

Scholes | 37 mins
Irwin | 72 mins (pen)

REFEREE

S Muhmenthaler | Switzerland

VISITORS

1.	Jerzy Dudek	7
6.	Fernando Picun	6
17.	Ulrich van Gobbel	9
15.	Bernard Schuiteman	6
7.	K. Van Wonderen	6
3.	Patricio Graff	8
14.	Paul Bosvelt	6
5.	Jean-Paul Van Gastel	6
11.	G. Van Bronckhorst	6
10.	Pablo Sanchez	7
18.	David Connolly	6

SUBSTITUTES

19.	Igor Korneev	7
	Bronckhorst	37 mins	
2.	George Boateng	7
	Sanchez	75 mins	
20.	Henk Vos	7
	Connolly	72 mins	
12.	Zsolt Petry	
16.	Geoffrey Claeys	

SCORERS

Vos | 83 mins

MATCH REPORT

United are getting the hang of this European football. Three games played, three games won and more goals scored at the halfway point than were scored in the whole of the group stage last season.

The pace of United's football unsettled the Dutch, but too often United's finishing let them down. Sheringham, Cole, Butt and Giggs were all guilty of misses that would have settled the match earlier. It was not a display to rival the one that dispatched Juventus, but then United were never in any risk of losing to last season's Dutch runners-up.

Scholes gave United the lead when he controlled Cole's knockdown and finished with a precise volley. But United could not relax until Denis Irwin stepped up to convert a penalty awarded for a foul on Sheringham.

United faced Feyenoord shorn of three central defenders, but on Gary Neville's performance you would never have known it. Neville impressively partnered Gary Pallister and was singled out for praise by Alex Ferguson. The new pairing was breached only once when Vos ran through to score, ensuring a nervy end to a game United had dominated.

IN THE PAPERS

"It might not have been a night of vintage football and glory, but at least it was a victory to savour in contrast to other English clubs' efforts. Manchester United's performance was an antidote to Liverpool's shambles, Newcastle's defeat and only a creditable draw by Aston Villa in Bilbao."
MIRROR

"Fergie's men looked like an unregistered charity as Feyenoord escaped what should have been their biggest massacre in years. United were the masterful destroyers of Juventus just three weeks ago, but lacked that clinical cutting edge in the encounter with the Dutchmen."
SUN

"United eventually beat Feyenoord comfortably enough last night to consolidate their lead over Juventus, but did not punish last season's modest runners-up in the Dutch league by the margin their superiority demanded."
GUARDIAN

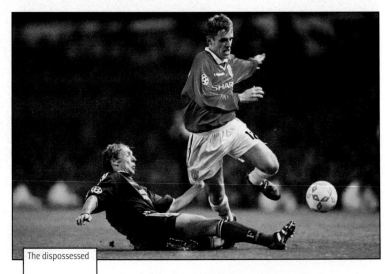

The dispossessed

Will Ryan be nobbled by Van Gobbel?

2–0: Irwin blasts in the penalty

FEYENOORD 1

MANCHESTER UNITED 3

HOME TEAM

1.	Jerzy Dudek	7
17.	Ulrich Van Gobbel	7
7.	Kees Van Wonderen	8
5.	Jean-Paul Van Gastel	7
15.	Bernard Schuiteman	7
14.	Paul Bosvelt	7
2.	George Boateng	7
11.	G. Van Bronckhorst	7
3.	Patricio Graff	6
19.	Igor Korneev	7
9.	Julio Cruz	5

SUBSTITUTES

24.	Clemens Zwijnenberg	
16.	Geoffrey Claeys	6
	Graff I 34 mins	
20.	Henk Vos	6
	Cruz I 76 mins	
12.	Zsolt Petry	
6.	Fernando Picun	

SCORERS

Korneev I 87 mins

REFEREE

Sandor Puhl I Hungary

VISITORS RATING

1.	Peter Schmeichel	7
2.	Gary Neville	8
3.	Denis Irwin	8
6.	Gary Pallister	9
21.	Henning Berg	7
7.	David Beckham	7
8.	Nicky Butt	8
11.	Ryan Giggs	8
10.	Teddy Sheringham	7
18.	Paul Scholes	8
9.	Andy Cole	9

SUBSTITUTES

15.	Karel Poborsky	6
	Scholes I 76 mins	
12.	Phil Neville	6
	Irwin I 82 mins	
20.	Ole G Solskjaer	6
	Cole I 76 mins	
13.	Brian McClair	
17.	Rai Van Der Gouw	
23.	Ben Thornley	
26.	John Curtis	

SCORERS

Cole I 31/44/73

MATCH REPORT

The nasty atmosphere that hung over this encounter could do nothing to wipe the smile from Andy Cole's face. He scored United's first hat-trick in the European Cup for 29 years to take his personal total to eight in the last three games and United to the brink of the quarter finals.

United's first rewarded Cole's persistence, but owed more to good fortune. As Cole chased a long pass from Gary Neville, Schuiteman's clearance deflected off Cole's thigh and over Dudek in the Feyenoord goal. For Cole's second, Sheringham played in Beckham behind the Feyenoord defence who crossed for Cole to shoot low past Dudek.

Cole's hat-trick finished off the best move of the game. Pallister advanced forward and exchanged a series of passes with Giggs who crossed from the left to leave Cole with an empty net to tap in to.

Furious at being so outplayed, Feyenoord began to lash out. Their aggression climaxed in Bosvelt's horrendous stamp on Denis Irwin's calf. On the sidelines, an incensed Ferguson exchanged angry words with the Feyenoord coach and at the final whistle ordered his players not to swap shirts.

IN THE PAPERS

Group B hug

"Andy's pace was a real threat to Feyenoord – like a dog out of the traps."
ALEX FERGUSON

"Look at me, Ma. I'm on top of the world!"

MANCHESTER UNITED 3
FC KOSICE 0

HOME TEAM

		RATING
1.	Peter Schmeichel	7
2.	Gary Neville	7
5.	Ronny Johnsen	8
6.	Gary Pallister	8
12.	Phil Neville	7
8.	Nicky Butt	8
7.	David Beckham	7
11.	Ryan Giggs	8
18.	Paul Scholes	9
10.	Teddy Sheringham	7
9.	Andy Cole	8

SUBSTITUTES

20.	Ole G Solskjaer	7
	Butt	54 mins	
21.	Henning Berg	7
	P Neville	75 mins	
15.	Karel Poborsky	7
	Giggs	75 mins	
13.	Brian McClair	
30.	Michael Twiss	

SCORERS

Cole | 40 mins
Faktor | og 85 mins
Sheringham | 90 mins

REFEREE

A Cakar | Turkey

VISITORS

1.	Ladislav Molnar	6
10.	Robert Semenik	7
4.	Ivan Kozak	7
2.	Marek Spilar	7
8.	Dusan Toth	7
13.	Miroslav Sovic	7
5.	Peter Dzurik	7
11.	Vladislav Zvara	7
6.	Vladimir Janocko	7
7.	Rusian Ljubarskij	7
9.	Jozef Kozlej	7

SUBSTITUTES

14.	Lubomir Faktor	6
	Zvara	80 mins	
18.	Albert Rusnak	7
	Janocko	31 mins	
15.	Marian Bochnovic	6
	Koslej	83 mins	
3.	Andras Telek	
17.	Radoslav Krai	

MATCH REPORT

Manchester United were installed as favourites for the European Cup after qualifying for the quarter finals with their fifth consecutive victory in Group B.

Such achievements glossed over a rather tepid performance. For 85 minutes, the sides were separated only by Andy Cole's first-half strike until Teddy Sheringham and an own goal finally flattered United.

The United faithful turned up for a party, but spent most of their time dodging misplaced shots into the crowd as United wasted a host of chances. Sheringham, Cole and Giggs all contributed some footage for those smarmy comedian's cock-up videos.

Cole opened the scoring five minutes before half-time after he ran onto a clever pass from David Beckham and fired the ball through Molnar's legs. Two months ago it would have hit the goalkeeper's knees, now Cole is getting all the luck.

United enjoyed more luck when the ball flew in off Faktor's legs for their second goal. But Teddy's stunning third goal owed nothing to luck and everything to genius. He advanced to the edge of the area before placing a curling shot into the corner.

IN THE PAPERS

"On the face of it, a 3–0 win against the worst team in the entire competiton is not quite what Alex Ferguson had in mind, not really. He would have wanted his Champions to progress through to the quarter finals in a flurry of goals, to send a message to the rest."
DAILY STAR

"Manchester United continued their progress in the Champions' League last night when his side won their fifth successive game to reach the quarter finals. They now go to Turin in a fortnight with their fate secured and Juventus in their sights."
TELEGRAPH

"There was one man at Old Trafford last night who reckoned he had seen the new Kings of Europe. Karol Pecze, a well-intentioned footballing type from Slovakia. But even the humble boss of whipping boys Kosice knows a real team when he sees one, and Alex Ferguson's team are not hard to spot."
SUN

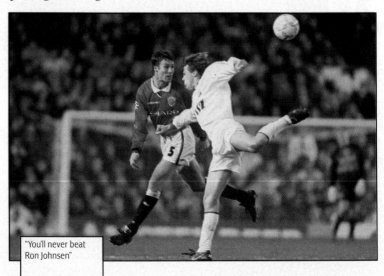

"You'll never beat Ron Johnsen"

Cole cracks the first

Sheringham curls the third

JUVENTUS 1
MANCHESTER UNITED 0

HOME TEAM

1.	Angelo Peruzzi	7
15.	Alessandro Birindelli	7
2.	Ciro Ferrara	7
13.	Mark Luliano	7
3.	Moreno Torricelli	7
7.	Angelo Di Livio	7
8.	Antonio Conte	7
21.	Zinedine Zidane	7
20.	Alessio Tacchinardi	7
18.	Daniel Fonseca	7
9.	Filippo Inzaghi	7

SUBSTITUTES

5.	Fabio Pecchia	7
	Tacchinardi I 45 mins	
4.	Paolo Montero	
6.	Manuel M Dimas	7
	Birindelli I 75 mins	
12.	Michel Rampulla	
31.	Salvatore Aronica	

SCORER

Inzaghi I 83 mins

REFEREE

G Veissiere I France

VISITORS   RATING

1.	Peter Schmeichel	8
2.	Gary Neville	6
6.	Gary Pallister	7
12.	Phil Neville	7
21.	Henning Berg	7
7.	David Beckham	7
5.	Ronny Johnsen	6
11.	Ryan Giggs	6
15.	Karel Poborsky	6
20.	Ole G Solskjaer	6
10.	Teddy Sheringham	6

SUBSTITUTES

13.	Brian McClair	6
	Poborsky I 80	
9.	Andy Cole	6
	Solskjaer I 74	
17.	Rai Van Der Gouw	
23.	Ben Thornley	
29.	John Curtis	

MATCH REPORT

On the verge of being ousted from the Champions' League, the Old Lady of Turin leapt from her deathbed. Filippo Inzaghi's late winner in Turin and Olympiakos' even later equaliser against Rosenborg allowed the Italians to slip in to the quarter finals by the narrowest of margins.

This was Man United's first defeat in the Champions' League this season. Gone was the swaggering confidence that had seen them win their first five group games and score 15 goals. Instead, United played below par and were, at times, over-run by the Italians.

Juventus had not failed to make the last eight in Europe for the last decade. It was a record they were keen to prolong and in the second half they swarmed all over the United goal. Only a combination of poor finishing and Schmeichel's brilliance kept them out. With six minutes remaining, United's luck ran out. Zidane crossed from the byline and Inzaghi was there to head into an unguarded net.

Inzaghissimo!

IN THE PAPERS

"Manchester United's proud reputation as the invincibles of Europe took some damage in Turin. It wasn't a write-off, it wasn't even serious. In fact, it happened in a formality of a match, but the sacrifice of that specially-earned aura must have hurt all the same."
SUN

"One year on, United are a confident, swaggering team heading for the quarter finals in March with a growing belief that they can add more silverware to their already bulging trophy cabinet."
STAR

"This was a night Manchester United may yet come to rue. Comfortably qualified for the quarter finals of the European Cup and coasting accordingly, they finally conceded a goal to Fillipo Inzaghi in a dramatic finale in the Stadio Deli Alpi last night and allowed Juve to join them in the last eight."
INDEPENDENT

"It was not that any of the United players disgraced themselves, just that at full strength and full throttle they would surely have put the Italians away comfortably as they are in the habit of pocketing the Premiership."
DAILY MAIL

"Juventus haven't just gone back since they gave England's finest a couple of master class lessons last season, they've gone to pieces. The selling of the goalscorers who win them titles has resulted in the poorest Italian Champions in living memory."
EXPRESS

Montero polices Johnsen

Czech this out!

MONACO 0

MANCHESTER UNITED 0

HOME TEAM

		RATING
1.	Fabien Barthez	6
18.	Willy Sagnol	7
5.	Franck Dumas	7
21.	Muhamed Konjic	8
17.	Philippe Leonard	8
15.	Sylvain Legwinski	8
4.	Martin Djetou	7
7.	John Collins	7
8.	Ali Benarbia	7
12.	Thierry Henry	8
24.	Victor Ikpeba	7

SUBSTITUTES

11.	Stephane Carnot	6
	Benarbia | 74 mins	
14.	Fabien Lefevre	6
	Henry | 78 mins	
22.	Robert Spehar	6
	Ikpeba | 60 mins	
16.	Stephane Porato	
3.	Christophe Pignol	

REFEREE

Manuel Diaz Vega | Spain

VISITORS

1.	Peter Schmeichel	8
2.	Gary Neville	6
5.	Ronny Johnsen	8
21.	Henning Berg	7
3.	Denis Irwin	7
7.	David Beckham	7
8.	Nicky Butt	7
18.	Paul Scholes	7
12.	Phil Neville	6
10.	Teddy Sheringham	7
9.	Andy Cole	7

SUBSTITUTES

13.	Brian McClair	7
	Irwin | 65 mins	
17.	Rai Van Der Gouw	
5.	David May	
32.	Michael Clegg	
20.	Ole G Solskjaer	

MATCH REPORT

Alex Ferguson decided not to gamble in Monte Carlo. The United manager kept his chips safely in his pocket to earn a goalless draw in the Stade Louis II. Though United fulfilled their task, they may well rue not registering an away goal.

"Boring" is how Peter Schmeichel described this game and few would disagree. Indeed, rarely has such a high profile game involving United been so devoid of incident.

Mindful of the dreadful state of the pitch and conceding a goal away to Borussia Dortmund in the knock-out stages last season, United set out to contain Monaco. A goal would be a nice bonus, but the priority was to leave the South of France without damage.

"We sacrificed what we are normally good at," said Alex Ferguson, "which is playing with risk. In the past, we've probably been naive, going full out to win matches away from home."

Sheringham and Cole could have taken the night off, so isolated were they up front. Monaco's goalkeeper Barthez made only one save all evening when he tipped over a Nicky Butt header. Schmeichel was the busier goalkeeper, saving efforts from Leonard, Spehar and Henry.

Oh–oh, 0–0, Monaco

IN THE PAPERS

"In this United performance there were echoes of England's scoreless draw in Rome, the result which assured Glenn Hoddle's team of qualification for the World Cup. Essentially, it was a game of patience, with Ferguson's players usually finding the right card in the right place at the right time. As an example of economic passing, sound tackling technique and closing down space efficiently, it could hardly have been bettered."

GUARDIAN

"Alex Ferguson willingly sacrificed a reputation in his ruthless pursuit of the one football prize that has become his life. Banished to oblivion were those deadly skilled cavaliers of Manchester United who have terrified Europe with their attacking arrogance. This was the night Fergie decided the princes and playboys of Monaco could go to hell as he chased the ultimate prize, the European Cup."

SUN

Eyes down
for the next
pothole

Fear of flying
Frenchmen

MANCHESTER UNITED 1
MONACO 1

HOME TEAM

	RATING
17. Rai Van Der Gouw	7
2. Gary Neville	6
12. Phil Neville	6
5. Ronny Johnsen	6
3. Denis Irwin	6
7. David Beckham	7
8. Nicky Butt	6
18. Paul Scholes	6
20. Ole G Solskjaer	7
10. Teddy Sheringham	5
9. Andy Cole	8

SUBSTITUTES

25. Kevin Pilkington	
4. David May	
13. Brian McClair	
21. Henning Berg	7
Scholes	45 mins	
19. Michael Clegg	8
G Neville	33 mins	

SCORERS

Solskjaer | 53 mins

REFEREE

Helmut Krug | Germany

VISITORS

1. Fabien Barthez	7
19. Willy Sagnol	7
5. Franck Dumas	8
21. Muhamed Konjic	8
17. Phillippe Leonard	7
4. Martin Djetou	8
7. John Collins	8
6. Djebril Diawara	7
8. Ali Benarbia	7
9. David Treseguet	8
24. Victor Ikpeba	7

SUBSTITUTES

16. Stephane Porato	
3. Christophe Pignol	
12. Thierry Henry	7
Ikpeba	60 mins	
11. Stephane Carnot	7
Bernarbia	67 mins	
18. Francisco Da Costa	7
Konjic	75 mins	

SCORERS

Treseguet | 5 min

MATCH REPORT

Manchester United's European dream is over for another year. Injuries and a discplined Monaco performance conspired to deny United passage to what they believed to be their destiny.

United started without such experienced performers as Schmeichel, Pallister, Giggs and Keane and were further weakened by the loss of Scholes and Gary Neville in the first half. As Ferguson said, "With a full-strength side we'd have beaten them."

United suffered the worst possible start when Treseguet gave Monaco the lead after only five minutes with a shot measured at 96 mph. Like Dortmund last season, to come back from such an early goal proved too great a challenge for United.

Ole Gunnar Solskjaer gave United hope with an equaliser after 53 minutes, volleying in a Beckham cross at the far post. This set up a frantic last 35 minutes as United searched in vain for a winner.

Try as they might, United could not get close enough to force a save from Barthez. United's semi-final exit at the hands of Borussia Dortmund last year was galling for the amount of missed opportunities, but this was notable for a lack of any sort of chances.

IN THE PAPERS

"They threw everything at Monaco but the kitchen sink – yet still the winner wouldn't arrive. Yes, Alex Ferguson's men played their hearts out, they went down fighting, but isn't that what English teams do? Aston Villa did the same the night before... and they're out of Europe, too."
DAILY STAR

"Manchester United's desperate desire to conquer Europe is to tantalise and torment Alex Ferguson's team for another year. It was denied them at an expectant Old Trafford last night by the French Champions of Monaco who took all of six minutes to destroy the hopes of those who packed out the Theatre of Dreams."
SUN

"In the Winter, Manchester United had stoked those European hopes with performances that showed they could compete with the best on the Continent. But last night against Monaco, drained of fluency and disfigured by injury, the dream ebbed away for another season."
EXPRESS

Solskjaer takes one touch too many

Ole beats Cole to the equalising shot

All that good work for nothing

EURO MEMORIES

All spent out
in Monaco

Going out of the 1996/97 European Cup to Borussia Dortmund at the semi-final stage was hard to take. If anything positive came from that narrow elimination it was that Manchester United were finally establishing themselves in Europe after some disappointing previous campaigns. With this in mind, hopes were high that United could go one better and reach the 1998 European Cup Final in Amsterdam. After a faultless start in this year's competition, in which United guaranteed their qualification to the quarter final stages with five straight victories, fortunes started to falter with a defeat in Turin. Two costly draws against AS Monaco led to our elimination on the away goals rule. It was no classic year in Europe for Manchester United but that's not to say there weren't any memories. Here's a selection of the good, the bad and the ugly...

● The 'stadium' in Kosice – it would have struggled to be passed fit for the Vauxhall Conference and yet it staged three Champions' League games.

● Kosice fans trying to sell match tickets to United fans for £200 when the face value was around a fiver. Your average Mancunian isn't quite a gullible as your typical Japanese tourist but then the locals weren't to know... they've never played us before.

● Coming from behind to beat Juventus 3–2. Probably the finest game of the season at Old Trafford.

● 3,000 Feyenoord fans at Old Trafford – the loudest away fans at Old Trafford all season.

● Bosvelts gruesome 'tackle' on Denis Irwin .

● United fans singing 'Ajax' to wind up Feyenoord fans – it worked.

● Andy Cole's hat-trick in Feyenoord.

● United being so confident of reaching the European Cup Final that they booked flights to Amsterdam in January.

1997/98

● The military-style operation launched by the Turinese Police to look after the 3,600 United fans after accusations of heavy-handed treatment by the same Police force a year previous.

● Juventus fans celebrating qualification to the quarter final stages in Turin after hearing that Olympiakos had equalised against Rosenborg in Athens – thus ensuring that the Italians qualified as one of the best runners-up to United.

● Inzaghi's 87th-minute goal in Turin that ruined our 100% Champions' League group record.

● Winning our group and being installed as favourites to win the European Cup.

● The red European kit shirt. Simple, red and understated – all the ingredients for a classic United shirt.

● Monaco fans. Possibly the most apathetic and affluent fans on earth.

● The pitch in Monaco, it's no excuse but it really was poor.

> ## "United had fire in their eyes when we played them at Old Trafford"
>
> ALESSANDRO DEL PIERO

● The 4,000 United fans singing, "Forever and ever," in Monaco – a loud and proud rendition if there ever was one.

● David Trezguet's exoceted goal for Monaco at Old Trafford which shattered our European dream.

● Suited Monaco fans celebrating in one Manchester 70s theme night disco after their draw at Old Trafford – they thought that all Mancunians were 20 years behind the time in our musical taste.

● The critics, whom, with the benefit of hindsight, were able to pinpoint why United didn't succeed in Europe. If only they had been so vociferous before the game then maybe United would have progressed further.

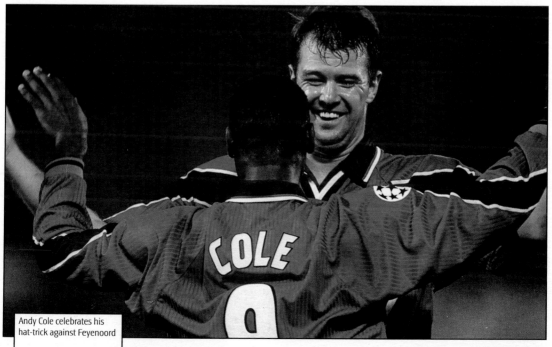

Andy Cole celebrates his hat-trick against Feyenoord

THE TEAM

DAVID BECKHAM

DAVID BECKHAM

PROFILE

Everyone, it seems, has an opinion about David Beckham. Unfortunately most of those opinions, like my mum's for instance, are not based on his outstanding footballing ability but on his relationship with one of the most famous women in the world, Spice Girl Victoria Adams.

> **"David Beckham is one of those players who can bring the crowd to the height of their emotions."**
> ALESSANDRO DEL PIERO

While David Beckham has the highest profile of any Manchester United player and has to put up with constant and unwarranted intrusions into his private life, it was actually on a football field that Beckham made his name.

The injury which ruled Roy Keane out for most of last season was to the detriment of Beckham more than any other player. With Keane out, Beckham's role changed from a wide player to a player who was constantly dragged into the middle of the field to chase. Ultimately, it compromised his creative play. Beckham's trade-mark spectacular goals were still evident and his free-kicks, such as the one that busted David James' net at Anfield, set him aside from his contemporaries as did another quality of Beckham's play: his pin-point, cross-field passes that are such a joy to watch.

Beckham's temperament could improve – at times he let himself down by dropping to the standards of those who were trying to rile him – but that should improve with age and guidance.

With a faultless work-rate and God's gift of so much natural talent, the future of David Beckham burns brightly. With any luck, he'll be an integral part in any Manchester United successes over the next decade.

FACT FILE

Born:
2 May 1975 | Leytonstone
Height: **6' 0"**
Weight: **11st 2lb**
Signed for United:
23 January 1993
Signed as a trainee:
8 July 1991
United League debut:
2 April 1995 |
Leeds United (h)
Previous clubs:
None

1997/98 RECORD
45(4) apps | 11 goals
MANCHESTER UNITED RECORD
129(18) apps | 31 goals
INTERNATIONAL RECORD
13 apps | 0 goals
Team: **England**
Debut: **September 1996 |**
Moldova (a)

BEST MOMENT OF 97/98

Two goals at Chelsea in the FA Cup to silence the Stamford Bridge morons

Smell that!

HENNING BERG

HENNING BERG

PROFILE

Alex Ferguson had tried to buy Blackburn's Norwegian centre half Henning Berg on more than one occasion before a £5-million bid was accepted in August 1997. The fee made Henning United's second costliest player and the most expensive defender in the country, but it was a price Fergie thought worth paying. He was convinced that United needed the stability in defence which they'd enjoyed for years with Bruce and Pallister.

> **"We're always going to be up there challenging for prizes. I can't ask for more."**
>
> BERG ON JOINING UNITED

Henning, a United fan who listed Coppell, Hill and Macari as his childhood heroes, actually spent a week on trial at Old Trafford in 1988. But, by his own admission, he wasn't quite ready for the top-flight and returned to Norway where he began to make impressions at Velerengen and SK Lillestrom, before Kenny Dalglish signed him for Blackburn in 1993. In 1994/95, Henning partnered Colin Hendry in the heart of Blackburn's defence as they pipped United to the title and he became a popular, if unsung member, of the Rovers set-up.

Once at Old Trafford, Berg appeared to settle immediately after his debut as a substitute at home to Southampton. Until Christmas, he was pretty much an ever-present in United's first XI.

With Berg flitting in and out of the side towards the end of the season, the Norwegian went public by saying that he thought his days at United could be numbered with the arrival of Jaap Stam from PSV Eindhoven.

FACT FILE

Born:
1 September 1969 | Eidsvell | Norway

Height: **6' 0"**

Weight: **12st 4lb**

Signed for United:
11 August 1997

Transfer fee:
£5 million

United League debut:
13 August 1997 | Southampton (h)

Previous clubs:
KFUM Oslo | Valerengen | SK Lillestrom | Blackburn Rovers

1997/98 RECORD
31(4) apps | 1 goal

MANCHESTER UNITED RECORD
31(4) apps | 1 goal

INTERNATIONAL RECORD
50 apps | 4 goals

Team: **Norway**

Debut:
May 1992 | Faroe Islands

Berg's greatest quality is his ability to man mark a dangerous attacker out of the game. But there have been times when he's been caught off-guard by attackers. With competition amongst the back four as intense as ever, it's up to Berg to make it difficult for the manager *not* to pick him next season.

BEST MOMENT OF 97/98

Getting in where the boots were flying to head United's first against Everton on Boxing Day

Never out of the limelight for long

NICKY BUTT

NICKY BUTT

PROFILE

Nicky Butt grows in stature as a United player with every season that passes but 1997/98 was possibly his best yet.

A first-team regular since the departure of Paul Ince in the summer of 1995, Nicky Butt steadily improved as a player alongside United's midfield general Roy Keane. When the United captain was ruled out for the rest of the season through a cruciate injury, some feared the United team would fall apart, particularly in the heart of the team. Butt had different ideas and, instead of wilting under the increased workload left by the absence of his inspirational midfield partner, revelled in the added responsibility, showing why he is generally regarded as one of England's brightest young stars. A fact not missed by England manager Glenn Hoddle who regularly called him up to the national squad.

> ## "Butty's been brilliant this year. You need someone like that who will win you the ball."
> RYAN GIGGS

Although renowned for his combative ball-winning style, Butt soon proved that there was much more to his game than tackling. As the main midfielder he passed and read the game in a way that few outside the club knew he could. For a time, during United's pre-Chrismas purple patch, the midfield quartet of Giggs, Beckham, Scholes and Butt were as powerful a combination as anything in Europe. Only United's injury crisis in the latter stages of the season prevented the Butt-commanded midfield from leading United to the title.

When, as expected, Roy Keane makes a successful return to the United midfield next season, it will be a far more mature and accomplished Nicky Butt he'll find playing alongside him.

And that can only be good news for Alex Ferguson and Manchester United.

"I'm Alan Partridge. Ah-haa!"

FACT FILE

Born:
21 January 1975 | Manchester
Height: **5' 10"**
Weight: **11st 3lb**
Signed for United:
23 January 1993
United League debut:
21 November 1992 | Oldham Athletic (h)
Previous clubs:
None

1997/98 RECORD

39(2) apps | 2 goals

MANCHESTER UNITED RECORD

131(12) apps | 11 goals

INTERNATIONAL RECORD

3 (2) apps | 0 goals
Team: **England**
Debut:
29 March 1997 | Mexico

BEST MOMENT OF 97/98

A crunching tacke to set up the fourth goal in United's 5–3 thrashing of Chelsea

ANDY COLE

ANDY COLE

PROFILE

Two months into last season and the pressure on Cole was as intense as it had ever been. Even some of the most pro-Cole supporters were beginning to have their doubts as the luckless forward missed chance after chance, a clear illustration that his confidence was shot. But then Cole's game started to click, the runs started to come off and the goals by which people will always measure his effectiveness started to go in. A hat-trick in the 7–0 demolition of Barnsley was a confidence booster if there ever was one. But it was his three goals in the 3–1 victory away at Feyenoord that showed Cole's finishing quality at the highest level.

> "I've got rid of the demons in my head. I used to have the weight of the world on my shoulders."
>
> ANDY COLE

Cole has won over many of his doubters, not just in view of his goalscoring record this season but for his faultless work that saw him chasing for 90 minutes up front. Cole is best when he's running at players, beating them and shooting on target, often from the most acute of angles. At times he's needed a quality forward player to complement his game and to

FACT FILE

Born:
15 October 1971 | Nottingham
Height: **5' 11"**
Weight: **11st 2lb**
Signed for United:
12 January 1995
Transfer fee:
£6.25 million
United League debut:
22 January 1995 | Blackburn Rovers (h)
Previous clubs:
Bristol City | Arsenal Newcastle United

1997/98 RECORD
41(3) apps | 24 goals

MANCHESTER UNITED RECORD
112(20) apps | 57 goals

INTERNATIONAL RECORD
0(2) apps | 0 goals
Team: **England**
Debut:
29 March 1995 | Uruguay (h)

develop an understanding with. But whether Alex Ferguson will splash out on a world-class striking partner for Cole remains to be seen. Last season was Cole's best at the club since he arrived from Newcastle in January 1995. A major new contract will keep him at the club well into the next century. Let the Andy Cole renaissance continue.

BEST MOMENT OF 97/98

A world-class finish to United's finest team move of the season at Ewood Park

Hatta boy, Andy!

RYAN GIGGS

RYAN GIGGS

PROFILE

Ryan Giggs is one of a just a handful of Manchester United players who deserve the tag 'world class' – a player who would walk into any club side in the world and improve the team. Giggs has been at the club since he was a kid and during the trophy-laden 1990s has played as crucial a role as anyone in United's success. Last season again saw Giggs produce the kind of quality form for which he has become renowned and many fans listed him as their player of the year. Giggs has that rare ability to tilt a game in United's favour with his blistering runs at opponents. His performances at Everton away and Juventus at home last season were two of his finest in a Red shirt as he tormented both defences to the point where they were chasing shadows.

> **"There are many great players out there but Ryan Giggs is something extraordinary."**
>
> JAAP STAM AFTER WATCHING GIGGS LIVE FOR THE FIRST TIME

The only problem with Giggs is that he's played so well that United are simply not the same without him. Like Cantona, with whom he linked up so well, Giggs is a match winner and when he's been injured, as he was at some crucial points last season, his absence has been sorely missed and cost the team dearly.

A fully-fit Ryan Giggs is crucial to any United successes over the next decade. Giggs is the player who the top European coaches always name-check and he's the one individual who consistently strikes fear into the opposition. More of the same please, Ryan.

FACT FILE

Born:
29 November 1973 | Cardiff

Height: **5' 11"**

Weight: **10st 7lb**

Signed for United:
29 November 1990

Signed as trainee:
9 July 1990

United league debut:
2 March 1991 | Everton (h)

Previous clubs:
None

1997/98 RECORD

34(1) apps | 9 goals

MANCHESTER UNITED RECORD

283(26) apps | 66 goals

INTERNATIONAL RECORD

21 apps | 5 goals

Team: **Wales**

Debut:
13 March 1993 | Belgium (h)

You're the man!

BEST MOMENT OF 97/98

Scoring United's third to clinch a famous win over Juventus

DENIS IRWIN

DENIS IRWIN

PROFILE

The fact that the most poignant image of Denis Irwin's season is of him buckling under a horror tackle from Feyenoord's Paul Bosvelt does injustice to his contribution in 1997/98. Once again he was the epitomy of consistency, United's ever-dependable left full back and Old Trafford's unsung hero.

At the start of the season some doubters predicted he'd be phased out of first team action, that Phil Neville was now ready to take his place at left back and that sooner or later he'd be exiled to the subs bench. Yet he figured in the first starting XI of the season away at Spurs, and apart from when he was sidelined by the injury sustained in Rotterdam, he was the regular choice at left back.

> **"It doesn't bother me that I don't get any attention. I just get on with my game and my life."**
> DENIS IRWIN

In fact it was the quiet Irishman that kick-started United's run of five successive Champions' League victories, with the opening goal of the campaign in the away trip to Slovakian Champions Kosice. His typical overlapping run and low finish put United on their way to an important 3–0 victory. It proved to be his only goal from open play last season, but certainly not the only time he got his name on the score sheet. After Teddy Sheringham had missed three consecutive penalties, it was the Eire international who was called on to take the responsibility from 12 yards. It was a role he had filled in the 1994/95 season as a stand-in for the suspended Eric Cantona, so he was the obvious choice this time around. He was only required to take two penalties but scored them both.

Irwin has made over 350 appearances in a United shirt and can be expected to add to that total next season in his own quiet, unassuming way.

FACT FILE

Born:
31 October 1965 | Cork

Height: **5' 8"**

Weight: **10st 8lb**

Signed for United:
8 June 1990

Transfer fee:
£625,000

United League debut:
**25 August 1990 |
Coventry City (h)**

Previous clubs:
**Leeds United |
Oldham Athletic**

1997/98 RECORD

31(4) apps | 3 goals

MANCHESTER UNITED RECORD

370(10) apps | 24 goals

INTERNATIONAL RECORD

47 apps | 2 goals

Team: **Republic of Ireland**

Debut:
**12 September 1990 |
Morocco (h)**

BEST MOMENT OF 97/98

Taking over the penalty job and scoring a vital one against Feyenoord at OT

The goalie's making me laugh

RONNY JOHNSEN

RONNY JOHNSEN

PROFILE

In his two full seasons at Old Trafford to date we've seen Ronny Johnsen develop into a first-class defender of international pedigree. Described last season by one United fanzine writer as the 'Norwegian Beckenbauer', Johnsen enjoyed a season of remarkable consistency in spite of playing in an unsettled defence. But then Johnsen is used to change. He played as a striker in Norway until the age of 24 before dropping into midfield and then back further still to his current central defensive position. With this experience in other positions, manager Alex Ferguson has made use of the tall Scandinavian's versatile nature by playing him in central midfield on occasion.

> **"It was not until I signed for United that I realised it was *the* biggest club in the world"**
>
> RONNY JOHNSEN

Costing just £1.5 million from Turkish side Besiktas in 1996, the signing of Johnsen turned out to be one of Fergie's best move and it's amazing that other top European sides weren't alerted to Johnsen's faultless distribution and reliability in making the final tackle. How many times did you see Johnsen give away a free kick last season? How many times did you see him lose possession? Not many.

Some thought that Johnsen would assume his international defensive partnership with Henning Berg when he signed for United from Blackburn for £5 million, but with May and Pallister vying for the same position and injuries playing their part, United's central defence was as unsettled as a Geordie looking at a football trophy. The arrival of record signing Jaap Stam is only going to add to the competition for those places. But Johnsen has the ability to make his place a regular one next season, as long as Michael Owen doesn't go diving into his ankles every time Man United play Liverpool.

BEST MOMENT OF 97/98

Ron's match-winning volley against Wimbledon in March

FACT FILE

Born: **10 June 1969** | **Sandefjord** | **Norway**

Height: **6' 2"**

Weight: **13st**

Signed for United:
10 July 1996

United League debut:
17 August 1996 | **Wimbledon (a)**

Previous clubs:
Besiktas (Turkey) | **Lillestrom SFK Lyn Oslo** | **IF Eik-Tonsberg**

1997/98 RECORD

26(4) apps | 2 goals

MANCHESTER UNITED RECORD

63(9) apps | 2 goals

INTERNATIONAL RECORD

31 apps | 1 goal

Team: **Norway**

Debut: **8 August 1991** | **Sweden (h)**

Ron shields his privates

ROY KEANE

ROY KEANE

PROFILE

Given the skipper's armband, Alex Ferguson expected Roy Keane's combative qualities and vocal on-pitch prescence to galvanise United's 1997/98 European Cup challenge. The initial omens were good. With United lacking sparkle up front in the early-season skirmishes, it was often Roy's drive that pulled them through tight games. A prime example was the come-from-behind win at home to West Ham. When most of his team-mates seemed to be dreaming of future battles in Europe, Roy concentrated on the matter in hand with manic intensity.

Married in summer 1997, Roy was also showing signs of settling down on the pitch but a fatal week in September summed up his ambiguous character. At Bolton, we were treated to the sight of Keano acting as peacemaker during the Nathan Blake–Gary Pallister sending-off incident.

> **"The games we have lost this season, we would never have lost them if Keane had been playing."**
> ALEX FERGUSON

Four days on, a less disciplined display against Chelsea showed Roy could still be rattled by opponents intent on winding him up. Three days later, disaster struck at Elland Road. A late challenge on Alf-Inge Haaland left Roy clutching his right leg. Diagnosed as a cruciate injury, his season was over before our European campaign had gathered momentum.

Stunning form in the Champions' League group stages and Premiership thrashings administered to Barnsley and co suggested the Irishman was not indispensable. However, when more injuries struck in the New Year and the pressure was on United's youthful team, Keane's influence was sorely missed. Alex Ferguson would later lament the lack of leadership in the side minus Roy, explaining that an "angry dressing room at half-time" wouldn't have done any harm.

Keane's rehabilitation was not rushed. Fergie sees him as the dynamic core of United's side for years to come. No risks could be taken with such a prize asset. By next season, Keane will be fighting fit and ready to frighten opponents to death yet again.

BEST MOMENT OF 97/98

Celebrating his deflected goal in style against West Ham at Old Trafford

FACT FILE

Born:
10 August 1971 | Cork

Height: **5' 10"**

Weight: **11st 1lb**

Signed for United:
19 July 1993

Transfer fee:
£3.75 million

United League debut:
15 August 1993 | Norwich City (a)

Previous clubs:
Cobh Ramblers | Nottingham Forest

1997/98 RECORD

10(0) apps | 2 goals

MANCHESTER UNITED RECORD

161(8) apps | 21 goals

INTERNATIONAL RECORD

38 apps | 3 goals

Team: **Republic of Ireland**

Debut: **22 May 1991 | Chile**

Hammers don't hurt 'em

GARY NEVILLE

GARY NEVILLE

PROFILE

In an era when players have freedom of movement between clubs and million-pound contracts are as disposable as tissues, Gary Neville's loyalty to United comes free. Gary is a dyed-in-the wool Red who knows what it's like to stand on the terraces at Old Trafford alongside success-starved fans. He grew up supporting United in the 1980s when the team limped along in Liverpool's shadow. In a short but spectacular career that has brought Premiership, FA Cup and international success, it is perhaps the disappointments his club brought Gary in youth which drive him on to continuously repel failure. He still feels defeat as keenly as the staunchest fan.

> **"Gary eats and sleeps the game. Talk about football and Nev knows everything."**
>
> EX-TEAM MATE DION DUBLIN

This year, Gary and brother Phil were both awarded the longest player contracts (seven-and-a-half years) ever given to United players. The Neville brothers attitude is simple: as long as United want them, they'll be here giving it everything.

Although Gary gets light-hearted stick from his team-mates for his fanatical devotion to football, he has the respect of every player from Brian McClair to John Curtis.

Gary is one of the first names on Fergie's teamsheet and he is already talked about as a future captain. Gary described wearing the United's captain's armband for the first time at Hillsborough in March as, "The greatest personal honour I've ever had... or ever could have." In his *Manchester Evening News* column, Gary Pallister predicted Gary would be the man most likely among United's younger brigade not just to become regular captain, but eventually manage the club! A 500–1 shot? Get your bets on now.

FACT FILE

Born:
18 February 1975 | Bury
Height: **5' 10"**
Weight: **11st 11lb**
Signed as Trainee:
8 July 1991
Signed as Professional:
23 January 1993
United League debut:
**8 May 1994 |
Coventry City (h)**
Previous clubs:
None

1997/98 RECORD
44(1) apps | 0 goals

MANCHESTER UNITED RECORD
148(9) apps | 1 goal

INTERNATIONAL RECORD
25 apps | 0 goals
Team: **England**
Debut:
3 June 1995 | Japan (h)

BEST MOMENT OF 97/98

Captaining the side for the first time at Hillsborough in March

Sharing a laugh with Casp and Ben

PHIL NEVILLE

PHIL NEVILLE

PROFILE

The intense competition for places in United's starting XI is highlighted by Phil Neville's situation over the past season. An established England international, Phil still struggled to shift Denis Irwin from the left back slot. Instead, Phil has shown considerable versatility, playing at right back and across the midfield. At first, Phil's venture into midfield was more of a makeshift measure by Fergie brought on by injuries to key men. But as the season wore on, Phil settled into the role in which he had excelled during his youth team days. He soon added intelligent running and no little skill to his assured tackling and natural competitiveness.

> ## "Coley ribs me about my lack of goals. He calls me 'Jigsaw' because I fall to pieces in front of goal."
> PHIL NEVILLE *BEFORE* HIS GOAL AT CHELSEA

Phil was mainly employed as a player to mop up the bits and pieces in midfield allowing Beckham, Giggs and Scholes to concentrate on attack. This paid off, most notably at Villa Park, when Phil came on as substitute for Brian McClair at half-time. A tepid 0–0 scoreline was converted into a 2–0 win as scorers Beckham and Giggs revelled in their freer roles.

One of the most amiable players at the club, Phil puts United's cause before anything else on the pitch as former team-mate and friend Keith Gillespie found out. At St James' Park, in Phil's words, "We kicked lumps out of each other... It's harder to kick a friend!"

Undoubtedly, one of the most memorable moments of the season was Phil's first competitive goal. At 11.46 am on 28 February 1998 after 89 goalless games, Phil broke his duck at Stamford Bridge. Jubilant strains of, "There's only one Phil Neville" rang out from the packed United end while Phil ran off towards the Chelsea fans in a joyous daze! A few more classic finishes like that and he'll be able to sharpen up his celebration technique.

FACT FILE

Born:
21 Janaury 1977 | Bury
Height: **5' 10"**
Weight: **11st 10lb**
Signed as trainee:
5 July 1993
Signed as professional:
1 June 1994
United League debut:
11 February 1995 | Manchester City (a)

1997/98 RECORD

32(7) apps | 1 goal

MANCHESTER UNITED RECORD

77(18) apps | 1 goal

INTERNATIONAL RECORD

9(1) apps | 0 goals
Team: **England**
Debut: **23 May 1996 | China**

BEST MOMENT OF 97/98

His clinical finish at Stamford Bridge... Cantona couldn't have done it better

"Alright, Jigsaw"

GARY PALLISTER

Squad Number: 6 | Defender

GARY PALLISTER

PROFILE

At the start of the 1997/98 season, Gary Pallister was written off as injury prone. They said that his suspect back would not hold out, that this would be the season his United career would draw to a close.

Once again he proved his critics wrong, and by the time his niggling back injury returned, in United's 1–0 win against Chelsea at Stamford Bridge, he had made more appearances in the season than any other player at the club.

> "Pally organises everything here and I'm very surprised he's not in England's starting XI."
>
> PETER SCHMEICHEL

Since the departure of Steve Bruce, Pally has been the senior central defender at Old Trafford, appearing totally comfortable playing alongside any of United's four other centre halves. In the air he is almost unbeatable and although his pace may not be what it was, he makes up for any loss of speed with good reading of the game and the excellent timing of his tackles. His contribution was a major factor in United ending the season with the tightest defence in the Premiership.

Some of his performances last season were as good as any he has given in his nine seasons at Manchester United. In fact, so good was his form, both domestically and in Europe, that it seemed a trip to France '98 with Glenn Hoddle's England squad would be a certainty. How he didn't make the final 22 will be a mystery to the majority of United fans.

Although the addition to the squad of £10.75 million Jaap Stam will have Pallister's critics writing him off again, if his track record in 1997/98 is anything to go by, he'll be around for some time to come.

And he'll be hoping to add to the 427 full appearances he's amassed for the club.

FACT FILE

Born:
30 June 1965 | Ramsgate

Height: **6' 4"**

Weight: **14st 13lb**

Signed for United:
28 August 1989

Transfer fee:
£2.3 million

United League debut:
**30 August 1989 |
Norwich City (h)**

Previous clubs:
**Darlington (loan) |
Middlesbrough**

1997/98 RECORD

42(0) apps | 0 goals

MANCHESTER UNITED RECORD

427(4) apps | 15 goals

INTERNATIONAL RECORD

22 apps | 0 goals

Team: **England**

Debut:
30 August 1988 | Hungary

BEST MOMENT OF 97/98

**Last-ditch tackle to stop
Inzaghi at Old Trafford**

Don't make me laugh

MANCHESTER UNITED
OFFICIAL REVIEW 97/98 **185**

PETER SCHMEICHEL

Squad Number: 1 | Goalkeeper

PETER SCHMEICHEL

PROFILE

Peter Schmeichel has more reason than most to be disappointed about the 1997/98 season. When Roy Keane's campaign ended prematurely at Elland Road, Schmeichel was the man Alex Ferguson chose to lead United towards European and domestic glory, the man who would lift the European Cup should United fulfil their potential. This *could* have been his dream season. All season Schmeichel was in fine form, proving he was still the best goalkeeper in the country – if not Europe – maybe even the world. At the time he was appointed skipper some questioned whether he would be able to lead the team from so far behind the play, but as United thumped in the goals during the pre-Christmas period, Schmeichel was left at the other end of the field admiring the lightening forward play of his team-mates.

> ## "We are not hated for the people we are, but for the success we've enjoyed."
>
> SCHMIKES ON THE ANTI-UNITED BRIGADE

His performances in the Champions' League were among his best in a United shirt. He did as much as anyone to ensure the team progressed to the quarter finals with five group match wins out of six. In the one game United did lose, in the Stadio Delle Alpi, he was the best United player, pulling off save after save, only to be beaten by a late Inzaghi header.

When the team needed their captain most, however, he was struck down by injury, damaging a hamstring in the home game against Arsenal. Just as he had missed the away European Cup semi final at Dortmund 11 months earlier, he was forced to sit in the stands as United went out on away goals to Monaco.

He did not lift any end-of-season silverware but still had every right to be proud of the way he led the team and maintained his own very high standards.

FACT FILE

Born:
18 November 1963 | Gladsaxe | Denmark
Height: **6' 4"**
Weight: **15st 13lb**
Signed for United:
6 August 1991
United league debut:
17 August 1991 | Notts County (h)
Previous clubs:
Brondby IF

1997/98 RECORD

44 apps | 0 goals
19 clean sheets

MANCHESTER UNITED RECORD

337 apps | 1 goal
157 clean sheets

INTERNATIONAL RECORD

98 apps | 0 goals

BEST MOMENT OF 97/98

Two wonderful saves from Pearce and Barnes' headers at St James' Park

United's backbone

PAUL SCHOLES

PAUL SCHOLES

PROFILE

If anything positive came out of Roy Keane's season-ending injury, then it had to be the form of Paul Scholes. He replaced Keane and linked up with Nicky Butt in United's midfield engine room with the same steely determination. Throughout the autumn, Scholes' form was simply magnificent. His first-half performance at Highbury where United were to lose 3–2 saw even Arsenal fans clapping in appreciation of his tidy footwork and clever passes that knitted together United's play.

> **"I could talk about Paul Scholes all day. There's not a player like him anywhere in the world."**
>
> GLENN HODDLE

But it wasn't only his form for United that was earning the plaudits. Scholesy's performance for England in the Le Tournoi during pre-season had established him as a cert in Glenn Hoddle's side and prompted comparisons with other eminent footballers, such as Mr Cantona himself.

The hectic post-Christmas schedule exposed the fallibility of a previously on-song United. The sheer number of games that he had played both at home and abroad also took its toll on Paul. He began to miss some great chances, like the one against Sheffield Wednesday, that a fully-fit Scholes would have put away with the usual combination of power and flair.

There's no need to worry too much, though. Paul Scholes is an outstanding talent with an attitude to match who still has many great years ahead of him. His creative play is as deceptive as his strength on the ball and the fact that he's a Manchester lad who has supported United since he was in nappies means he always gives 110%. Another glorious prospect.

FACT FILE

Born:
16 November 1974 | Salford

Height: **5' 7"**

Weight: **11st**

Signed for United:
23 January 1993

Signed as Trainee:
8 July 1991

United League debut:
24 September 1994 | Ipswich Town (a)

Previous clubs:
None

1997/98 RECORD

36(5) apps | 9 goals

MANCHESTER UNITED RECORD

84(44) apps | 37 goals

INTERNATIONAL RECORD

6 apps | 3 goals

Team: **England**

Debut:
24 May 1997 | South Africa (h)

BEST MOMENT OF 97/98

A beautifully-taken goal in United's 7–0 win over Barnsley. Class personified

Nice 'n' kneesy

TEDDY SHERINGHAM

TEDDY SHERINGHAM

PROFILE

Viewed in isolation, Teddy Sheringham's transfer from Tottenham to United in summer 1997 was an absolute steal. An established partner in England's SAS strikeforce snapped up for just £3.5 million on a three-year contract was bright business, but Cantona's departure cast a huge shadow. Even an international star of Euro '96 would struggle to meet the impossible expectations of United fans reared on five years of Cantona-inspired success.

Teddy got off to an unfortunate start, missing a penalty in front of an unforgiving White Hart Lane crowd, who chanted "Judas" at their former hero. Two further penalty misses saw him confined to the "dole queue as far as penalties are concerned," according to Fergie.

> **"Having played at all levels, after all I've seen through my career, to finish off here is great."**
>
> TEDDY SHERINGHAM

Lacklustre early-season performances also failed to convince hardcore United fans of Teddy's ability to inspire match-winning performances on a regular basis.

Unlike his crowd-pleasing French predecessor at United, Teddy's teamworking attributes tend to endear him more to players and managers. "I'm not the type of player who goes past four players and drills it in the top corner," admits Teddy. "But I know when I'm on song, I do an efficient job for the team."

It took a superb headed equaliser in United's home win over Juventus to persuade some supporters of his big-game potential. Teddy followed up with vital contributions to thrashings of Sheffield Wednesday, Chelsea, Feyenoord, Blackburn and Chelsea which temporarily earnt United the 'best team in Europe' tag.

Despite this, some fans made Teddy a scapegoat for our European Cup exit and League decline. Unfair and unreasonable, but for some supporters he isn't Cantona, and that's that.

FACT FILE

Born:
2 April 1966 | Highams Park
Height: **5' 11"**
Weight: **12st 5lb**
Signed for United:
June 1997
United League debut:
10 August 1997 | Tottenham Hotspur (a)
Previous clubs:
Tottenham Hotspur | Nottingham Forest | Millwall

1997/98 RECORD
37(4) apps | 14 goals

MANCHESTER UNITED RECORD
37(4) apps | 14 goals

INTERNATIONAL RECORD
30(8) apps | 9 goals
Team: **England**
Debut:
1993 | Poland

Proud to be United

BEST MOMENT OF 97/98

His brilliant equaliser against Arsenal at Highbury

OLE GUNNAR SOLSKJAER

OLE GUNNAR SOLSKJAER

PROFILE

Ole Gunnar's second year at Old Trafford proved to be more frustrating than fulfilling for the likeable Norwegian. After sensationally announcing his arrival in English football by becoming United's top League scorer with 18 goals in his first season, Ole Gunnar took a more peripheral role in 1997/98.

His woes started in a pre-season 'friendly' at home to Inter Milan when Massimo Paganin's studs crunched his ankle. As a result, the striker was sidelined for almost two months. His return as substitute against Chelsea proved the lay-off had not blunted his sharpness in front of goal. With United 2–1 down with minutes remaining, Solskjaer coolly converted the equaliser.

> "When I think back to my first season, I was just walking on clouds. Now I know what it's all about."
>
> OLE GUNNAR SOLSKJAER

Having recovered full fitness, Ole Gunnar was faced by another obstacle – Andy Cole. In a complete role reversal of the previous season, the much-maligned Goal King was living up to his soubriquet and Solskjaer couldn't get a look in. It was a testimony to the changing fortunes of United's two hit-men that scoring two goals in a 6–1 win over Sheffield Wednesday couldn't prevent Solskjaer from being dropped from the team to play Feyenoord three days later.

Ole Gunnar didn't sulk. Instead he sought to maintain his form in the Reserve team. A four-goal salvo against Everton in April 1998 made him favourite to finish as the Reserves top-scorer.

In the second half of the season, his first-team opportunities increased, but Cole's consistent form in the central striker's role meant Solskjaer often played as a makeshift left winger. Although he acquitted himself well, goals were harder to come by. Ole Gunnar will be looking to re-establish his centre-forward credentials next season. A seven-year contract will keep Ole Gunnar at Old Trafford until 2004. Expect total commitment and loads more goals.

BEST MOMENT OF 97/98

His sublime curling equaliser against Chelsea at OT

FACT FILE

Born:
26 February 1973 | Norway
Height: **5' 9"**
Weight: **11st 10lbs**
Signed for United:
23 July 1996
United League debut:
25 August 1996 |
Blackburn Rovers (h)
Previous clubs:
Molde | FK Clausenengen

1997/98 RECORD
19(10) apps | 9 goals

MANCHESTER UNITED
52(23) apps | 28 goals

INTERNATIONAL RECORD
11 apps | 6 goals
Team: **Norway**
Debut:
December 1995 | Jamaica

Delighted to be United

MICHAEL CLEGG

PROFILE

Manchester United's production line of quality full backs rolls on. 1997/98 saw the continuing upward curve of 20-year-old Michael Clegg's career adding healthy competitive pressure on Denis Irwin and the Neville brothers.

Consistently praised by youth coaches for his dedication, Michael's first-team performances this season prove he can make the step to senior level.

A headed goal against Inter Milan in pre-season was a good start, but Mike had to content himself with a series of substitute non-appearances in the first half of the season. United's post-Christmas injury crisis gave him more opportunities. Strong in the tackle and rapid on the overlap, Cleggy impressed against Barnsley in the FA Cup. He was also called upon in the second half of the European Cup quarter final against Monaco and his stinging shot and intelligent runs were bright spots on a dismal night.

Watch out for another Clegg coming through the United ranks. Younger brother Steve plays for United's Under–16s.

FACT FILE

Born:
3 July 1977 | Tameside
Height: **5' 8"**
Weight: **10st 12lb**
Signed as trainee:
5 July 1993
Signed Professional:
1 July 1995
United League debut:
23 November 1996 | Middlesbrough (a)

1997/98 RECORD

3(4) apps | 0 goals

MANCHESTER UNITED RECORD

8(4) apps | 0 goals

Squad Number: 14 | Forward

JORDI CRUYFF

PROFILE

Even the most sceptical fans started to believe the Jordi Cruyff comeback stories when the Dutchman dazzled in pre-season and played the first three games of the League campaign.

But then the spectre of injury reared its ugly head again, with ankle ligament damage forcing a painful substitution at Leicester City. Cruyff's chance to cement a strike partnership with Teddy Sheringham had gone and he knew it. Kicking himself wasn't advised on medical grounds, and rightly so.

More bad news was to come in the shape of a ruptured thigh, suffered in a charity friendly in December. Then there was the fractured right fibula, sustained in a substitute appearance against Derby County in February. It's a catalogue of woe that could deflate anybody, but Jordi is still determined to succeed at Old Trafford in the two years he has remaining on his contract.

FACT FILE

Born:
9 February 1974 | Amsterdam
Height: **6' 0"**
Weight: **11 st**
Signed for United:
9 August 1996
Transfer fee:
£1.5 million
United League debut:
17 August 1996 | Wimbledon (a
Previous clubs:
Barcelona

1997/98 RECORD:

4(3) apps | 0 goals

MANCHESTER UNITED RECORD:

19(9) apps | 3 goals

JOHN CURTIS

PROFILE

There was an air of inevitability about John Curtis' League debut last October. The Lilleshall graduate had been odds-on for the big time since May 1995 when he helped United to win the FA Youth Cup. Even then, at 16 years old, he looked old enough and wise enough to take senior football in his stride, a maturity borne of captaining England at junior level.

Still, the big day was no less thrilling for the defender, who played throughout United's biggest win of the season, a goal difference-boosting 7–0 victory over Barnsley.

"I thought I did okay," he says. "I just played everything as simply as I could."

John's second League start became something of an ordeal when he was asked to mark Overmars of Arsenal. There was no shame in coming off second best; on that form, the Gunner would have demolished many men of greater experience in the very same way.

FACT FILE

Born:
3 September 1978 | Nuneaton
Height: **5' 10"**
Weight: **11st 7lb**
Signed as trainee:
10 July 1995
Signed as professional:
23 September 1995
United League debut:
25 October 1997 | Barnsley (h)
1997/98 RECORD:
4(5) apps | 0 goals
MANCHESTER UNITED RECORD:
4(5) apps | 0 goals

DAVID MAY

PROFILE

Following on from the season 1996/97, which was undoubtedly his finest since joining the club from Blackburn in 1994 for a £1.2 million fee, David May experienced a season of disappointment in 1997/98.

It wasn't that May played poorly when selected – far from it – it was that injury played havoc with his season. And with three other international centre-halves vying for two positions, May had to wait until March just to make his first League start of the season.

As is the case for Henning Berg, Ronny Johnsen and Gary Pallister, the arrival of Jaap Stam, the world's most expensive defender, will make May's quest for a regular first-team position all the more difficult. But as we saw in 1996/97, May has the ability to make a place his own. After all, the fans don't sing, "David May, Superstar, he's got more medals than Shearer" for no reason.

FACT FILE

Born:
24 June 1970 | Oldham
Height: **6' 0"**
Weight: **12st 10lb**
Signed for United:
1 July 1994
Transfer fee:
£1.2 million
United League debut:
20 August 1994 | QPR (h)
Previous clubs:
Blackburn Rovers
1997/98 RECORD
9(2) apps | 0 goals
MANCHESTER UNITED RECORD
81(13) apps | 8 goals

BRIAN McCLAIR

PROFILE

Any player that makes nearly 400 full appearances and scores 126 goals for Manchester United over an 11-year period will be remembered for his contribution for a long, long time. Brian McClair is no exception. McClair arrived in the summer of 1987 from Glasgow Celtic for a £850,000 fee and promptly scored 24 League goals in a 31-goal haul in his first season – the first player to break the 20-goal League barrier since George Best. Choccy's given us many magic moments: his goals at City in '90, Legia Warsaw away in '91, against Red Star Belgrade in the same year, in the Rumbelows Cup Final in '92, and Anfield in '93 to name but a few. We'll not forget the clashes with Nigel Winterburn either, him captaining a team of fledglings against Port Vale in '94, nor his Testimonial against Celtic in '97 when 43,743 showed their appreciation for his services in the red shirt. Cheers for the memories, Choccy, and best wishes for the future.

FACT FILE

Born:
8 December 1963 | Airdire
Height: **5' 10"**
Weight: **12st 12lb**
Signed for United:
1 July 1987
Transfer fee:
£850,000
United League debut:
15 August 1987 |
Southampton (a)

1997/98 RECORD:

6(14) apps | 0 goals

MANCHESTER UNITED RECORD

395(73) apps | 126 goals

Squad number: 28 | **Midfielder**

PHIL MULRYNE

PROFILE

Life seems to be moving faster for Phil Mulryne on the international stage than it does on the domestic front. And when you consider his goalscoring debut for Northern Ireland against Belgium in February 1997, and the fact that he's captained his country's Under-21 side, it's surprising how little he has played for Manchester United's first team. But that's more a reflection of United's strong squad than it is of Phil's abilities. Nicky Butt, David Beckham and Ryan Giggs are just three names who block his path.
A debutant in the 2–0 Coca-Cola Cup defeat at Ipswich, Phil later came on as sub in the 5–1 FA Cup Fourth Round mauling of Walsall and made his first League start at Barnsley on the last day of the season.
Encouraging signs, but there was more work to be done in the Pontin's League where Phil became a regular alongside Brian McClair in the Reserves' midfield.

FACT FILE

Born:
1 January 1978 | Belfast
Height: **5' 7"**
Weight: **10st 13lb**
Signed as trainee:
11 July 1994
Signed as professional:
17 March 1995
United debut
Coca-Cola Cup | 14 October 19
| Ipswich Town (a)

1997/98 RECORD:

2(1) apps | 0 goals

MANCHESTER UNITED RECORD:

2(1) apps | 0 goals

Squad Number: 22 | Forward

ERIK NEVLAND

PROFILE

    If Ole Gunnar Solskjaer's first season was way ahead of schedule, then Erik Nevland's went much more according to plan. Plenty of Reserve team games and goals, a couple of sub appearances in the first team and some starts in the Cups – it was probably what Fergie had in mind for Ole Gunnar 12 months earlier.

    Not that Erik was complaining. He arrived last summer from Viking Stavanger, well prepared to wait, and to listen and learn from the wealth of experience and talent around him. In his favour was that three compatriots were already at Old Trafford; when Erik came off the bench against Walsall to join Ole, Henning Berg and Ronny Johnsen, it was the first time that four Norwegians had appeared in the same Manchester United side.

Erik prematurely ended his English season in April, to rejoin Stavanger on loan for the start of their League campaign.

FACT FILE

Born:
10 November 1977 | Stavanger
Height: **1.76 m**
Weight: **71 kg**
Signed for United:
1 July 1997
United League debut:
19 January 1998 |
Southampton (a)
Previous clubs:
Viking Stavanger
1997/98 RECORD:
2(3) apps | 0 goals
MANCHESTER UNITED RECORD:
2(3) apps | 0 goals

Squad Number: 25 | Goalkeeper

KEVIN PILKINGTON

PROFILE

    Again, there were no giant leaps or bounds for Kevin Pilkington during 1997/98, even if he did pack a suitcase for Glasgow in April. The Reds' Reserve shot-stopper kept Celtic's bench warm as the Bhoys scripted one of Scotland's more interesting title races. Back home, he might have done much the same for Manchester United, particularly with Peter Schmeichel's fitness faltering. But the job of deputy is still Raimond Van Der Gouw's, and consequently Kevin's best route to the top still looks like a permanent transfer.

    There was at least a Christmas present of two first-team games for the 1992 Youth Cup winner. With Rai and Peter both unavailable, Kevin stepped in to face Everton and Coventry City.

    "It's a bit frustrating in my position," said Kev, after his brief recall. "Once you get the taste of first-team action, you just want to keep doing it."

FACT FILE

Born:
8 March 1974
Height: **6' 1"**
Weight: **13st 1lb**
Signed for United:
1 July 1992
United League debut:
19 November 1994 |
Crystal Palace (h)
1997/98 RECORD:
2 apps | 1 clean sheet
MANCHESTER UNITED RECORD:
6(2) apps | 2 clean sheets

KAREL POBORSKY

PROFILE

After a frustrating 18 months at Old Trafford, Karel Poborsky left for Portuguese giants Benfica at the turn of the year.

The Czech Republic international never reproduced his spectacular Euro '96 form that had persuaded Alex Ferguson to spend £3.5 million on him. He was expected to be the natural succesor to Andrei Kanchelskis on United's right wing, but the emergence of David Beckham and his own indifferent form left him spending most of his time on the bench.

The inevitable withdrawl of Karel's work permit at the end of the season gave Ferguson no choice but to accept Graeme Souness' bid in late December.

At Benfica Poborsky rediscovered his form and promptly scored four goals in his first five games. In a bizarre twist, Benfica, a club in dire financial straits, still hadn't paid a single penny to United come April and the transfer as in the hands of UEFA.

FACT FILE

Born:
**30 March 1972 |
Jindiachuv-Hradec**
Height: **5' 8"**
Weight: **11st 2lb**
Signed for United:
24 July 1996
United League debut:
**21 August 1996 |
Everton (h)**
1997/98 RECORD
7(9) apps | 2 goals
MANCHESTER UNITED RECORD
29(19) apps | 6 goals
INTERNATIONAL RECORD
25 apps | 1 goal
Team: **Czech Republic**
Debut: **23 February 1994 |
Turkey (a)**

Squad Number: 23 | Midfield

BEN THORNLEY

PROFILE

After having to sit back and watch his youth team contemporaries, Butt, Beckham and co establish themselves in the first team, this was the season where Ben Thornley at last got the chance to show what he could do.

The hamstring injury Ryan Giggs sustained in February gave Ben an extended run in the team. Against West Ham and Arsenal he displayed his trickery on the wing, but it was against Wimbledon that he showed the threat he can pose to defences on the wing. Late in the game he ran from his own half, jinked past Chris Perry and delivered a perfect cross for Beckham to nod back for Paul Scholes to score.

In 1998, Ben made strenuous efforts to rekindle the potential he once showed as the star of the 1992 youth team, enlisting for extra training with Brian Kidd. Despite this, his future was still uncertain by summer.

FACT FILE

Born:
21 April 1975 | Bury
Height: **5'10"**
Weight: **11st 12lb**
Signed as trainee:
8 July 1991
Signed Professional:
23 January 1993
United League debut:
**26 February 1994 |
West Ham United (a)**
1997/98 RECORD
2(5) apps | 0 goals
MANCHESTER UNITED RECORD
5(8) apps | 0 goals

RAI VAN DER GOUW

PROFILE

Until this season, Rai Van Der Gouw was still something of an unknown quantity at Old Trafford. But after his performances in the Spring of 1998, United's faithful can rest assured they have an excellent back-up for Peter Schmeichel.

Called up for the Champions' League quarter final second leg against Monaco, there was nothing Rai could do about David Trezeguet's 96 mph rocket after only five minutes, but for the next 85 minutes the Dutchman confidently repelled Monaco's attacks to keep United in the game.

He kept a clean sheet against Wimbledon in March to keep United in the hunt for the title and then, on as a substitute for Schmeichel, gave his finest display yet in the frantic game against Newcastle. United were being held 1–1 and while desperately searching for an equaliser, were leaving their goal exposed. They need not have feared for Van Der Gouw produced two memorable saves from Alan Shearer and Ketsbaia.

FACT FILE

Born:
24 March 1963 |
Oldenzaal | Holland
Height: **6' 2"**
Weight: **13st 1lb**
Signed Professional:
1 July 1992
United League debut:
21 September 1996 |
Aston Villa (a)
Previous Clubs:
Go Ahead Eagles |
Vitesse Arnhem

1997/98 RECORD
5(1) apps | 4 clean sheets
MANCHESTER UNITED RECORD
10(2) apps | 5 clean sheets

RONNIE WALLWORK

PROFILE

Ronnie Wallwork saw just 26 minutes of League action with United in 1997/98, but many hours more in the lower divisions. The young Mancunian enjoyed two loan spells in the Nationwide League, the first with Second Division side Carlisle United.

"I learned a lot down there," says Ronnie, one of Manchester United's ex-Lilleshall recruits. "The games were more physical but I got on with it and I believe I did well."

After two months in Cumbria, Ronnie returned to Old Trafford, only to leave again almost immediately for Stockport County. It was another more than useful experience, even if the die-hard Red had to taste the rare pain of losing to Manchester City in a 4–1 thrashing at Maine Road. It was a far cry from Ronnie's United debut when he came on as sub for Gary Pallister, with the team already six goals to the good against Barnsley.

FACT FILE

Born:
10 September 1977
Height: **5' 10"**
Weight: **12st 12lb**
Signed as trainee:
11 July 1994
Signed as professional:
17 March 1995
United League debut:
25 October 1997 |
Barnsley (h)

1997/98 RECORD:
0(1) apps | 0 goals
MANCHESTER UNITED RECORD:
0(1) apps | 0 goals

WES BROWN

PROFILE

For all the recent success of Manchester United's youth academy, the club has yet to produce a home-grown centre half. That could all change with Wes Brown, the gifted Mancunian who's quietly developing into one of the country's most promising young defenders. A graduate of the FA's School of Excellence at Lilleshall, he's kept a sure footing on the England ladder, playing most recently for the nation's Under-18 side. Certainly his cool temperament is suited to the international game and it would serve him equally well in United's front line.

Wes was again an A team championship winner this season, despite missing several matches due to a hernia operation and also a bout of tonsilitis. He returned to form and fitness in time for United's trip to Italy, where he broadened his experience by playing against Parma and AC Milan in a world youth tournament.

Despite all the medals, caps and foreign trips, the strong and speedy defender has kept his feet firmly on the ground and will focus in 1998/99 on nailing a regular place in United's Reserve team. A fine reader of the game, he's set to frustrate forwards throughout the Pontin's League and beyond.

FACT FILE

Born:
16 March 1979 | Manchester

Height: **6' 1"**

Weight: **12st 2lb**

Signed as trainee:
8 July 1996

Signed Professional:
4 November 1996

1997/98 RECORD

RESERVES
4(1) apps | 0 goals

A TEAM
16(1) apps | 1 goal

B TEAM
0 apps | 0 goals

WAYNE EVANS

PROFILE

Ryan Giggs now has another Welsh compatriot to replace the brother he lost in Mark Hughes. From Camarthen comes Wayne Evans, a composed playmaker who's already represented the principality as captain of the Under-15 side.

Always a mature presence on the field, Wayne earned himself an early call into the B team ranks, playing nine times as a schoolboy 'guest' in the 1996/97 title-winning season. Consequently he became something of a leader for the first-year apprentices in 1997/98, appearing regularly in the B team.

"As an attack-minded player, Wayne's work on the ball is first class," says coach Neil Bailey. "He's a terrific prospect."

Like Richard Wellens, Wayne could probably score a few more goals from midfield. He managed just three of the B team's century this season, all three coming in the first two months of the campaign. However, nobody should question his contribution to the approach play, least of all prolific team-mates like Ian Fitzpatrick and Paul Wheatcroft who have both profited from his accurate passing.

As a second year apprentice, Wayne is hoping to find himself a place in the A team in 1998/99, and seal his pro status.

FACT FILE

Born:
23 October 1980 | Camarthen

Height: **5' 9"**

Weight: **9st 10lb**

Signed as trainee:
30 June 1997

1997/98 RECORD

RESERVES
0 apps | 0 goals

A TEAM
3(4) apps | 0 goals

B TEAM
21(2) apps | 3 goals

DAVID HEALY

PROFILE

Prolific, 20-plus goalscorers might be something of a rarity in Manchester United's first team, but at Youth level, the club seems to be annually blessed with them. Following on from Paul Scholes and Alex Notman comes David Healy, a young man of similar build and the same sharp eye for goal. Healy hails from Northern Ireland, the nation of George Best, Sammy McIlroy and Norman Whiteside to name just three United legends. To emulate them would be a proud moment for any young Ulsterman, and David has already set his sights in that direction.

He started out with 25 goals in his first year, many of them match winners in a championship season for the B team. This season, he's been just as reliable in front of goal, whenever he's found room in a crowded A team attack. In one spell this season, he managed eight goals in eight games to help the A team clinch their umpteenth Lancashire League title on the trot.

"You can never lose your concentration when you play against David," says youth coach Neil Bailey. "His finishing is excellent."

David stepped up another grade in April of this year when he came on a sub for Ole Gunnar Solskjaer in a 2–0 Reserves win over Birmingham.

FACT FILE

Born:
5 August 1979 | Downpatrick

Height: **5' 8"**

Weight: **10st 2lb**

Signed as trainee:
8 July 1996

1997/98 RECORD

RESERVES
0(1) apps | 0 goals

A TEAM
11(5) apps | 12 goals

B TEAM
7(1) apps | 7 goals

RICHARD WELLENS

PROFILE

For the closest thing to Roy Keane at Youth level, read Richard Wellens. The combative midfielder is making a name for himself, and not just in the little black books that referees carry around. Like his first team icon, there's more to Richard's game than fire in his belly and an uncompromising will to win. He's also very skilful and is equally adept at distributing the ball as he is at stealing it away from overpowered opponents.

"He's very talented," says Richard's former youth coach Eric Harrison. "He has great control and quick feet."

Those feet were put to good use in the first season of his apprenticeship, spurring on the B team to their first Lancashire League Division Two title for nine years. He also played in the Lancashire Youth Cup-winning side.

This season he's been a mainstay of the A team's midfield. Goals have been scarce, although he did manage to salvage a point last October when he equalised in a gritty game against Blackburn Rovers. Sadly, his cards and cautions have occurred more frequently, testament to his quick temper.

"There's nothing wrong with him being fiery," adds Eric Harrison, "but his aggression needs to be more controlled."

FACT FILE

Born:
26 March 1980 | Manchester

Height: **5' 9"**

Weight: **10st 7lb**

Signed as trainee:
8 July 1996

Signed Professional:
2 May 1997

1997/98 RECORD

RESERVES
1 app | 0 goals

A TEAM
24 apps | 3 goals

B TEAM
0 apps | 0 goals

ALEX FERGUSON

PROFILE

    Alex Ferguson doesn't like losing. Manchester United's capitulation in the Championship and their failure to progress past the quarter final stage of the Champions' League hurt like hell. The sight of Arsene Wenger lifting United's trophy will be an image burnt into Ferguson's memory as he seeks to regain Premiership supremacy.

    "I know I speak for the players when I say we are hurting," said Ferguson after the season. "Failure will make us better. I will look into where we went wrong and examine my own contribution. We must all stand up and be counted."

    Maybe if United had swept the board this year Ferguson would have begun to wind down, but failure has made him as hungry as ever. Even before the season's climax Ferguson dismissed talk that he would soon be retiring.

    "In the position I am in now, defeat changes me a little bit. Losing the Premiership this season will change me a little bit because I will want to get things done again. This is one of the great things about football. It is a never-ending process."

    In his inquest, Ferguson entertained many reasons for United's turn of the year decline. Complacency? "Maybe we have got to look at our current team and ask, 'Have we got the same hunger right through the team as we had two years ago?' You have to acknowledge that the team of 1996 or 1994 would not have lost any of the games we lost this season."

    The loss of Keane? "The games we have lost this season, we would never have lost if Keane was playing. I think there has been a lack of leadership because of the youthfulness of the side."

    Lack of depth in the squad? "The possibility of the loss of Ryan Giggs is something we should have thought of and done something about at the start of the season. As it was, we had an imbalance when Giggs was out of action. The problem for me is that, when my 11 best players are fit, it is hard for me to go and take two good players who are the same quality as them."

    The signing of Jaap Stam for a world record fee of £10.75 million before the season had finished demostrates Ferguson's hunger is still there.

FACT FILE

Born:
31 December 1941 | Govan

Previous clubs as player:
**Dunfermline Athletic
Glasgow Rangers | Falkirk
Ayr United**

Previous teams as manager:
**East Stirling | St Mirren
Aberdeen | Scotland**

HONOURS WITH MANCHESTER UNITED

**FA Cup 1990 | 1994
European Cup Winners'
Cup 1991
European Super Cup 1991
Football League Cup 1992
FA Premier League 1993 | 1994
1996 | 1997
FA Charity Shield 1990 | 1993 |
1994 | 1996 | 1997**

AF in control

BRIAN KIDD

PROFILE

It was no surprise to see Brian Kidd linked with jobs in Barcelona and Juventus this season. After all, what assistant manager in world football has four titles and two FA Cups on his CV?

Kiddo has a huge reputation on the continent. Juventus' coach Marcelo Lippi regularly meets with him and Glenn Hoddle enquired about him joining England's World Cup campaign.

United chairman Martin Edwards swiftly ended talk of Kidd leaving Old Trafford by claiming, "Brian Kidd is happy here and he'll be at Manchester United until he retires." Nothing would please Collyhurst-born Kiddo more. He once modestly described himself as, "Just a fan who works here."

Brian Kidd has played a major role in Manchester United's return to greatness in the Nineties, but prefers to remain in the background.

"I am just a matter of fact guy. I prefer it that way. I don't need the fuss. It doesn't bother me at all that I'm not in the spotlight. Let's be honest, the Boss is now a celebrity. I have no desire to be in the headlines, with my name up in lights, it's definitely not for me. But please God, let me be at United until I retire."

While Kidd might not blow his own trumpet, his charges, United's players, are more than happy to. "He's called the Legend by the rest of us for obvious reasons," said Gary Pallister. "Because if he wanted to, he could get out the big one, that very special medal from the 1968 European Cup."

Brian Kidd plays a leading role in fostering the team spirit at Old Trafford. "Our way is a we and us method," he says. "It keeps everyone knitted together here. The camaraderie is what counts for us."

While Alex Ferguson is the public face of United, Brian Kidd is happy on the training ground. And he is looking forward to taking a leading role in the new Youth Academy United are planning to open at Carrington next year.

FACT FILE

Born:
29 April 1949 | Manchester
United League debut:
19 August 1967 v Everton (a)
MANCHESTER UNITED PLAYING RECORD
255 apps | 70 goals

INTERNATIONAL PLAYING RECORD

2 apps
Team: **England**

Other clubs as player:
**Arsenal | Manchester City
Everton | Bolton Wanderers
Atlanta Chiefs, USA
Fort Lauderdale Strikers, USA
Minnesota Kicks, USA**

Managerial/coaching career:
**Preston North End |
Manchester United B team,
1989 | Manchester United
Youth Development, 1990 |
Manchester United assistant
manager, 1991**

"Let me go on, Boss. Show 'em how it's done!"

MANCHESTER UNITED
RESERVES

TEAM REPORT

SCORERS

Alex Notman	11
Ole Gunnar Solskjaer	9
Erik Nevland	8
Ben Thornley	6
Brian McClair	4
Michael Twiss	4
Phil Mulryne	3
Jordi Cruyff	2
Chris Casper	1
Terry Cooke	1
Andy Cole	1
Karel Poborsky	1
John O'Kane	1
David Brown	1
Jamie Wood	1
owngoal	1

United Reserves raced to the line in a superb second half of the season, only to finish second behind Leeds United. The "bonus" for coach Jim Ryan was seeing his team finish as top scorers in the League for the third year running.

"That was really pleasing," he says. "We've played a lot of good, flowing football. If you play the right kind of football, you get the results in the end."

It was a valiant effort by the Reds, who seemed to be well off the pace during the long winter slog. Conditions were never worse than at a swampy Hednesford Town, home to Birmingham City's Reserves. The match was pure farce, and the Brummies had the last laugh when Kevin Francis poked home the winner from out of the mud.

"I thought we'd live to regret playing there," says Jim. "But it was from that Birmingham game that we had a pleasing run. In a couple of games, we had mostly young players in the team, and still we came back from being a goal down both times."

The younger element of the squad sharpened their resilience in February, when they represented Manchester United in a world youth tournament in Viareggio, Italy.

"That was very beneficial," the coach reflects. "One of our emphases over there was not to concede goals, and we only lost two to goalkeeping mistakes. When we came home, we only conceded four

PONTIN'S LEAGUE 1997/98   RESULTS

Date	Opponent	H/A	Score	Date	Opponent	H/A	Score
14 Aug	Leeds United	Away	0-3	11 Dec	Blackburn Rovers	Away	1-3
20 Aug	Blackburn Rovers	Home	2-2	30 Dec	Leeds United	Home	1-1
25 Aug	Aston Villa	Home	1-0	7 Jan	Aston Villa	Away	1-0
10 Sep	Sheff. Weds	Home	4-0	14 Jan	Birmingham City	Away	3-4
22 Sep	Derby County	Away	4-0	4 Feb	Sheffield Wednesday	Away	2-0
29 Sep	Tranmere Rovers	Home	1-2	9 Mar	Stoke City	Away	2-1
7 Oct	Everton	Away	2-3	21 Mar	Derby County	Home	2-1
13 Oct	Nottingham Forest	Home	1-1	25 Mar	Liverpool	Home	0-1
27 Oct	Liverpool	Away	2-2	30 Mar	Preston North End	Away	6-1
12 Nov	Stoke City	Home	4-2	8 Apr	Birmingham City	Home	2-0
24 Nov	Preston North End	Home	5-2	22 Apr	Everton	Home	7-0
2 Dec	Tranmere Rovers	Away	1-0	29 Apr	Nottingham Forest	Away	1-0

PONTIN'S LEAGUE PREMIER DIVISION

Leeds United	24	15	3	6	50	27	48
Manchester United	24	14	4	6	55	29	46
Blackburn Rovers	24	11	7	6	41	33	40
Aston Villa	24	10	7	7	34	24	37
Birmingham City	24	9	7	8	33	29	34
Stoke City	24	10	4	10	35	41	34
Everton	24	9	6	9	33	32	33
Derby County	24	10	3	11	34	38	33
Preston North End	24	10	3	11	32	48	33
Liverpool	24	8	5	11	32	43	29
Nottingham Forest	24	7	5	12	37	51	26
Tranmere Rovers	24	4	9	11	38	48	21
Sheffield Wednesday	24	4	7	13	25	37	19

goals in seven games."

If goals in the right end were hard to come by in Italy – they only scored one – the Reserves had no such trouble on English soil. Preston North End and Everton both tasted the Red attack in full effect, shipping 13 strikes between them to the likes of Ole Gunnar Solskjaer, Alex Notman and Michael Twiss.

"Our football quality was high in both games," purrs Jim. "We scored some fantastic goals."

Notman scored one of the best, a 30-yard rocket at Preston. A second goal in that excellent match took the young Scot's tally to 11, making him the Reserves' top scorer in his first full season.

"The new lads who came in have done well," affirms their proud coach. "Danny Higginbotham comes to mind, Michael Twiss, Alex Notman, Wes Brown, Richard Wellens has had some games... overall, they've improved through the season. That's what you're hoping for when young players come to you in August."

Some of the young players took time out to sample League football on loan in the lower divisions. Ronnie Wallwork played for Carlisle United and Stockport County, Grant Brebner went home to Edinburgh to play for Hibernian, and Paul Teather joined Bournemouth.

"Paul was having quite a successful period there before he fractured his cheekbone," says Jim. "He then had to miss the last part of a good season."

Happily Paul and Terry Cooke, who suffered a cruciate injury in September, will have fully recovered in time for the start of 1998/99 season.

Michael never gets his knickers in a Twiss

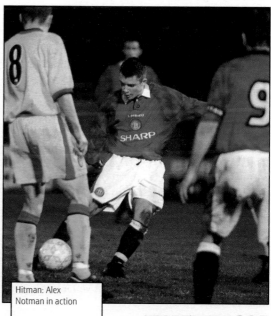

Hitman: Alex Notman in action

MANCHESTER UNITED
YOUTH TEAMS

At the time of going to print some teams had not completed all their fixtures, but United's positions in the League were guarant

TEAM REPORTS

A TEAM: Manchester United's third team romped home again in their title race, with a new pair of hands keeping a grip on the reins. Dave Williams stepped into Eric Harrison's sizeable shoes in September, and swiftly set about the twin aims of retaining the Lancashire League championship and bringing on the stars of the future.

"The A team have had a terrific season," says Dave, a former senior coach with Leeds United, Everton and Wales. "Working with young players has been a new experience for me, and quite a challenge, but I've enjoyed it."

Like last season, the A team were well into October before they tasted defeat for the first time. Prior to that 0–2 reversal at Wrexham, they'd turned in some steely performances, such as a 2–1 win at Liverpool and a 3–2 derby victory over Manchester City. For Dave, the pick of the many highlights came in early February when Blackburn were becoming something of a thorn in United's side.

"Blackburn have had a good season all round," comments Dave. "Reaching the final of the FA Youth Cup, and flying high in the A and B leagues. But we went there and won 4–1 with a very, very good performance. We took the game by the throat from the first minute and didn't allow Blackburn to get off the deck."

YOUTH TEAM: The A team's League success helped to compensate for the season's big disappointment, losing to Blackburn in the FA Youth Cup. United battled back from 2–0 down in the replay at Old Trafford, only to lose 3–2 via an owngoal in extra-time. Their bid for a third successive Lancashire Youth Cup also ended in extra time, this time in the semi final against Tranmere who scraped through 4–3.

B TEAM: United's youngest trophy-hunters came home empty-handed at

A-TEAM SCORERS

David Brown	16
David Healy	12
Jamie Wood	10
Alex Notman	6
Jonathan Greening	5
Stuart Brightwell	4
Tommy Smith	4
D Higginbotham	3
Neil Mustoe	3
Richard Wellens	3
Jordi Cruyff	2
Andrew Duncan	2
Ryan Ford	2
Mark Wilson	2
George Clegg	1
Grant Brebner	1
Wes Brown	1
Gavin Naylor	1
Graeme Tomlinson	1
John Thorrington	1

B-TEAM SCORERS

Paul Wheatcroft	25
Luke Chadwick	17
Ian Fitzpatrick	13
George Clegg	10
Lee Whiteley	10
David Healy	8
Dominic Studley	5
John Thorrington	5
Wayne Evans	3
Jason Hickson	3
Lee Roche	2
Michael Ryan	2
Michael Stewart	2
Stephen Cosgrove	1
Ryan Ford	1
Thor Kristjansson	1
Gareth Strange	1
Ben Muirhead	1

LANCASHIRE LEAGUE DIVISION ONE

	P	W	D	L	F	A	Pts
Manchester United A	30	22	6	2	80	29	72
Everton A	28	15	7	6	66	34	52
Crewe Alex. Reserves	27	16	4	7	67	39	52
Blackburn Rovers A	30	13	9	8	61	36	48
Oldham Athletic A	30	14	6	10	49	40	48
Bury A	29	13	9	7	44	41	48
Burnley A	30	13	6	11	55	55	45
Liverpool A	29	13	5	11	43	42	44
Manchester City A	30	11	8	11	47	39	41
Bolton Wanderers A	29	12	5	12	36	38	41
Tranmere Rovers A	30	10	7	13	57	67	37
Wrexham A	30	10	4	16	59	78	34
Morecambe Reserves	30	7	11	12	41	56	32
Stoke City A	29	8	6	15	37	48	30
Preston North End A	29	3	6	20	22	64	15
Marine Reserves	30	4	3	23	24	82	15

LANCASHIRE LEAGUE DIVISION TWO

	P	W	D	L	F	A	Pts
Blackburn Rovers B	33	26	4	3	105	27	82
Everton B	35	25	6	4	88	33	81
Tranmere Rovers B	35	21	8	6	77	49	71
Blackpool A	35	21	4	10	65	48	67
Manchester United B	36	21	3	12	110	57	66
Wigan Athletic A	36	18	5	13	60	56	59
Stockport County A	36	17	6	13	101	81	57
Oldham Athletic B	36	17	6	13	53	43	57
Wrexham B	36	15	5	16	52	55	50
Manchester City B	36	15	4	17	70	62	49
Liverpool B	35	14	6	15	66	57	48
Crewe Alexandra A	34	14	6	14	62	62	48
Carlisle United A	35	11	8	16	54	68	41
Chester City A	35	11	6	18	69	82	39
Burnley B	35	11	6	18	52	73	39
Rochdale A	35	10	7	18	50	74	37
Bury B	36	9	4	23	33	87	31
Marine Youth	35	4	4	27	39	87	16
Morecambe A	36	3	6	27	36	141	15

Date	Opponent	Venue	Score		Date	Opponent	Venue	Score
23 Aug	Crewe Alexandra Res.	Away	3-1		20 Dec	Bury A	Home	3-2
30 Aug	Stoke City A	Home	1-1		20 Jan	Wrexham A	Home	4-1
13 Sep	Morecambe Reserves	Home	3-1		24 Jan	Bolton Wanderers A	Away	2-1
16 Sep	Liverpool A	Away	2-1		31 Jan	Manchester City A	Home	1-1
20 Sep	Manchester City A	Away	3-2		7 Feb	Blackburn Rovers A	Away	4-1
27 Sep	Tranmere Rovers A	Home	5-0		21 Feb	Oldham Athletic A	Home	0-0
4 Oct	Bury A	Away	4-0		28 Feb	Burnley A	Home	3-1
18 Oct	Blackburn Rovers A	Home	1-1		13 Mar	Morecambe Reserves	Away	4-2
25 Oct	Wrexham A	Away	0-2		28 Mar	Everton A	Away	2-4
1 Nov	Preston North End A	Away	2-1		31 Mar	Oldham Athletic A	Away	1-1
8 Nov	Liverpool A	Home	3-1		4 Apr	Everton A	Home	1-0
15 Nov	Tranmere Rovers A	Away	3-1		14 Apr	Marine Reserves	Away	4-0
22 Nov	Bolton Wanderers A	Home	1-0		18 Apr	Burnley A	Away	2-2
29 Nov	Preston North End A	Home	4-0		25 Apr	Crewe Alexandra Res.	Home	3-0
6 Dec	Marine Reserves	Home	9-0		27 Apr	Stoke City A	Away	2-1

Date	Opponent	Venue	Score		Date	Opponent	Venue	Score
16 Aug	Chester City A	Home	5-1		13 Dec	Wrexham B	Away	0-1
23 Aug	Crewe Alexandra A	Away	2-0		20 Dec	Morecambe A	Home	6-1
30 Aug	Burnley B	Away	6-1		10 Jan	Crewe Alexandra A	Home	2-3
7 Sep	Marine Youth	Home	5-2		24 Jan	Blackburn Rovers B	Home	3-1
13 Sep	Morecambe A	Away	9-2		31 Jan	Everton B	Away	0-0
17 Sep	Oldham Athletic B	Home	3-4		7 Feb	Manchester City B	Home	2-1
20 Sep	Rochdale A	Home	7-1		14 Feb	Bury B	Away	3-0
24 Sep	Stockport County A	Home	6-1		21 Feb	Liverpool B	Home	0-1
27 Sep	Liverpool B	Away	6-3		28 Feb	Stockport County A	Away	5-5
4 Oct	Everton B	Home	0-3		14 Mar	Blackpool A	Away	1-2
11 Oct	Carlisle United B	Away	4-1		21 Mar	Burnley B	Home	5-1
18 Oct	Marine Youth	Away	3-2		28 Mar	Wigan Athletic A	Home	1-2
25 Oct	Tranmere Rovers B	Away	4-5		4 Apr	Blackpool A	Home	1-2
1 Nov	Blackburn Rovers B	Away	0-4		11 Apr	Wigan Athletic A	Away	4-0
15 Nov	Tranmere Rovers B	Home	1-1		15 Apr	Wrexham B	Home	0-1
22 Nov	Rochdale A	Away	2-1		18 Apr	Bury B	Home	0-1
29 Nov	Oldham Athletic B	Away	2-0		22 Apr	Carlisle United B	Home	4-0
6 Dec	Manchester City B	Away	3-2		25 Apr	Chester City A	Away	5-1

the end of a long, hard season, despite banging in a century of goals in Lancashire League Division Two. Tellingly, they were already halfway towards that milestone after their first 12 games.

"The end of the season has been a bit disappointing, given the way we started," says coach Neil Bailey. "We were scoring goals left, right and centre, and some of the performances were really good. It's towards the end that we've had one or two blanks, losing games one-nil, and that's cost us." If the B team's shooting boots only failed them at the wrong time, it was in defence that problems recurred more frequently. Crucial lapses of concentration created some crazy scorelines, notably a 5–5 draw at Stockport and a 4–5 defeat by Tranmere.

"Entertaining games, but they don't do anything for the coach!" remarks Neil, recalling some stressful moments on the sideline. "You don't mind sometimes if the opposition score good goals, but quite often they're down to our own errors. Hopefully the players will learn how to eliminate those silly mistakes and next year turn those defeats into victories."

The victorious A team

THE OPPOSITION

LIVERPOOL

TEAM PROFILE

Liverpool just can't cut the mustard like they used to be able to – to the great satisfaction of many United fans who grew up thinking that Liverpool won the League and United didn't. On their day, Roy Evans' side are capable of passing teams to death and on paper they certainly have the individuals to be challenging for honours. McManaman and Ince would get into any Premiership side outside of Manchester 16 and in Michael Owen the Scousers have unearthed a gem (although Ronny Johnsen may not be so forthcoming in sharing that opinion).

For Liverpool fans, brought up on a staple diet of success and more success, times are hard. But as Manchester United found out in 26 Championship-free years, no team has a divine right to win the League.

Liverpool's inconsistency needs to be addressed if they are to achieve their first League Championship since 1990 because, by their own fans' admission, Liverpool aren't a great team. It won't be long before some young United fans make a banner that reads: "Have you ever seen the Scousers win the League?"

ONE TO WATCH

MICHAEL OWEN

TEAM LINE-UP

David James, Rob Jones, Bjorn Tore Kvarme, Jason McAteer, Mark Wright, Phil Babb, Steve McManaman, Oyvind Leonhardsen, Robbie Fowler, Jamie Redknapp, Karlheinze Riedle, Neil Ruddock, Patrik Berger, Michael Thomas, Paul Ince, Michael Owen, Mark Kennedy, Stig Bjornebye, Dominic Matteo, Tony Warner, Danny Murphy, David Thompson

FACT FILE

Stadium:
Anfield | Anfield Road Liverpool | L4 0TH

Capacity: **45,362**

Manager: **Roy Evans**

Record Attendance:
2 February 1952 | 61,905 v Wolverhampton Wanderers | FA Cup

Club number: **0151 263 2361**

Tickets: **0151 260 8680**

Ticket Prices:
Adult: £18
Family: £24-£27

Nearest BR station: **Kirkdale**

ARSENAL

TEAM PROFILE

Credit where it's due, Arsenal are quality and Arsene Wenger fully deserves his Manager of the Year award. Wenger swaggered into Highbury's antiquated marble halls and proceeded to remove 100 years of the 'Boring Arsenal' tradition. He brought in quality players like Vieira, Overmars, Petit and Anelka to compliment a defence that have played together since the start of the century. Or so it seems.

Wenger's Highbury overhaul raised a few eyebrows, but he brought in players who would draw blood to see Arsenal win. Players who have got as much pride in the Gunners as the staunchest Clock Ender. Players who achieved a deserved League double over Manchester United as they went on to win the League Championship for the first time since 1991.

By April of last season, Arsenal reminded many of the exciting Manchester United team of 1994: solid at the back, creative and strong in midfield with fast wingers and a proven scorer up front in Denis Bergkamp.

Fair play Arsenal... but don't expect any favours when United play you next season.

ONE TO WATCH

DENNIS BERGKAMP

TEAM LINE-UP

David Seaman, Lee Dixon, Nigel Winterburn, Patrick Viera, Steve Bould, Tony Adams, David Platt, Ian Wright, Nicolas Anelka, Dennis Bergkamp, Marc Overmars, Christopher Wreh, Alex Manninger, Martin Keown, Ray Parlour, Emmanuel Petit, Gilles Grimandi, Remi Garde, Mattthew Upson, Louis Boa-Morte, John Lukic, Scott Marshall, Stephen Hughes

FACT FILE

Stadium:
Highbury | Avenell Road | London N5 1BU

Capacity: **38,500**

Manager: **Arsene Wenger**

Record Attendance:
9 March 1935 | 73,285 v Sunderland | Div 1

Club number: **0171 704 4000**

Tickets: **0171 704 4040**

Ticket Prices:
Adult: £15-£31
Child/OAP: £7.50-£8.50

Underground: **Arsenal or Highbury & Islington**

LEEDS UNITED

TEAM PROFILE

George Graham's first full season in charge at Elland Road saw him lead the club to what was, after recent years of under achievement, a respectable League position.

Such has been Leeds progress under Graham

that they are now regarded as one of the Premiership's hardest teams to beat. Nigel Martyn has established himself as England's second choice goalkeeper and he can take much of the credit for their miserly record of conceding goals. Leeds' main problem, however, is their play at the opposite end of the pitch where they have had difficulty finding the back of the net on a regular basis.

ONE TO WATCH
JIMMY FLOYD HASSELBAINK

The signing of Jimmy Hasselbaink proved an astute one and he ended the season as the Yorkshire club's top scorer. But they will have to provide him with a quality strike partner if Leeds are to challenge for honours next season.

Their main hopes of a trophy in 1997/98 evaporated with their exit to Wolverhampton Wanderers in the FA Cup quarter final, but the Elland Road supporters – whose numbers mysteriously swell by thousands when United visit – will be hoping that, with a few summer signings, they can improve on the progress made last season.

TEAM LINE-UP

Nigel Martyn, Gunnar Halle, David Wetherall, Lucas Radebe, David Robertson, Gary Kelly, David Hopkin, Bruno Ribeiro, Alf-Inge Haaland, Harry Kewell, Rodney Wallace, Robert Molenaar, Derek Lilley, Mark Beeney, Lee Bowyer, Jimmy Floyd Hasselbaink, Lee Sharpe, Mark Jackson, Ian Harte, Martin Hiden

FACT FILE

Stadium:
Elland Road | Leeds | West Yorkshire | LS 11 OES

Capacity: **40,000**

Manager: **George Graham**

Record Attendance:
15 March 1967 | 57,862 v Sunderland | FA Cup

Club number: **0113 226 6000**

Tickets: **0113 226 1000**

Ticket Prices:
Adult: £16-25
Concessions: £8–£16.50

Nearest BR station:
Leeds City

CHELSEA

TEAM PROFILE

It was an eventful season at Stamford Bridge, on and off the pitch. With all seemingly going well at the club – through to the Cup Winners' Cup quarter finals, one step from Wembley in the Coca-Cola Cup and with an outside chance

of the Premiership – Chelsea announced the termination of manager Ruud Gullit's contract. Most football pundits predicted their demise. They were wrong.

Under the guidance of new manager Gianluca Vialli, Chelsea improved on their 1997 FA Cup success by winning the Coca-Cola Cup and reaching the European Cup Winners Cup final. However, under Vialli, their Premiership form was anything but consistent and only towards the end of the season, seemingly bouyed by their Cup success, did they put a good run of League results together.

ONE TO WATCH
ROBERTO DI MATTEO

TEAM LINE-UP

Ed De Goey, Dan Petrescu, Celestine Babayaro, Frank Leboeuf, Steve Clarke, Bernard Lambourde, Gustavo Poyet, Gianluca Vialli, Mark Hughes, Dennis Wise, Michael Duberry, Kevin Hitchcock, Graeme Le Saux, David Lee, Roberto Di Matteo, Danny Granville, Andy Myers, Tore Andre Flo, Frank Sinclair, Paul Hughes, Eddie Newton, Gianfranco Zola

FACT FILE

Stadium:
Stamford Bridge | Fulham Road | London SW6 1HS

Capacity: **32,000**

Manager: **Gianluca Vialli**

Record Attendance:
12 October 1935 | 82,905 v Arsenal | Division One

Club number: **0171 385 5545**

Tickets: **0891 121 011**

Ticket Prices:
£16-£50

Nearest Underground:
Fulham Broadway

Inconsistency prevented Chelsea from sustaining a serious title challenge, and if they are to make a genuine attempt at the title it is a problem they will have to solve. They have a fine squad of players and an abundance of forward talent but they need to learn to save some of their Cup performances for the Premiership.

ASTON VILLA

TEAM PROFILE

Great things were expected of Villa at the start of the 1997/98 season but once again they failed to capitalise on the undoubted talent at their disposal. When the club's record summer signing Stan Collymore 'came home' to the club he supported as a boy, joining quality players like Dwight Yorke, Julian Joachim, Gareth Southgate and Mark Draper, most pundits tipped them to finish in the top five. However, Villa struggled to find consistency and Collymore couldn't fulfill the expectations of the Villa faithful.

Despite progress in the UEFA Cup, they found themselves at the wrong end of the Premiership and it was no real surprise when Brian Little resigned as manager.

New manager John Gregory turned things around in the Premiership almost straight away, instilling pride and passion into a team which looked devoid of ideas. Even Collymore's form improved. Despite going out of the UEFA Cup on away goals, Premiership security had been achieved. Villa can now concentrate on making the most of the undoubted talent assembled at the club.

ONE TO WATCH

UGO EHIOGU

TEAM LINE-UP

Mark Bosnich, Gary Charles, Steve Staunton, Gareth Southgate, Ugo Ehiogu, Ian Taylor, Mark Draper, Savo Milosevic, Dwight Yorke, Stan Collymore, Julian Joachim, Michael Oakes, Alan Wright, Fernando Nelson, Simon Grayson, Lee Hendrie, David Hughes, Riccardo Scimeca, Lee Collins, Neil Davis, Darren Byfield, Richard Walker, Matthew Gent

FACT FILE

Stadium:
Villa Park | Trinity Road Birmingham | B6 6HE

Capacity: **39,500**

Manager: **John Gregory**

Record Attendance:
2 March 1946 | 76,588 v Derby County | FA Cup

Club number: **0121 327 2299**

Tickets: **0891 121 848**

Ticket Prices:
£7–£18

Nearest BR station:
Witton or Aston

LEICESTER CITY

TEAM PROFILE

Martin O'Neill is a respected figure in football. He says little but what he does say counts and he's built a Leicester team that get the respect they deserve. At the start of the season the Foxes sat proudly near the top of the League and with the prospect of a UEFA Cup tie against Athletico Madrid to saviour, things were looking up at Filbert Street. Although Leicester's sortie into Europe was a brief one and they slipped slightly as the season went on, O'Neill's side earned a reputation for being difficult to beat. Alongside Champions Arsenal, Leicester were the only other side to chalk up a victory at Old Trafford last season as United found it tough to combat their physical approach to the game. Emile Heskey has continued to impress, as has Muzzy Izzet, Neil Lennon and ex-United junior Robbie Savage. All these players have age on their side and, under Martin O'Neill's wise guidance, should be able to build on their top ten finish next season. This in itself will be a challenge for a club who are limited to gates of just under 21,000 until their new stadium is built.

ONE TO WATCH

MATT ELLIOT

TEAM LINE-UP

Kasey Keller, Julian Watts, Steve Walsh, Mustafa Izzet, Neil Lennon, Scott Taylor, Garry Parker, Emile Heskey, Robbie Savage, Pontus Kaamark, Stuart Campbell, Spencer Prior, Matt Elliot, Rob Ullathorne, Ian Marshall, Graham Fenton, Sam McMahon, Stephen Guppy, Stuart Wilson, Tony Cottee, Stephen Wenlock, Stefan Oakes, Ian Andrews, Theo Zagorakis

FACT FILE

Stadium:
City Stadium | Filbert Street Leicester | LE2 7FL

Capacity: **21,000**

Manager: **Martin O'Neill**

Record Attendance:
18 February 1928 | 47,298 v Tottenham | FA Cup

Club number: **0116 291 5000**

Tickets: **0116 291 5232**

Ticket Prices:
Adult: £13.50–£22 OAP/child: £7–£11

Nearest BR station:
London Road

BLACKBURN ROVERS

TEAM PROFILE

Roy Hodgson's first season at Ewood Park has to be judged a success – despite the lack of trophies in the grand oak boardroom at Ewood. After pipping United to the League in 1995, Rovers' fortunes declined as they slipped right

down the table and inconsistency became their hallmark. Hodgson, fresh from managing Inter in Milan, arrived and imposed qualities that resulted in a swift improvement in results. Chris Sutton's Anglo-Scottish partnership with Kevin Gallacher is continuing to provide goals and the emergence of

ONE TO WATCH
CHRIS SUTTON

youngsters like Damien Duff has encouraged the residents of the Lancashire valleys even further.

Jack Walker, the man responsible for pumping the money into Blackburn which lead to the success in 1995, is still around at Ewood Park and the club recently announced plans to develop one side of their ground that will raise the capacity to 40,000. Looking at the calibre of the players at the club, not to mention a fine stadium that's about to get even better, it's safe to assume the club who attracted under 6,000 ten years ago have come a long way in a short time. Expect another top eight finish from Blackburn and the possibility of a good Cup run.

TEAM LINE-UP

Tim Flowers, Callum Davidson, Jeff Kenna, Tim Sherwood, Colin Hendry, Tore Pederson, Stuart Ripley, Kevin Gallacher, Chris Sutton, Martin Dahlin, Jason Wilcox, John Filan, Anders Andersson, Garry Flitcroft, Billy McKinlay, Gary Croft, Patrick Valery, Stephane Henchoz, Damien Duff, Marlon Broomes, Tony Williams, Alan Fettis, James Beattie

FACT FILE

Stadium:
Ewood Park | Blackburn | Lancashire | BB2 4JF

Capacity: **31,367**

Manager: **Roy Hodgson**

Record Attendance:
2 March 1929 | 61,783 v Bolton Wanderers | FA Cup

Club number: **01254 698 888**

Tickets: **0891 121014**

Ticket Prices:
£16-23

Nearest BR station:
Blackburn

COVENTRY CITY

TEAM PROFILE

After investing heavily in a batch of quality players, it was a great mystery as to why Coventry City had not been able to shrug off their perennial strugglers tag... until last season. The Sky Blues started the season in their usual

substandard fashion and yet another battle with relegation looked inevitable. That is until Gordon Strachan's talented side hit a rich vein of form around Christmas time which carried them through to the end of the season and their first mid-table finish in years.

Manchester United were on the receiving end of the Sky Blues battling quality at Highfield Road in

ONE TO WATCH
DION DUBLIN

December. With five minutes to go, the Reds were coasting to a 2–1 victory until the precocious talents of ex-Red Dion Dublin and Darren Huckerby combined for two goals and a fine win. It was Coventry's first win in 17 games against United but, as their subsequent form proved, it was no fluke.

With a dedicated manager, an ambitious chair-man and a multitude of promising young-sters, that Eton Boat song may well get a few more airings to toast a rare Sky Blue success.

TEAM LINE-UP

Steve Ogrizovic, Richard Shaw, David Burrows, Paul Williams, Liam Daish, Gary Breen, Darren Huckerby, Noel Whelan, Dion Dublin, Gary McAllister, John Salako, Paul Telfer, Magnus Hedman, Trond Soltvedt, George Boateng, Willie Boland, Marcus Hall, Martin Johansen, Mike O'Neill, Andy Ducros, Simon Haworth, Roland Nilsson, Scott Howie, Gavin Strachan

FACT FILE

Stadium:
Highfield Road | King Richard Street | Coventry | CV2 4FW

Capacity: **23,662**

Manager: **Gordon Strachan**

Record Attendance:
29 April 1967 | 51,445 v Wolves | Division Two

Club number: **01203 234 0000**

Tickets: **0891 12 10 66**

Ticket Prices:
£8-£22

Nearest BR station:
Coventry

DERBY COUNTY

TEAM PROFILE

Derby County will be hoping to build upon the success of last season's campaign, which held out the prospect of European football returning to the club for the first time in over 20 years.

However, if the Rams are to continue their improvement and mount anything resembling a Championship challenge they will need a great deal more consistency.

ONE TO WATCH

PAULO WANCHOPE

There were times last term when manager Jim Smith must have been tearing out what little hair he has left. Getting stuffed 5–0 at home to Leeds was bad enough, but Derby also contrived to lose at Crystal Palace in April to hand the low-flying Eagles their first home win of the season.

On the other hand, the Rams gave Champions Arsenal their biggest thrashing of the year and Pride Park was frequently delighted by the swashbuckling interplay between the rubber-limbed Paulo Wanchope and the Italians, Baiano and Stefano Eranio.

Derby's problems are in defence and the signing of a top-class centre back to play alongside Igor Stimac is a priority. Still, with their dodgy back line and vibrant attack, Derby are sure to be one of the most entertaining teams United will face.

TEAM LINE-UP

Russell Hoult, Gary Rowett, Chris Powell, Darryl Powell, Dean Yates, Igor Stimac, Robin Van Der Laan, Dean Sturridge, Paulo Wanchope, Rory Delap, Ron Willems, Lars Bohinen, Marc Gridge-Wilkinson, Jacob Laursen, Lee Carsley, Steve Elliot, Stefano Eranio, Mart Poom, Christian Dailly, Mauricio Solis, Deon Burton, Robert Kozluk, Jon Hunt, Francesco Baiano

FACT FILE

Stadium:
Pride Park | Derby | DE24 8XL

Capacity: **30,139**

Manager: **Jim Smith**

Record Attendance:
20 September 1969 | 41,826 v Tottenham | Division One

Club number: **01332 667503**

Tickets: **01332 209209**

Ticket Price:
Adult: **£18–£23**
Child: **£9–£11**

Nearest BR station:
Derby

WEST HAM UNITED

TEAM PROFILE

After narrowly avoiding relegation in 1996/97, West Ham were a transformed side last season and some excellent results in the run-in kept them in the European frame.

Manager Harry Redknapp must take much of the credit. He relaxed his hard-line "Buy British" policy by bringing Israeli international Eyal Berkovic and French striker Samassi Abou to Upton Park. Both proved themselves to be more committed to the West Ham cause than the previous year's foreign intake.

ONE TO WATCH

JOHN HARTSON

Just as important to the East Enders' renaissance was the emergence of youngsters Rio Ferdinand and Frank Lampard Junior. Arguably, a bigger factor still was the form of John Hartson. A centre forward in the Geoff Hurst mould, Hartson would surely have been the Premiership's top scorer if he hadn't missed so many games through suspension.

With their neat, fluid passing, West Ham are guaranteed to be one of the most attractive teams United face this season. But it's unlikely the Reds will be relishing their trip to Upton Park; this is the one London ground where we never seem to win.

TEAM LINE-UP

Ludek Miklosko, Tim Breacker, Julian Dicks, Steve Potts, Richard Hall, David Unsworth, Trevor Sinclair, Paul Kitson, John Hartson, Steve Lomas, Rio Ferdinand, John Moncur, Stan Lazaridis, Frank Lampard, Ian Pearce, Andy Impey, Craig Forrest, Scott Mean, Samassi Abou, Lee Hodges, Emmanuel Omoyinmi, Chris Coyne, Eyal Berkovic, Neil Finn, Bernard Lama, Lee Boylan

FACT FILE

Stadium:
Boleyn Ground | Upton Park London E13 9AZ

Manager: **Harry Redknapp**

Capacity: **26,012**

Record Attendance:
17 October 1970 | 42,322 v Tottenham

Club number: **0181 548 2748**

Tickets: **0181 548 2700**

Ticket Prices:
Adult: **£18–£31**
Child: **£9–£14**

Nearest BR station:
Upton Park

SOUTHAMPTON

TEAM PROFILE

Tipped by just about everybody for relegation last season, Southampton surprised probably even themselves by finishing in a mid-table spot. Saints' manager David Jones rather enjoyed himself as he handed out generous portions of humble pie to the doubters.

Jones had every reason to feel satisfied with his first season in charge, having transformed the Saints' prospects with some astute signings. Carlton Palmer and Kevin Richardson arrived to stiffen the midfield, while £2 million-man David Hirst formed an effective strike partnership with Egil Ostenstad. The Saints boss also swooped to bring his old Stockport goalkeeper Mark Jones (no relation) to the Dell in yet another value-for-money deal.

One disappointing aspect of the season for Southampton fans, however, was the up-and-down form of Matthew Le Tissier. No change there, then.

No doubt, Southampton will be seen by many as relegation candidates again this season. Having watched the Reds lose their last three League games down at the Dell, some uncharitable Man United fans may be hoping this is the year the Saints sink. For our part, we wish the plucky seasiders well.

ONE TO WATCH
KEVIN DAVIES

TEAM LINE-UP

Paul Jones, Jason Dodd, Lee Todd, Carlton Palmer, Ken Monkou, Claus Lundekvam, Matt Le Tissier, Matthew Oakley, Egil Ostenstad, Richard Dryden, Neil Moss, John Beresford, Frances Benali, Kevin Davies, Kevin Richardson, Darryl Flahaven, Andy Willians, Duncan Spedding, Steve Basham, Stig Johansen, David Hughes, David Hirst

FACT FILE

Stadium:
The Dell | Milton Road | Southampton | SO 15 2XH

Manager: **Dave Jones**

Capacity: **15,250**

Record Attendence:
8 October 1969 | 31,044 v Man United | Division One

Club number: **01703 220 505**

Tickets: **01703 337 171**

Ticket Prices:
Adult: £16-20
Child: £7

Nearest BR station:
Southampton Central

SHEFFIELD WEDS

TEAM PROFILE

When the Reds stuffed Sheffield Wednesday 6–1 at Old Trafford last season it was not so much the final straw for David Pleat's managerial reign at the South Yorkshire club, more like a giant haystack landing on him from a great height.

Pleat was immediately sacked, to be replaced in the Hillsborough hotseat by none other than Mr Bojangles himself, Ron Atkinson. The former United boss showed that his Midas touch had not deserted him, guiding the Owls away from the danger zone with four consecutive wins.

Big Ron's top priority was to stop Wednesday leaking goals. To this end he stiffened his back four with a raid on Goodison Park, signing both Earl Barrett and Andy Hinchcliffe from Everton to play alongside Des Walker and John Newsome.

Atkinson will be looking for a top-half finish this season, and he has the squad to achieve it. In midfield, Peter Atherton, Mark Pembridge and Petter Ruudi provide solidity to complement the flair of Paolo Di Canio. Up front, Andy Booth forms a potent partnership with overhead kick specialist Benito Carbone.

ONE TO WATCH
PAOLO DI CANIO

TEAM LINE-UP

Kevin Pressman, Peter Atherton, Ian Nolan, Mark Pembridge, Jon Newsome, Des Walker, Guy Whittingham, Benito Carbone, Andy Booth, Paolo Di Canio, Graham Hyde, Matt Clarke, Stephen Nicol, Patrick Blondeau, Ritchie Humphreys, Lee Briscoe, Dejan Stefanovic, Scott Oakes, Wayne Collins, Adem Poric, Manuel Agogo, Petter Rudi, Bruce Grobbelaar

FACT FILE

Stadium:
Hillsborough | Penistone Road | Sheffield | S6 1SW

Manager: **Ron Atkinson**

Capacity: **39,880**

Record Attendence:
2 February 1952 | 61,905 v Wolves | FA Cup

Club number: **0114 221 2121**

Tickets: **0114 221 2400**

Ticket Prices:
Adult: £9–£21
OAP/child: £6–£12

Nearest BR station:
Sheffield Midland

WIMBLEDON

TEAM PROFILE

After reaching the semi finals of both Cup competitions and finishing a respectable eighth in the League the previous season, Wimbledon were tipped to do well in 1997/98. Even the cynics who normally predict the Dons to finish in the bottom three, for possibly the first time ever, tipped them to have a great season. As usual they were wrong.

Partly due to injury and partly because of their inability to hit the back of the net, Wimbledon were hugely disappointing and found themselves struggling to avoid the drop. It seemed whenever one key player returned from injury another would promptly limp off to the treatment room. Players like Robbie Earle, Efan Ekoku and Jason Euell were missing for long periods of the season.

Despite having the threat of Nationwide football hanging over them, the fans had their minds on other more pressing concerns. Like where the club would be playing their home matches in future. Having avoided relegation, and if they can keep their key players fit, then Wimbledon shouldn't find 1998/99 as big a struggle as last season.

ONE TO WATCH

MICHAEL HUGHES

TEAM LINE-UP

Neil Sullivan, Kenny Cunningham, Alan Kimble, Dean Blackwell, Ben Thatcher, Ceri Hughes, Robbie Earle, Andy Roberts, Marcus Gayle, Chris Perry, Paul Heald, Alan Reeves, Michael Hughes, Neil Ardley, Duncan Jupp, Andy Clarke, Jason Euell, Peter Fear, Carl Cort, Carl Leaburn, Mark Kennedy

FACT FILE

Stadium:
Selhurst Park | London | SE25 6PY

Manager: **Joe Kinnear**

Capacity: **26,000**

Record Attendance:
3 February 1996 | 32,852 v Man United | Premier League

Club number: **0181 771 2233**

Tickets: **0181 771 8841**

Ticket Prices:
Adult: £10–£17
Child: £5–£8

Nearest BR station:
Selhurst or Thornton Heath

NEWCASTLE UNITED

TEAM PROFILE

One of the big surprises of last season was the decline in the League fortunes of Newcastle United. Kenny Dalglish's team had finished runners-up to United in 1997 and many of 'the greatest fans in the world' thought this would be their year. How wrong could they have been?

Newcastle's European aspirations started with a bang with victories over Barcelona and a credible draw in Kiev but soon fizzled out as they failed to qualify for the quarter final stages. In the League, what started out as another solid Championship-chasing campaign had soon disintegrated into farce as Newcastle tumbled right down the table. Troubles off the pitch made the headlines for all the wrong reasons and injuries to key players like Shearer didn't help the Geordie cause. Just when it seemed that Newcastle United were ready to self-combust, the first team strung together a decent Cup run that carried them all the way to the Twin Towers and relegation was avoided.

Expect a much stronger challenge in the League from Newcastle United this season.

ONE TO WATCH

ALAN SHEARER

TEAM LINE-UP

Shay Given, Warren Barton, David Batty, Darren Peacock, Steve Howey, Rob Lee, Ian Rush, Alan Shearer, John Barnes, Gary Speed, Stuart Pearce, Temuri Ketsbaia, Shaka Hislop, Jon-Dahl Tomasson, James Crawford, Keith Gillespie, Steve Watson, Bjarni Gudjonsson, Pavel Srnicek, Des Hamilton, Alessandro Pistone, Phillipe Albert, Patrick Kelly

FACT FILE

Stadium:
St James' Park | Barrack Road | Newcastle | NE1 4ST

Manager: **Kenny Dalglish**

Capacity: **36,610**

Record Attendance:
3 September 1930 | 68,386 v Chelsea | Division One

Club number: **0191 201 8400**

Tickets: **0191 261 1571**

Ticket Prices:
to be confirmed

Nearest BR station:
Newcastle Central

TOTTENHAM HOTSPUR

TEAM PROFILE

This time round Tottenham fans will be desperately hoping they don't have to endure another season like last year. Faced with the prospect of sliding out of the top flight for the first time in over 20 years, Spurs just got their act together in time.

At times the goings-on at White Hart Lane would not have looked out of place in a West End farce. No sooner had Gerry Francis made way for new manager Christian Gross then former boss David Pleat was also back on the scene. Confusion about who was in charge only increased when Jurgen Klinsmann returned to North London clutching an unusual contract guaranteeing him a first-team place.

However, this season should be a better one for the Lillywhites. After all, Gross can call on the services of a whole team of full internationals. With strikers like David Ginola, Les Ferdinand and Chris Armstrong Spurs will always score goals, and the long-awaited return of Darren Anderton will increase the supply to the front.

The defence remains Spurs' biggest problem. Sol Campbell needs better support and Gross will surely be badgering Alan Sugar to release funds for this vital area.

ONE TO WATCH

DAVID GINOLA

TEAM LINE-UP

Ian Walker, Dean Austin, Justin Edinburgh, David Howells, Colin Calderwood, Gary Mabbutt, Ruel Fox, Allan Nielsen, Darren Anderton, Les Ferdinand, Chris Armstrong, Stephen Carr, Espen Baardsen, David Ginola, Ramon Vega, Clive Wilson, John Scales, Steffen Iverson, Jose Dominguez, Andy Sinton, Sol Campbell, Neale Fenn, Stephen Clemence, Jurgen Klinnsman

FACT FILE

Stadium:
White Hart Lane | Tottenham | London | N17 OAP

Manager: **Christian Gross**

Capacity: **33,208**

Record Attendance:
5 March 1938 | 75,038 v Sunderland | FA Cup

Club number: **0181 365 5000**

Tickets: **0891 335 566**

Ticket Prices:
£16-£35

Nearest BR station:
White Hart Lane or Northumberland Park

EVERTON

TEAM PROFILE

Poor old Everton. Once a proud member of the Big Five, the Merseysiders spent most of last season battling against the drop. Then again, it wasn't a new experience for the Toffees who, over the past five years, have developed a

Coventry-style ability to pull themselves back from the brink of the relegation abyss.

How manager Howard Kendall – now in his third spell at Goodison Park – must pine for the glory days of the mid-1980's, when Everton won the title twice. Quite why his side were so dire last year is a bit of a mystery; with players of the calibre of Duncan Ferguson, Nicky Barmby, Michael Madar and Slaven Bilic at the club, Everton should have been mid-table at least.

One plus point from an otherwise forgettable campaign was the breakthrough of a crop of youngsters into the first team. Dreadlocked winger Danny Cadamateri was the pick of the bunch, but defender Michael Ball and fresh-faced midfielder John Oster also made good impressions.

Kendall's problem is that these players are merely promising, and need another couple of years to mature. You can't win anything with kids!

ONE TO WATCH

DUNCAN FERGUSON

TEAM LINE-UP

Danny Williamson, Dave Watson, Mickael Madar, Terry Phelan, Nick Barmby, Duncan Ferguson, Donald Hutchison, John Spencer, Craig Short, Paul Gerrard, Peter Beagrie, Gareth Farrelly, John Oster, Mitchum Ward, Gavin McCann, Carl Tiler, Michael Ball, Graham Allen, Richard Dunne, Slaven Bilic, Danny Cadamateri, Thomas Myhre, John O'Kane

FACT FILE

Stadium:
Goodison Park | Goodison Road | Liverpool | L4 4EL

Manager: **Howard Kendall**

Capacity: **40,280**

Record Attendance:
18 April 1948 | 78,299 v Liverpool | FA Cup

Club number: **0151 330 2200**

Tickets: **0151 330 2300**

Ticket Prices:

Adult: £16

Child: £8

Nearest BR station:
Kirkdale or Lime Street

NOTTINGHAM FOREST

TEAM PROFILE

Few managers have more experience of promotion campaigns than Dave Bassett, so it was hardly a surprise that Forest waltzed back into the Premiership last season.

Bassett, though, is nothing but a realist and will know that his side are likely to struggle among the big boys. The goalkeeping position is a major concern: opposition strikers will surely be licking their lips at the thought of facing the error-prone Dave Beasant. The whole defence has a rickety look, although Colin Cooper is a classy stopper.

ONE TO WATCH
PIERRE VAN HOOIJDONK

The picture looks brighter elsewhere on the pitch. In midfield Stone, Gemmill and Bart-Williams provide the sweat, while Andy Johnson (a £2.2-million signing from Norwich) adds a dash of creativity. Up front, the pairing of a rejuvenated Kevin Campbell and the dangerous Pierre van Hooijdonk looks good for goals – although they'll be hard-pressed to match their joint tally of over 50 strikes last season.

For the most part, this is the Forest side which limped out of the Premiership at the end of the 1996/97 season. But there are some new faces. Watch out for Thierry Bonolair, a full back who likes to rampage forward in the manner of the much-missed Stuart Pearce.

TEAM LINE-UP

Marco Pascolo, Dave Beasant, Des Lyttle, Thierry Bonalair, Alan Rogers, Steve Chettle, Colin Cooper, Jon Hjelde, Craig Armstrong, Chris Bart-Williams, Scott Gemmill, Thomas, A Johnson, D Johnson, Steve Stone, Ian Woan, Allen, Kevin Campbell, Pierre Van Hooijdonk, Dean Saunders, Ian Moore, Guinan, Stephen Howe

FACT FILE

Stadium:
City Ground | Nottingham | NG2 5FJ

Manager: **Dave Bassett**

Capacity: **30,602**

Record Attendance:
2 March 1946 | 76,588 v Derby County | FA Cup

Club number: **0115 952 6000**

Tickets: **0115 952 6002**

Ticket prices:
to be announced

Nearest BR station:
Nottingham Midland

MIDDLESBROUGH

TEAM PROFILE

It was another rollercoaster of a season on Teeside last time round as Middlesbrough regained their Premiership place at the first attempt, but also had to endure yet more Wembley misery in the Coca-Cola Cup Final.

ONE TO WATCH
PAUL MERSON

Seeing their side lose 2–0 to Chelsea beneath the Twin Towers was an experience straight out of the film *Groundhog Day* for the Boro' fans, as only ten months earlier Bryan Robson's men had lost by the same score to the same team in the FA Cup Final.

Never mind. Robbo said all along that promotion was far more important than Cup success. His team retains the heart of the side that last appeared in the top flight – particularly in defence where Pearson, Kinder, Vickers and Festa form a solid-looking back four.

Of course, there are changes from the side which went down whinging about their deducted points. Gone are the star Brazilians and the tiresome Ravanelli. In their place much will be expected from Merson, Branca and the up-and-coming Armstrong. Above all, Boro fans will be praying Gazza stays fit and produces his best form

TEAM LINE-UP

Marlon Beresford, Andy Dibble, Ben Roberts, Steve Baker, Gianluca Festa, Curtis Fleming, Craig Harrison, Vladimir Kinder, Nigel Pearson, Robbie Stockdale, Steve Vickers, Clayton Blackmore, Fabio, Craig Hignett, Neil Maddison, Alan Moore, Robbie Mustoe, Phil Stamp, Andy Townsend, Paul Gascoigne, Alun Armstrong, Mikkel Beck, Paul Merson, Marco Branca

FACT FILE

Stadium:
Cellnet Riverside Stadium | Middlesbrough | TS3 6RS

Manger: **Bryan Robson**

Capacity: **30,304**

Record Attendance:
19 October 1996 | 30,215 v Tottenham | Premiership

Club number: **01642 877 700**

Tickets: **01642 877 745**

Ticket Prices:
to be announced

Nearest BR station:
Middlesbrough

CHARLTON ATHLETIC

TEAM PROFILE

Charlton fans have needed a warped sense of humour over the years. Some of them still argue the greatest achievement of their 1997/98 season was selling striker Carl Leaburn to Wimbledon and getting paid £300,000 for the privilege! Anyone who had spent a decade wincing at the profligacy of the non-goalscoring Leaburn knows what I mean.

Joking aside, the way Alan Curbishley cajoled an inexperienced side into the play-off picture was extraordinary considering the quality of Charlton's competitors. Lacking the lavish budgets of rival managers such as Bryan Robson and Peter Reid, Curbs refused to be intimidated. Homegrown talent was nurtured and every penny of the £1.7 million he spent last season was spent wisely. Even the £8 million that will flood his funds for new players should Charlton make the Premiership won't alter his attitude. Expect a similar policy to that adopted by Martin O'Neill at Leicester and perhaps similar results.

Apart from the odd weed-smoking scandal (ironic as Charlton boasts one of the best drug-education programmes in football), Charlton is a low-profile club nowadays but their stylish play lit up the First Division in 1997/98. Clive Mendonca's goals and Shaun Newton's enterprising wing play particularly impressed, but Alan Curbishley will need to buy committed players to survive a season in the Premiership.

ONE TO WATCH
SHAUN NEWTON

FACT FILE

Nickname: **Addicks**

Stadium:
The Valley | Floyd Road | London | SE7 8BL

Capacity: **16,000**

Club number: **0181 333 4000**

Tickets: **0181 333 4010**

Manager:
Alan Curbishley

IPSWICH

TEAM PROFILE

No-one who saw George Burley's face after United hammered his Ipswich side 9–0 at Old Trafford in 1995 would begrudge him Ipswich's Coca-Cola Cup win over the Reds last year. Classy Argentinian left back Mauricio Taricco completed a 2–0 win with a rasping 25-yarder. United fans didn't care much, but 25,000 gleeful Ipswich fans did.

Burley has moulded a useful side on a low budget and Ipswich are producing the finest homegrown talent outside of the Premiership. 20-year old goalkeeper Richard Wright has represented England at schools, youth and Under-21 level. The precocious midfield talents of 19-year old Keiron Dyer make him comparable to David Beckham according to ex-United youth David Johnson.

In fact, Johnson's £1-million mid-season transfer from Bury to Portman Road was probably *the* major factor in Ipswich's promotion push. David challenged Phillips and Van Hooijdonk at the top of the First Division goalscoring charts.

A lacklustre attitude cost him his chance at OT, but the new, fitter Johnson received his first England B cap in April.

If Ipswich don't make it through the play-offs, it's doubtful whether Burley will be able to keep the likes of Dyer, Johnson and Wright from the clutches of Premiership cradle snatchers.

ONE TO WATCH
DAVID JOHNSON

FACT FILE

Nicknames: **Blues; Town**

Stadium:
Portman Road | Ipswich | Suffolk | IPI 2DA

Capacity: **22,675**

Club number: **01473 400500**

Tickets: **01473 400555**

Manager:
George Burley

SHEFFIELD UNITED

TEAM PROFILE

Sheffield United stumbled into the play-offs after an eventful season. Only Birmingham City's failure to beat Charlton Athletic on the final day of the season granted the Bramhall Road club a possible route to the Premiership.

To make the play-offs was an

admirable achievement after their season had threatened to be derailed by the mid-season sale of their two strikers, Brian Deane to Benfica and Jan Aage Fjortoft to Barnsley. The departure of manager Nigel Spackman did little to boost morale, either.

STAR PLAYER

MARCELLO

Steve Thompson came in and steadied the ship, but Sheffield United's collection of hard-working players need a couple of superstars if they are to make it past their play-off rivals and then survive a challenging season in the Premiership.

The FA Cup proved to be a welcome diversion from the grind of the promotion race and the Blades were just a game away from a coveted tie at Wembley. Though they succumbed to Newcastle United in the semi final at Old Trafford after a battling display, the Cup run-in showed the team at their heroic best: David Holdsworth's spectacular volley against Coventry to rescue United in the last minute of the quarter final and Alan Kelly's penalty shoot-out saves in the replay.

Losing in the last minute of last season's play-off final to Palace hurt the Blades. They don't want to go through that again.

FACT FILE

Nickname: **Blades**

Stadium:
Bramall Lane Ground, Sheffield S2 4SU

Capacity: **30,200**

Club number: **0114 221 5757**

Tickets: **0114 221 1889**

Manager:
Steve Thompson

SUNDERLAND

TEAM PROFILE

Sunderland manager Peter Reid may not count Mary Whitehouse among his fans – his expletive-packed team talks during a television documentary series earlier this year would have made Roy 'Chubby' Brown blush – but for the Sunderland faithful he is a messiah.

If Sunderland are succesful in the play-offs, this will be the second time Peter Reid has led the Wearsiders into the Premiership and the former Manchester City boss will be praying it doesn't all end in tears, again.

ONE TO WATCH

KEVIN PHILLIPS

The trouble is that this is pretty much the same Sunderland side which fell out of the top division on the last day of the 1996/97 campaign, so you don't need to be Nostradamus to predict another season of struggle for the north-easterners.

If Sunderland are to survive they will require regular goalkeeping heroics from the flamboyant Frenchman Lionel Perez; stout defending from the likes of Michael Gray and Jody Craddock; consistently dynamic midfield displays from captain Kevin Ball, Lee Clark and Allan Johnston; and a steady flow of goals.

The main difference for Sunderland this season has been Kevin Phillips. Phillips is the goalscorer Sunderland lacked last season. With a tally of 31 goals in the 1997/98 campaign, he very nearly overtook Brian Clough's club record of 33 goals in a season.

FACT FILE

Nickname: **Rokermen**

Stadium:
Stadium of Light | Sunderland | SR5 1SU

Capacity: **42,000**

Club number: **0191 551 5000**

Tickets: **0191 551 5000**

Manager:
Peter Reid

Other titles available from Manchester United Books

0 233 99178 6	Manchester United in the Sixties by Graham McColl	£12.99
0 233 99340 1	Manchester United: The Insider Guide	£9.99
0 233 99359 2	Sir Matt Busby: A Tribute by Rick Glanvill	£14.99
0 233 99045 3	Cantona on Cantona by Eric Cantona	£14.99
0 233 99047 X	Alex Ferguson: Ten Glorious Years	£9.99
0 233 99368 1	A Will to Win: The Manager's Diary by Alex Ferguson with David Meek	£6.99
0 233 99362 2	Odd Man Out: A Player's Diary by Brian McClair with Joyce Woolridge	£6.99
0 233 99417 3	The Official Manchester United Quiz Book	£9.99
0 233 99148 4	David Beckham: My Story	£12.99

All these books are available from your local bookshop or can be ordered direct from the publisher.

This season's videos from VCI

MUV27	Champions Again! Season Review 1996/97	£13.99
MUV28	Alex Ferguson's Ultimate United	£13.99
MUV29	David Beckham: Football Superstar	£13.99
MUV32	Au Revoir Cantona	£10.99
MUV33	300 Manchester United Premiership Goals	£10.99
MUVM5001	Manchester United on Video Vol 5 No 1	£7.99
MUVM5002	Manchester United on Video Vol 5 No 2	£7.99
MUVM5003	Manchester United on Video Vol 5 No 3	£7.99
MUVM5004	Manchester United on Video Vol 5 No 4	£7.99

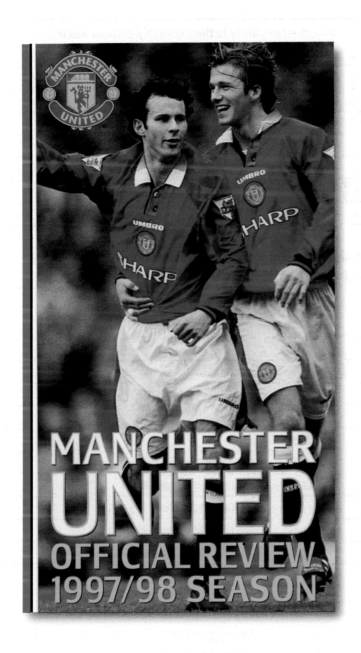

MANCHESTER UNITED

Manchester United Football Club
Old Trafford | Manchester | M16 ORA

Chairman & Chief Executive
C M Edwards

Directors
J M Edelson
Sir Bobby Charlton CBE
E M Watkins LLm
R L Olive

Manager
Alex Ferguson

Secretary
Kenneth Merrett

USEFUL TELEPHONE NUMBERS

General enquiries	**0161 930 1968**
Ticket information	**0161 872 0199**
Development Association	**0161 872 4676**
	0161 873 8378
	0161 873 8379
Commercial Department	**0161 872 3488**
Membership Office	**0161 872 5208**
Executive Suite	**0161 872 3331**
United Megastore	**0161 848 8181**
United Superstore	**0161 872 3398**
Mail Order Hotline	**0161 877 9777**
Club Call	**0891 121 161**
Subscriptions to official magazines ***manchester united*** and **Glory Glory Man United**	**0990 442 442**